Humane Politics and Methods of Inquiry

Humane Politics and Methods of Inquiry

Ithiel de Sola Pool

edited by Lloyd S. Etheredge

Transaction Publishers
New Brunswick (U.S.A.) and London (U.K.)

First paperback printing 2016

This book is printed on acid-free paper that meets the American National Standard for Permanence of Paper for Printed Library Materials.

Library of Congress Catalog Number: 00-020761
ISBN: 978-1-56000-401-1 (cloth); 978-1-4128-5709-3 (paper)
eBook: 978-1-4128-2571-9
Printed in the United States of America

Library of Congress Cataloging-in-Publication Data

Pool, Ithiel de Sola, 1917-
Humane politics and methods of inquiry / edited, and with an introduction by Lloyd S. Etheredge.
p. cm.
Includes bibliographical references and index.
ISBN 1-56000-401-0 (cloth : alk. paper)
1. Social sciences—Data processing. 2. Social sciences—Computer simulation. 3. Social sciences—Forecasting. II. Title.
U61.3 .P66 2000
300—dc21 00-020761

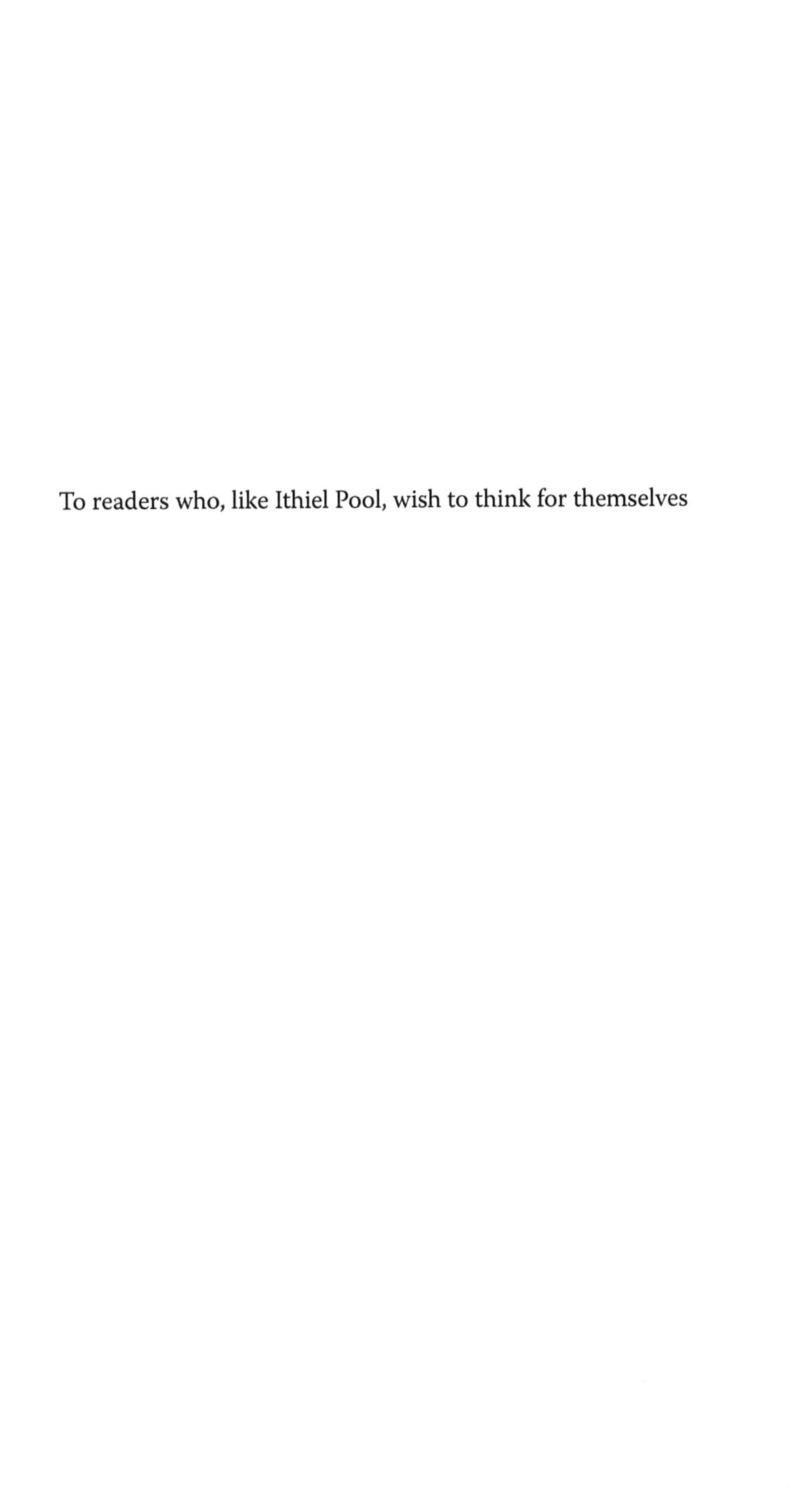

To readers who, like Ithiel Pool, wish to think for themselves

Contents

List of Tables

List of Figures

Preface

This volume emphasizes pioneering contributions of Ithiel de Sola Pool to the development of social science research methods that are likely to be more widely used in the years ahead. The reader also may wish to consult a companion volume that focuses on his contributions to understanding the social and political effects of new communications technology: Lloyd S. Etheredge (ed.), *Politics in Wired Nations: Selected Writings of Ithiel de Sola Pool* (New Brunswick, NJ: Transaction Publishers, 1998). The earlier volume includes a bibliography of his writing and a brief biography.

I have many debts in the preparation of this volume, to Ithiel's former colleagues and students, to Mrs. Jean Pool, and to others acknowledged in the earlier volume. To the Policy Science Center Inc., a nonprofit foundation founded at Yale Law School in 1948 by Ithiel Pool's former teacher and friend, Harold Lasswell, which has provided a professional home for the vision to unite science and the humanities in a commitment to public policy. And also to David Thorburn at MIT and the Markle Foundation for the invitation to present an earlier draft of the paper, "What's Next? The Intellectual Legacy of Ithiel de Sola Pool," included here, at a symposium at MIT in the spring of 1997.

Lloyd Etheredge

Acknowledgements

"Symbols, Meaning, and Social Science," by Ithiel de Sola Pool first appeared in *Symbols and Values: An Initial Study* (1954) edited by Lyman Bryson, Louis Finkelstein, R.M. MacIver, and Richard McKeon. New York: Harper and Brothers. Reprinted by permission.

"Content Analysis and the Intelligence Function," by Ithiel de Sola Pool first appeared in *Politics, Personality, and Social Science in the Twentieth Century: Essays in Honor of Harold D. Lasswell,* (1969) edited by Arnold A. Rogow. Chicago: University of Chicago Press. C 1969 by The University of Chicago Press. All rights reserved.

"Scratches on Social Science: Images, Symbols, and Stereotypes," by Ithiel de Sola Pool first appeared in *The Mixing of Peoples: Problems of Identity and Ethnicity* (1978), edited by Robert I. Rotberg. Stamford, CT: Greylock Publishers.

"The Simulmatics Project," by Ithiel de Sola Pool and Robert Abelson first appeared in *Public Opinion Quarterly* 25, no. 2 (Summer 1961). Reprinted by permission.

"A Postscript on the 1964 Election," by Ithiel de Sola Pool, Robert P. Abelson, and Samuel L. Popkin first appeared in *The American Behavioral Scientist* 8, no. 9 (May 1965). Reprinted by permission.

"The Kaiser, the Tsar, and the Computer: Information Processing in a Crisis," by Ithiel de Sola Pool and Allan Kessler first appeared in *The American Behavioral Scientist* 8, no. 9 (May 1965). Reprinted by permission.

"The International System in the Next Half-Century," by Ithiel de Sola Pool reprinted by permission of *Daedalus,* Journal of the American Academy of Arts and Sciences, from the issue entitled "Toward the Year 2000: Work in Progress," Summer 1967, Vol. 96, No. 3.

"The Art of the Social Science Soothsayer," by Ithiel de Sola Pool first appeared *in Forecasting in International Relations: Theory, Methods, Problems, Prospects* (1978), edited by Nazli Choucri and Thomas

W. Robinson. San Francisco, CA: W.H. Freeman and Company. Reprinted by permission.

"Hindsight and Foresight: The Case of the Telephone," by Ithiel de Sola Pool, reprinted from *The Social Impact of the Telephone*, 1977. Copyright 1973, MIT Press.

"Contacts and Influence," by Ithiel de Sola Pool and Manfred Kochen, reprinted from *Social Networks* 1, no. 1 with kind permission from Elsevier Science—NL, Sara Burgerhartstraat 25. 1055 KV Amsterdam, The Netherlands.

"Some Facts about Values," by Ithiel de Sola Pool first appeared in *PS* 3, no. 2 (Spring 1970). Reprinted by permission.

"What Ferment?" by Ithiel de Sola Pool first appeared in *Journal of Communications* 33, no. 3 (Summer 1983). Reprinted by permission.

"How Powerful is Business?" by Ithiel de Sola Pool first appeared in *Does Big Business Rule America* (1981), edited by Robert Hessen. Washington, DC: Ethics and Public Policy Center. Reprinted by permission.

"Human Subjects Regulations on the Social Sciences" first appeared in *Science and Public Policy III* (1983), edited by Frances S. Sterett, Annals of the New York Academy of Sciences, volume 403. Reprinted by permission.

Introduction

Ithiel de Sola Pool was one of the most original thinkers in the development of the social sciences. These papers introduce research methods that he helped to invent and that are especially suited for: (1) Wider applications, now that more powerful computers are available; (2) Integrating the sensibilities of the humanities more fully into social science; and (3) Studying the social and political effects of new communications technology. They also present his belief that social science adds a new dimension (beyond what is provided by the humanities and natural sciences) that can improve decision making in democracies and produce more humane politics.

The research methods include:

- the computer-assisted analysis of the content of communications;
- computer simulations (e.g., of Presidential elections and of crisis decision making in international politics);
- forecasting the future of international politics and methods to forecast the impacts of new telecommunications technology;
- the rigorous analysis of domestic and global contact networks and the so-called "small world" phenomenon.

A final section concerns challenges to the use of social science to create more humane politics. These include:

- the question of value neutrality;
- the unexpected tenacity and competition of simple ideological ideas;
- the challenge of deconstruction from the humanities;
- the threats of governments and a bureaucratized society to the health of universities and the progress of social science.

In the final chapter, I will draw upon Ithiel Pool's work and discuss several new ways in which methods in this volume can be applied to current problems of informed decision making and more humane politics.

* * *

Today, the social sciences are taken for granted as part of American universities and undergraduate education. The title of this book, linking social science research methods to more humane politics, may want explaining.

Social science is primarily a twentieth-century, and an American, invention. The movement grew at the University of Chicago in the 1930s, partly in response to the historical circumstances: the domestic political turmoil and unexpected collapse of the economy in the Depression, and the international rise of Communist and Nazi movements that began to threaten another global conflict within two decades of the unexpected and murderous trauma of World War I. The search for new methods to apply human intelligence effectively was spurred, too, by the anxiety that the traditional humanities-based education of ruling classes was not sufficient: the most civilized countries in Europe and their leaders were part of the problem.

In recent decades it has become fashionable for outside critics from the humanities to portray social scientists as technocratic and unconcerned with freedom. This is an ahistorical misreading of the origins. To Ithiel Pool's generation of founders, it was axiomatic that people were entrapped in traditional identities and, often, manipulated by their societies. During World War I and again in the 1930s and 1940s, hundreds of millions of people were marching to war under the leadership of national demagogues and their use of new mass communications technology for propaganda. After World War II, the end of colonialism and the modernization (often violent) of traditional societies, and the communist dictatorships in Russia, China, and Eastern Europe (held in place, in part, by totalitarian control of the media) made the battle for human freedom a strong (implicit) motivation for research. They believed that social science could be liberating and provide an independent, steadier, truer, and more realistic framework for democratic decision making than was provided by the world politics they inherited.

In later sections I will return to the idea that the invention and development of social science can contribute to democratic decision making and humane politics. However, there is an important caveat: Ithiel Pool was, in social science terms, a "soft" determinist. He did not believe that inventions (like research methods for social science) automatically force or assure specific effects, although they can make them possible, easier, or more likely. It is the decisions of individuals about what to *do* with inventions that create the future. And this caution (and implicit invitation) also applies to the potential benefits of social science research methods.

May 1998

Part I

The Analysis of Communications

Editor's Introduction

"Content analysis is a systematic and rigorous way of doing what humanistic students of ideas and behavior have always done, namely, to look at what symbols are used in a body of text. Such observations of the flows of symbols become content analysis or social science if some attention is paid to the procedures of observation."[1]

—Ithiel Pool [pp. 21–22, below]

"In its contribution to man's life in society, content analysis is at one with all the social sciences. In general it may be said that the social sciences are the humanities of our era. In previous times scholars considered it part of their role to be teachers of princes. They saw themselves as taming the violence of man's untutored nature by instilling in their young charges the quality of reason and the humane heritage of the liberal arts.

Today the social sciences are our best tools for understanding each other's human passions, motives, and plans. They are our most effective instrument for handling man's greatest problem, organized violence. . . . It is the social sciences that best help us understand the conditions by which a group may achieve consensus, the basis of psychopathological disturbances, the needs of minorities for respect. . ."

—Ithiel Pool [pp. 19–20, below]

The scientific analysis of political communications arose as the new technologies of mass communications (newspapers, radio, motion pictures) were used by governments for propaganda, by revolutionary leaders to organize mass followings, and by democracies for daily politics and policy discussion. Content analysis, as it is called, was an evolving set of methods to observe and understand the public political process, including the spread of emotion-charged ideas and words ("symbols") across national boundaries.

Content analysis also promises deeper and more powerful insights than merely observing the surface of what is being said. Ithiel Pool, Harold Lasswell, Nathan Leites, Alexander George, Irving Janis, and many other social science pioneers who were Pool's contemporaries were fascinated by psychoanalysis and underwent personal psychoanalysis. They were never persuaded to promote Sigmund Freud's particular clinical hypotheses, but they were hooked on the possibility of making inferences, from streams of talk, about the deeper organizing principles, images, and emotions that lay behind it. They hoped, someday, to both listen—and understand—individuals, group behavior, and even the logic of other cultures more powerfully by new methods that could be made explicit and steadily improved.

In the beginning, Ithiel Pool counted words (e.g., emotionally-charged political symbols like "democracy.") And in the so-called RADIR Project he and his associates recorded 105,000 occurrences of 415 symbols in 20,000 editorials from five countries across a sixty-year period. The work (conducted from 1948–1953) was done by hand: eventually, they set aside further research because the available technology was too laborious and expensive, and computers lacked the power and memory to analyze such large datasets with sophistication. Today, improvements in scanning technology, and the growing power and memory of desktop computers, make it feasible to convert thousands (and even millions) of words to electronic form at affordable cost. Content analysis is a method whose time has come. But the unprecedented quantity of data available raised then—and especially raises today—the question of what should be counted, and how inferences should be made?[2]

"Symbols, Meaning, and Social Science"

The first selection explores the problem of inference. As Ithiel describes, it can be useful to count words, obtain frequency distributions, and know that the word "democracy" began to capture imaginations in a certain historical period, and that it become so highly esteemed that almost everybody began to claim their political loyalties as "democratic" and to describe their revolutions as "democratic" or a "people's" revolution. But this initial statistical analysis only begins to understand what is being said, and what is being heard, when we observe that the term is used. The analysis of co-occurrences, that Pool recommends to his audience, is one of the tasks that is becoming feasible on a large scale.

"Content Analysis and the Intelligence Function"

Harold Lasswell, an early leader in the development of content analysis, was Ithiel Pool's teacher at the University of Chicago. During World War II, Ithiel Pool worked as Lasswell's research assistant in

Washington, DC to study Nazi propaganda. They continued a lifelong friendship. This second selection is drawn from a volume honoring Harold Lasswell's work: It provides a good historical overview of the development of content analysis and a discussion of the vision, that they shared, of producing a more thoughtful and well-informed basis for democratic decision making, and a humane politics, than the domestic and world politics, aswirl with demagoguery, impassioned rhetoric, and the threat of violence that they had inherited.

"Scratches on Our Minds: Beliefs, Stereotypes, and Images"

In applied settings (e.g., advertising) marketing researchers pay keen attention to the properties, flow, and change of images. The early social sciences, however, favored the concept of "attitude" as a more central explanation in social psychology. Thus many attitudes are measured [e.g., the extent of agreeing or disagreeing with a statement, on a 7–point scale.] but the types and properties of imagery (e.g., that ideologues have of government) still remain relatively *terra incognito.* This third selection honors the work of several theorists, including the former journalist Harold Isaacs whose interviewing methods, emphasis upon images, and (resulting) astute psychological observations Ithiel Pool admired.

Especially, Ithiel Pool felt that attention to images (going deeper than words alone) could enrich the explanatory power of social science by including—in a readily accessible way—some of the dynamics investigated by psychoanalysts.[3] Isaacs' observations about unrecognized splitting of national stereotypes (e.g., fond images of India and Indians might co-occur with suspicion of China and the Chinese) alerted Pool's clinical sensibility.[4]

Notes

1. For a related discussion see Robert E. Lane, *The liberties of wit: Humanism, criticism, and the civic mind.* (New Haven: Yale University Press, 1961).
2. The interested reader should consult, for more extensive discussions, Ithiel de Sola Pool (ed.), *Trends in content analysis* (Urbana, IL: University of Illinois Press, 1959), and especially Pool's summary essay, partly reproduced in Lloyd S. Etheredge (ed.), *Politics in wired nations: Selected writings of Ithiel de Sola Pool.* (New Brunswick, NJ: Transaction Publishers, 1998), pp. 119–158 and the useful overviews by Ole Holsti, especially "Content analysis," in G. Lindzey and E. Aronson (eds.) *Handbook of social psychology* (Reading, MA: Addison—Wesley, 1968), vol. 2, pp. 596–692 and his *Content analysis for the social sciences and humanities.* (New York: Random House, 1969).

3. See also Lloyd S. Etheredge (ed.), *op. cit.,* pp. 10–11 and Ithiel de Sola Pool and Irwin Shulman, "Newsman's fantasies, audiences, and newswriting," reprinted in *ibid.,* pp. 29–45.
4. It would be straightforward to suggest that similar rules of "splitting" hero v. villain properties may exist in ideological images in domestic politics. For example, liberal activists imagining a benevolent government paired with the evil image of selfish businessmen; conservatives holding the heroic image of businessmen entrepreneurs paired with the evil image of a restrictive do-nothing government bureaucracy.

1

Symbols, Meanings, and Social Science

Introduction

This paper deals with meanings in the natural language—that is, the language used by ordinary men in everyday parlance. How can we go about studying what a vague value symbol like democracy means to the men who use it? In this paper we propose that one way to study the meaning of a symbol to those who use it is to tabulate the syndromes of other symbols in which it occurs. This procedure, which we shall illustrate with reference to symbols referring to the value, democracy, is a kind of content analysis designed to facilitate the empirical study of values.[1]

It is a commonplace that the word, "democracy," means all things to all men. The Soviets call their tyranny a democratic dictatorship, while we defend individual freedom in the name of democracy. We hear about so-called democratic art and democratic education. Even some churches explain their time-honored doctrines as expressions of democracy.

When a word comes to be used this loosely purists or pedants are tempted to discard it. They call it "meaningless" or "nonsense." They dismiss it as simply a camouflage for personal preferences. They assert that "democratic" is simply a synonym for "desirable," and "undemocratic" a synonym for "undesirable."

This position is clearly wrong. When John Doe uses the word, "democratic," he is almost always adding some bits of information which would be lost if he used the word "undesirable" instead. If he says that he opposes regressive taxes because they are undemocratic, we suspect the following bits of information which we would not have suspected if

From *Symbols and Values: An Initial Study* (1954), edited by Lyman Bryson, Louis Finkelstein, R.M. MacIver, and Richard McKeon.

he had simply said that they are *undesirable.* We suspect that relative equality is a fairly important value to John Doe. We suspect that he considers economic equality as relevant to political status. We suspect that he is more concerned with or aware of the political effects of regressive taxes than of their effects on the level of national income. If he had used the word, "undesirable," we could not have confidently guessed any of these things. In short, given some knowledge of the context, the word, "democracy," imparts to us some vague bits of information.

For an empirical study of meanings the problem is to determine and specify the meanings which men in any given context embody in a given symbol. That is a different problem from that of establishing philosophical truths about democracy, and from the problem of determining what coherent and logical thinkers mean by it. It is rather to establish what groups of laymen vaguely and implicitly mean by it.

For scholars this is a relatively new kind of problem. It is a kind of problem which emerged historically together with the modern democratic state and with social science. The simultaneous emergence of these three things—modern democracy, the empirical study of language and social science—is no chance coincidence. Each contributes in its way to the others.

Until modern times, scholars were not concerned with the crude, ignorant, banal statements of their "inferiors." In aristocratic and class societies wherein the intellectual development of an elite rested upon the life draining labor of a mass, only elite expressions seemed worthy of study. The linguistic problem for scholars was to find formulations in which statesmen, priests, and scholars could make effective, correct, and unambiguous statements and relate such statements one to another. The result was grammar, rhetoric, and logic, all disciplines concerned with the correct use of language. They are all disciplines which enable trained men to reach the goal of proper communication according to established norms. The Platonic dialectic sought to discover the norms by critically examining the actual usage of intellectuals, then called sophists. The Aristotelian method sought the norms in nature, partly independently of actual usage. But whether proper usage and semantic clarity were sought by consulting the authority of wise men or by studying nature, or both, the goal was still a normative one. The goal was to iron the bugs out of a specialized language by introducing more sophistication into its use by educated men.

Interest by scholars in the sayings and opinions of the humble became prominent first in the practical arts. In them, as Edgar Zilsel pointed out, it led in the sixteenth century to the development of modern science. In the sixteenth century, and whenever else in the history of civilization the buds of science have opened up, we can find the explanation in a reorientation by trained intellectuals toward the practical artisans. Science emerged when these two social strata began communicating. That is to say, it emerged when the scholar trained in the process of generalization came to feel it proper to be interested in the practical problems of the artisan and informed himself of the artisan's lore of factual knowledge. From 1550 on, this process can be traced regarding such practical matters as pumping water, map making, determining longitude, etc.

Natural science thus emerged in the Renaissance when scholars began to listen to some of the things which artisans had to say. It was only much later that scholars became interested also in the style in which the masses talked. The arts and disciplines of expression were the last strongholds of aristocratic attitudes. In the seventeenth and eighteenth centuries—though with exceptions—literature was the concern of the drawing room while science was the hobby of the burghers. I do not mean to minimize the exceptions—Milton is one outstanding one. But the remarkable study by Robert Merton of *Science, Technology, and Society in 17th Century England* establishes the statistical validity of this generalization. Interest in poetry and interest in science were negatively, not positively correlated. Men who grew up in the hothouse of Puritanism and commercialism went one way; those who were nurtured in aristocratic conservative climates went the other. Indeed, even today, teachers of language and literature still often reveal aristocratic values when they talk about good form and correct speech. But alongside of the persistence of such prissy standards there has emerged, during the past century, a new set of interests in what living people do say.

The emergence of this new approach can be dated by changes in dictionary making. In the seventeenth and eighteenth centuries the function of the dictionary was to set correct usage. It aimed to purify the language. The great dictionaries were often the products of official academies of the top literati who became the arbiters of usage. In Italy, the Accademia della Crusca issued its *Vocabolario* in 1612, which long was the standard of the language. In France, the Académie Française published the first edition of its dictionary in 1694. In England, where no academy existed, the original intent of Johnson's *Dictionary* was the same, though the product was quite different. Thus these early dictionaries all had a common origin in a desire to set good usage.

The nineteenth century saw a change. In 1854, Jacob and Wilhelm Grimm published their dictionary of the German language which sought to register language as it was, not to make it is it ought to be. The new approach was well expressed by Dean Trench three years later in a paper on "Some Deficiencies in Existing English Dictionaries." He said, "A dictionary is an *inventory* of *the language*. . . . It is no task of the maker of it to select the *good* words. . . . He is an historian, . . . not a critic."

In the century since then great progress has been made in the empirical study of language. The latest dictionary, the Thorndike-Barnhart, is based upon the now familiar technique of word counts, The pocket edition contains the 30,000 most frequently used words as established in counts of over 30,000,000 words. The importance of different meanings (or definitions) is estimated on the basis of the Lorge-Thorndike *Semantic Count of English Words.* Semantic counts have been or are being made for French, German, Russian, and other languages. Grammar, too, has become statistical in such works as Charles C. Fries's, *American English Grammar.*

The same interest in the empirical study of popular communication may be seen in other fields. In the past century philology has come of age, but so have psychiatry and social science. These sciences, too, are largely ways of viewing the flow of the natural language. They involve a learned reinterpretation of the significance of common statements. What we said before about the origins of natural science may be equally said about them. When scholars with a generalizing tendency began to pay attention to the characteristics of what people said, the result was social science.

The growth of interest in popular speech, in philology, and in social science were simultaneous and intertwined, for most social facts worth studying are embedded in a process of communication. One cannot define social science as the study of communication, for some social factors are not thoughts, attitudes, or values.

Population is one such fact and technology another. We should not denigrate inquiries into such facts, even when the inquiries eschew the study of people's attitudes toward, or interpretations of the facts. But we may fairly assert that well over 80 percent of the topics social scientists investigate involve at least one variable consisting of statements, or attitudes, or beliefs.

We may therefore summarize what the psychiatrists and social scientists have done in the past century by saying they have become interested in the attitudes, opinions, and forms of expression of ordinary men.[2] When they paid attention to these banal and intellectually arid verbalizations they recognized new and interesting dimensions of the flow of language. Psychoanalysts have learned to read unconscious personal meanings in the subject's choice of metaphors or topics. Marx tried to read class and economic meanings into ideological statements. While this attempt succeeded only in part, it provided cues for later sociologists who have learned to identify the social functions of myths and attitudes.

What all these social scientists do is to use the subject's statements as data. They are not interested per se in the truth, logicality, brilliance, originality, or correctness of the subject's statement. When a subject says *A* they want to know what event *B* is likely also to occur or to have occurred.

B may be another statement or it may be a completely non-symbolic fact such as the explosion of a bomb. The social scientist studying symbols may relate them to other symbols or to non-symbols, but in either case he observes the symbols as social events. In other words, he is interested in the operational implications of event *A*, event *A* in this case being a symbol emission.

In simplest language, the social scientist asks what follows from statement *A*. The logician also asks what follows from statement *A*, but the logician and the social scientist mean very different things. The logician is concerned with what *logically* follows, what *correctly* follows, what is *implied by* statement *A*. The social scientist wants to know what events are apt to happen along with statement *A*. These other events may be the emission of the statements which logically follow or they may be something quite different. Thus the logician's problem and the social scientist's, though parallel and often verbally confused with each other, are actually quite different. Each asks what follows from symbol *A*. Each also asks what does symbol *A* mean to those who use it. But the meaning of meaning is different for each.

This brings us to the heart of our problem, and to the end of a rather discursive introduction. We want to explore the meaning of meaning as viewed by the social scientist studying symbols. Without getting off into endless controversies on the meaning of meaning, we may simply assert that in some sense to a normative logician or grammarian or phoneticist, the meaning of a symbol is a consistent body of norms about how it may be used. What is its meaning to a social scientist?

Meaning in the Social Sciences

A social scientist may define the meaning of a symbol to a given person as the sum of the contexts in which that person will use that symbol. The usages need not be consistent or "proper," but in so far as the usages occur in predictable contexts the symbol has meaning for the man who uses it and that meaning is an important fact to the social scientist.

As we noted above, the social scientist is interested in all the correlates—both verbal and nonverbal—of a symbolic event, but among these correlates, meaning is an important class. It is the class of correlates contained in propositions that if symbol *A* occurs, symbols *B, C, D, . . . N* will also occur in given relations, with given probabilities. Let us illustrate the point. Citizen Doe expresses the view that true freedom lies in obedience to the law. This is a symbol event about which a social scientist can say a number of things. From this symbol event he may infer some traits of the emitter. The emitter is probably an educated man. Furthermore most probably his education was either Continental, Rousseau or Hegel being major influences, or else it was legal. He is probably conservative. His personality may have traits of what is now often called the authoritarian type. These surmises about a particular case are illustrative inferences from general propositions and are obviously only probabilities, the probabilities varying with the proposition. Here, however, we are not interested in the confidence of the inference but only in its subject matter.

All the surmises above related symbol event *A* to some trait of the emitter other than the meaning with which he used the word, "freedom." We can also make surmises which relate symbol event *A* to meaning events. Having made the above remark about freedom, Citizen Doe is also likely to assert that true freedom is positive, not negative, that it is freedom "to," not freedom "from," that a human being develops fully only in society and that freedom is therefore social, that society is more than the sum of its parts, and that liberty is not license.

All of these are statements which commonly occur in the symbol flow of men who make the statement that freedom lies in obedience to law, and so these are all facets of the meaning of the symbol, freedom, to such men. Its meaning to them is fully defined only by the entire list of statements these men might make containing the symbol, freedom, with probabilities assigned to each statement.

This description of meaning as viewed by the social scientist is simply a complex expression of what the modern dictionary maker or grammarian does. He tries to determine the circumstances in which a word is actually used. To take two simple examples: Is a glider an airplane? Is a helicopter an airplane? The answers can be determined by whether in context of discussion of gliders or helicopters the word, "airplane," is used. If the word is readily used it is an airplane; if not used then it is not.

The same method and the same considerations apply in defining a word like "democratic." If we want to determine how a given person or group uses the word we can investigate where they use it and where they do not. We can ask whether they use it when discussing the incidence of taxes, the prevalence of civil liberties, the practice of elections, etc. When they discuss a corrupt plebian political machine controlling large masses of ignorant votes, do they call it "undemocratic and corrupt," or do they call it "democratic and corrupt"? If such a machine is considered undemocratic, then democracy is obviously being taken to mean effective autonomy for the individuals in the mass as well as adherence to parliamentary rules of the game. If the machine is called democratic, democracy is being taken to refer rather to social stratification, and the dominance of plebeians. Where men feel that a word applies, and where they feel that it does not apply is their definition of it.

This observation, although banal, has implications for social science that have seldom been fully realized. On the whole, social scientists have shied away from the study of meaning. They have preferred to explore correlates of verbal events more easily objectified than their meaning. Social scientists can tell you some fascinating things about a respondent who says, "I am a Republican." They can tell you the probabilities that he will be in any given income group, ethnic group, region, etc. They cannot tell you much, however, about what other sentences he may utter in which the word, "Republican," occurs. In other words they cannot tell you what the concept, "Republican," means to him.

Now if what we have said above is true, then meaning need not remain a topic too difficult for social scientists to study. Objective empirical studies of meaning can be conducted if social scientists will begin to collect data about the constellations in which symbols occur in ordinary speech. Let me cite one suggestive, although partial and incomplete, finding of research along these lines. At the Hoover Institute on War, Revolution, and Peace, Stanford University, we have recently been conducting studies of trends in the values which animate contemporary politics.

The editorials in the *New York Times*, the *Times* of London, *Le Temps*, and *Izvestia* were analyzed by counting the occurrence of some 400 key symbols and in each case the judgment made of the symbol. (The results of these studies are reported in the Hoover Institute Studies.) Among the symbols counted were such terms as "freedom," "independence," "anarchy." "laissez-faire," "individualism," and so on. Also among the symbols counted were such terms as "authority," "discipline," "order," "dictatorship," "tyranny," and so on.

Ordinarily one would assume that it would make little difference which set of terms one tabulated: the symbols of freedom or the symbols of authority. Logically they are alternative modes for expressing the samc idea. A libertarian asserts himself to be for liberty and/or against tyranny. An authoritarian asserts himself for discipline and/or against anarchy.

In the English and American papers this logical expectation proved to prevail. The study covered sixty years. In the course of the sixty years there were considerable shifts in editorial attitudes toward liberty and authority. When a shift occurred either in the direction of greater libertarianism or in the direction of greater authoritarianism, the shift was registered as one would expect, both in the symbols of liberty and in the symbols of authority.

In the Russian editorials, however, this was not the case. In the Russian papers when the editorials registered more affect in favor of liberty they often simultaneously registered more affect in favor of authority. When they registered less fervor for liberty, they often also registered less fervor for authority.

Now, as already stated, this is a fragmentary result, but still it is startling. It could be the cue for a series of thorough studies of this topic which might establish the real implications of the finding. If the finding held up in a series of samples, Bolshevik and non-Bolshevik alike, it would suggest that Russian usage of the symbol, freedom, had a different significance to the user than Western usage, and more important, that the Russian value structure was different, too.

With our present limited findings we can only speculate, but such speculation is worthwhile in that it suggests what a fuller study might confirm. Western usage, if our results may be believed, indicates a relatively stable and well rationalized attitude toward the value, freedom, which though emotionally charged is not the target of great ambivalence. The contradictory Russian usage implies, on the contrary, that freedom is a tremendously charged and also threatening concept. While very much desired it arouses guilt and fear which must be warded off by assertion of contradictory reactive symbols. Behind these contradictory symbols lies a struggle between fervently desired but incompatible values. Perhaps freedom is a value so fraught with danger in that culture that it arouses great anxiety and cannot be consistently accepted.

Let me cite another example of an empirical analysis of meaning from the same study—a finding about the meaning of the word, "democracy." It is fairly well recognized that there is an Eastern and Western or Continental and Liberal conception of democracy. The one stresses equality, the other personal freedom. This statement is, however, a gross oversimplification. How complex the intellectual history of democracy is may be seen in the UNESCO symposium, *Democracy in a World of Tensions.*[3] Disregarding the complications, we may fairly assert that throughout its history the concept, democracy, has implied several values which though partly interdependent are partly in conflict. Freedom and equality are among these values. Freedom is impossible without some measure of equality, yet when each is free to achieve what he can men do not remain equal but some advance beyond the others. This is one of the dilemmas of equality and freedom.

This paper is not the place to consider the proper and logical resolution of this long-discussed dilemma. We are here concerned only with empirically observing which horn of the dilemma various people have seized upon and how hard, that is, how they have interpreted democracy.

The Hoover Institute content analysis sheds some light on this question, but it reveals that three constellations of other symbols appeared in modern editorials along with the symbol, democracy, not just the two already noted. These included symbols of freedom, and symbols of the masses, but also symbols of constitutional government.

The last of these interpretations of democracy, which is often overlooked in discussions of the Eastern and Western conceptions, was indeed stressed least. Freedom and equality were more commonly associated with democracy. More important, and more distressing than the low total stress on constitutional government, is the fact that in discussions of democracy the mechanisms of constitutional government were decreasingly stressed over the past sixty years. The popular associations of the word, "democracy," are increasingly coming to be freedom and equality without reference to the regularized political framework which may provide for them. This represents in important, but not much noticed, change in the meaning of the term, democracy.

It might also be added that the count supported the belief that the strongest association of the symbol, democracy, in the West is personal freedom, while in Russia it is the masses. The Eastern and Western conceptions turned out as expected.

These instances illustrate how a value system may be described by tabulating what symbols are associated with what other symbols. The psychoanalysts have shown how closely intertwined and well integrated are a man's public symbol system with his private. If we do not impose upon our subjects the conditions of free association they will suppress the private symbols, but the public symbols will still form a repetitive and integrated whole worthy of study. This is a task for sociologists, political scientists, and historians. We can tabulate which symbols appear with which others in a symbol flow. The regular associations of any given symbol tell us what values that symbol implies to the speakers or writers studied. The total structure of their value system may be expressed by a series of equations which express the functional interrelationships of different symbols. Each equation states the probability that any one symbol, X, will appear if any one other symbol, Y, appears. The full series of equations represents the subject's value system. The technical problems involved in empirical studies of the values embedded in the flow of symbols in the natural language are great, but with the aid of precise analysis of linguistic constellations they are not insurmountable.

Notes

1. It should be noted that we use the word, "symbol," here in the way that certain philosophers use the word, "sign." We do so following most social science usage. The social scientist usually focuses on signs which are symbolic in most of the senses in which that word is used. By loose extension he generally continues to talk about symbols in referring to any sign or even sign vehicle.
2. Cf. Hans Speier, "Historical development of public opinion," *American Journal of Sociology*, LV, 1950, p. 4.
3. Richard McKeon, ed., *Democracy in a world of tensions* (Chicago: University of Chicago Press, 1951).

2

Content Analysis and the Intelligence Function

To his colleagues, the work of Harold Lasswell symbolizes the movement of the study of man toward science. But as with many of the makers of modern social science, a closer look reveals profound moral concerns that guided his professional career.[1] (It has often been noted that many leading social scientists are sons of ministers.) The study of man has been for Harold Lasswell not a matter of idle curiosity but a tool for promoting the dignity of man.

Content analysis was promoted by Lasswell not because of fascination with numbers but for its "contribution . . . to the special objectives of humane politics."[2]

In its contribution to man's life in society, content analysis is at one with all the social sciences. In general it may be said that the social sciences are the humanities of our era. In previous times scholars considered it part of their role to be teachers of princes. They saw themselves as taming the violence of man's untutored nature by instilling in their young charges the quality of reason and the humane heritage of the liberal arts.

Today the social sciences are our best tools for understanding each others human passions, motives, and plans. They are our most effective instrument for handling man's greatest problem, organized violence. It is the social sciences that give us the most reliable information about where riots will breed, how criminals can be controlled, whether insurgents will maintain rule of a university or a village, and how nuclear war can be avoided. It is the social sciences that best help us understand the conditions by which a group may achieve consensus, the basis of psychopathological disturbances, the needs of minorities

---

From *Politics, Personality and Social Science in the Twentieth Century: Essays in Honor of Harold D. Lasswell* (1969), edited by Arnold A. Rogow.

for respect. It is the social sciences that are now the best agency for civilizing statesmen.

The education of statesmen is but the latest of a series of functions that the humanities have abandoned to scientific disciplines. Philosophers used to observe and interpret nature, but since the seventeenth century they have abandoned that exercise to men of empirical science. They used to help men in their daily problems of disease, love, war, and farming by knowledge of stars, omens, magic, and potions, but these pretensions they abandoned at about the same time.

Even more recently the humanists have left the field of policy. But now the seer has been replaced as the prince's counselor by the operations analyst. Only the expressive, aesthetic function remains as the undisputed domain of the humanist. Today it has fallen to the policy scientist, as Harold Lasswell has called him, to moderate the action of the specialists in violence. It is the policy scientist who by the practice of intelligence tames the exercise of naked force in the practices of government and preserves respect for the humanity of man.

The importance of instruments of conciliation and moderation is increasingly great in our time, for since 1914 we have lived in an era of unprecedented violence. Our era opened on a note of confidence in democracy. Tocqueville eighty years before World War I, Marx seventy years before it, Ostrogorski a decade before it, and numerous other writers on modern civilization saw equality and democracy as the onrushing wave of the future. Mass organizations were being formed.[3] Mass participation in politics was growing. Social distinctions of status and right were being leveled.

After World War I, however, most social theorists, including Weber and Lasswell, became preoccupied with a new set of problems that grew out of their concern that democratic society might destroy itself. Led by demagogues who manipulated ideology, the mass movements that were the expression of democracy were imposing straitjackets of dogma on society. In Weber's formulation charismatic leaders create machines led by professionals which threaten to bring a dark night of rule by an absolute ethic that does not count costs. In Lasswell's formulation agitators and other political leaders who project complex private motives onto public objects may manipulate symbols of identification, demand, and expectation so as to establish garrison states that deny shared respect to their people. To these theorists democracy seemed far from a sure thing, and the conditions for its achievement and preservation were a major question for the social sciences to tackle. Much of Lasswell's writing in the 1930s and 1940s concerned the "developing science of democracy."

In 1942 Harold Lasswell wrote a piece with that title in a *Festschrift* for his mentor, Charles E. Merriam:

> The developing science of democracy is an arsenal of implements for the achievement of democratic ideals. We know enough to know that democracies do not know how to live; they perish through ignorance.... Without knowledge, democracy will surely fail.[4]

Furthermore, as he wrote elsewhere in the same year:

> Modern procedures do make it possible for the first time in the history of large scale social organization to realize some of the aims of democracy. Social and psychological sciences have developed procedures that are capable of reporting the facts about the thoughts and feelings of our fellow men.[5]

Content analysis is one of these procedures:

> We can actually study the thoughts and feelings of each of the major divisions of modern social structure and perfect means of making them fraternally intelligible to one another. . . . By examining the channels of public communication, we may determine the degree to which even the opportunity exists of taking the other fellow into proper account.[6]

Thus, content analysis could, in Lasswell's view, contribute to the objective of humane politics:

> The aim of humane politics is a commonwealth in which the dignity of man is accepted in theory and fact. Whatever improves our understanding of attitudes is a potential instrument of humane politics. Up to the present, physical science has not provided us with means of penetrating the skull of a human being and directly reading off his experiences. Hence, we are compelled to rely upon indirect means of piercing the wall that separates us from him. Words provide us with clues.[7]

Content analysis is a systematic and rigorous way of doing what humanistic students of ideas and behavior have always done, namely, to look at what symbols are used in a body of text. Such observations of the flow of symbols become content analysis or social science if some attention is paid to the procedures of observation. Content analysis is only a portion of the intelligence function that makes democratic and rational decision making possible.

Of seven functions which Lasswell distinguishes as taking place in the process of decision—intelligence, recommendation, prescription, innovation, application, appraisal, and termination[8]—it is the intelligence function that offers the content analyst or other man of learning the opportunity to humanize the exercise of power. The intelligence function is the bringing of knowledge of the conditions and consequences of his action to the consciousness of the decision maker. It includes the devices of interviewing, experimentation, espionage, participant observation, analysis, model building, introspection, computation, the census—everything that if done with rigor and objectivity deserves to be called broadly scientific.

The social scientist, including the content analyst, brings a new and more effective method of observation to bear on the perennial subject of human behavior. There are many ways of studying human behavior. There is the rationalistic approach used by the economist and moral philosopher of the nineteenth century. There is the developmental approach of the historian. There is the quantitative scientific approach of the empirical sociologist. There is the documentary institutional approach of the traditional political scientist. There is the individual psychodynamic approach of the psychologist.

Content analysis, as a rigorous, usually quantitative way of describing that part of human behavior which consists of symbol flows, belongs among the more empirical, positivistic ways of producing intelligence about men's attitudes, expectations, and values. It has been a particularly controversial manifestation of the scientific spirit because its object of study, symbol flows, comes so close to the heart of the humanists' own domain of study. The pretensions of the social scientists in encroaching upon the humanists' expertise in interpreting ideologies, doctrines, and value systems seemed particularly intolerable and philistine to those who disapproved of the social scientists' arrogation to themselves of a dominant role in the intelligence function. Content analysts have been repeatedly attacked on several grounds. Their critics have asserted that intellectual processes are too complex to be treated quantitatively, that in counting manifest symbols the content analyst disregards the nuances of meaning which can only be ascertained from the context, that content analysts naively count each symbol as having equal significance.

Perhaps in reaction to these attacks on their legitimacy, practitioners of content analysis have often gone to great lengths to prove how truly scientific they are. They have modeled their work on a prevailing ideal of what science should be.

The dominant image of science in the period since 1935, in which content analysis has been developed, is that of classical mechanics. This is not, however, the only image of science available to social scientists. Earlier social scientists often viewed their role as similar to that of naturalists; they wished to classify and document the variety of human societies and institutions. Other nineteenth century social scientists had an evolutionary image of what science was all about. They sought to formulate laws of history or trace the stages of the origins of institutions. But the dominant image today is certainly that of Galilean physics.

In this image of science, the scientist first formulates some universal proposition stating that the more (or less) of X there is, the more (or less) of Y there will be. He then performs some critical observation to prove the proposition. Needless to say, very little of social science, or for that matter natural science, fits that model. The scientist who describes in detail the steps in an adolescent's initiation into a society or the reproductive organs of a platypus is not behaving that way. Nor does the explorer, whether he is an anthropologist or ornithologist, follow that pattern. The formulator of a theoretical model, whether its elements are called ego, id, and superego, or electron, proton, and neutron, works outside the Galilean model, as does the inventor of a projective test or a laser. The world of science is a full one; it comprises many arts and devices. Nonetheless, most of the students of Lasswell, though not Lasswell himself, have valued content analysis mainly as a means to somehow approximate some externally derived image of science in their study of textual flows. For example, Richard Merritt, who has made some of the most interesting uses of content analysis in recent years, makes this methodological preference explicit:

> Ideally, the analyst formulates his hypotheses (as well as their alternatives) for testing at the onset of his project. Content analysis is useful only when the researcher has questions of a quantitative nature—how often? how much? how many? with what covariance? . . . The task of the analyst is to frame his questions so that quantitative data can answer them clearly, directly, and simply.[9]

A similar methodological preference is expressed by Robert North and his colleagues:

> The attempt to construct and rigorously to test hypotheses in the field of political science . . . has led many investigators on an intensive search for relevant and adequate data. . . .
>
> The following tentative hypothesis might he considered strictly for illustrative purposes:
>
> "If the incoming volume of messages for State A increases sharply over a brief time span, then the key decision-makers of A, as the recipients of this volume of messages, will perceive a sharp rise in hostility."[10]

Certainly, one thing that makes content analysis interesting is its usefulness in the testing of scientific hypotheses. Content analysis, because it does generate quantitative measures that arc reasonably independent of the idiosyncratic subjectivity of the observer, is a convenient observational tool for experiments designed to test hypotheses. An observational device, however, is not itself science. It may be useful for science, but an observational device that is useful in science may also be used in many other ways. Telescopes are used for recreation, for navigation, and for education, as well as for science. Content analysis also has many possible uses, including the scoring of psychological tests (e.g., for need achievement), the prediction of political behavior (e.g., in wartime intelligence), the comparison of propaganda from different sources, etc.

In some of Harold Lasswell's writings a number of different ways of thinking are distinguished for which content analysis may be relevant, but only one is, strictly speaking, scientific. Among these non-scientific modes of thought are goal (or normative) thinking, trend thinking, and projective thinking.[11]

> Many students of politics, confronted by the ambiguity of existing language, grow pessimistic about the possibility of science. Perhaps, therefore, it is worth emphasizing the point that exact methods of observation yield certain advantages now, quite apart from the contribution they may ultimately make to a highly systematic science of democracy.[12]

Among these other applications of content analysis, Lasswell, as we have already noted, rates the normative ones highly.

> The democratic ideal includes a decent regard for the opinions and sensibilities of our fellows. The moralists who have championed this ideal in the past have made no progress toward the discovery

> of methods appropriate to the understanding of the thoughts and feelings of others. The instrumentation of morals has had to await reliable methods of observation. . . . This much is clear: Whether or not the methods of scientific observation contribute to the eventual completion of a systematic science of democracy, they are certain to contribute here and now, to the practice of democratic morals.[13]

Documentation of trends by content analysis may also be useful in letting us know where we stand, but trend thinking by itself has limitations.

> While trend information is indispensable, it is not sufficient to enable us to mould the future. Trends have a way of changing direction; and often we can contribute to these changes. . . . A trend is not a cause of social change; it is a register of the relative strength of the variables that produce it.[14]

That is why scientific knowledge, if we can achieve it, is more interesting and powerful.

> The laws and propositions of science state invariant interrelations. We do not have scientific knowledge when we know, for example, that there was a trend toward world war in 1939; it is only when we can, by comparing war periods, relate war to conditioning factors that we have science. When we look toward the future our aim is not a draw of fatalistic series of trend curves. . . . To extrapolate in this way is necessary, but it is a prelude to the use of creative imagination and of available scientific knowledge in deciding how to influence the future.[15]

But for those interested in policy, like Harold Lasswell, scientific knowledge too has limitations as well as advantages. It is, for one thing, ahistorical. Scientific knowledge is a better instrument for understanding than the merely empirical reporting of trends, but it too is only an input to actions designed to change the course of history.

Lasswell's perspective is intensely historical. Time and discontinuities over time play a central role in his thinking, as they must in that of anyone concerned with policy.

> It is not enough to project scientific generalizations into the future. Scientific propositions avoid time; they treat time where it enters as a factor whose routine of interaction with other variables (at a specified magnitude) is *invariant*. . . .
>
> The mystic and the scientist share a curious ultimate bias against time.[16]

If one introduces time into one's mode of thinking along with goals, trends, and scientific uniformities, one is engaged in what Lasswell calls a "developmental construct."

> Trend and factor (scientific) thinking are requisite to projective thinking, which is concerned with future events. The question is, if we assume that no policy changes will be introduced, how will things turn out? Projective thinking is carried on by the use of developmental constructs, which we characterize as theoretical models of significant cross sections of past and future. Goals . . . are . . . points of departure for these constructs.[17]

Lasswell illustrated the notion of a developmental construct most fully in a gloomy article entitled "The Garrison State and Specialists on Violence" (1941).[18] Lasswell saw around him the collapse of the democracy which had been the focus of his value system. War, communism, and fascism were on the march. Depression seemed endemic to the democratic nations and there were fewer of them every year. The article is a strange one, for it breathes defeat on every page. For once in his life Lasswell was writing not about how to achieve the dignity of man, but rather how to adapt oneself to a society that denied it. While he starts without a commitment to a prophecy of doom, he soon admits to believing that it is the most probable course.[19]

What is this garrison state that Lasswell thought would probably overwhelm us? It is a state in which "specialists on violence are the most powerful group in society":

> The trend of our time is away from dominance of the business man, and toward the supremacy of the solider.

This trend of growing violence and growing oppression cast such a pall in 1941 that at the conclusion of his essay Lasswell did not ask how the garrison state could be prevented, but how the defeated democrats could live with it.

> It is clear that the friend of democracy views the emergence of the garrison state with repugnance and apprehension. He will do whatever is within his power to defer it. Should the garrison state become unavoidable, however, the friend of democracy will seek to conserve as many values as possible within the general framework of the new society.[20]

From the perspective of twenty-five years later this air of pessimism seems at least premature. Yet it would be hard to argue that Lasswell's construct was wrong. Whether the world is moving toward garrison states seems just as much a matter of both possibility and doubt today as it did twenty-five years ago. A quarter century has neither put the nightmare to rest nor has it confirmed it. It is certainly turning out to be true that military dictatorships are a normal mode of rule in the Third World of developing nations. There the military turn out to be the only well-organized social grouping. Even there, however, military rule seems to be a passing phase. Military dictatorships are fragile. They are ambivalent about retaining power. They are often committed to development, and as development does occur, businessmen once more come to the fore. Japan and Mexico are star examples.

In the communist world 700 million people have fallen under the veterans of the Long March and the businessmen have disappeared. But in the West the shadow of fascism has passed and the ideal of democracy is a norm more unquestioned than ever. Few indeed are the nations that are not a little ashamed of their departures from democracy. They try to deny them in their propaganda even if they do not change.

In Western democracies, however, arms budgets grow ever larger, though not as a steadily growing percentage of the gross national product. That varies. Nuclear weapons, hardly dreamed of in 1941, are with us. Defense plays an unprecedented part in our politics. Yet a businessman from a motor company has defeated the military establishment of the world's greatest military power, which is also the world's greatest democracy, and has made the military carry on their planning in a strictly businesslike style.

It is hard indeed to judge Lasswell's article on the garrison state even with our advantage of a quarter century of hindsight. For our purpose here, however, it is not necessary to judge it. We cite it as the clearest example of what Lasswell means by a developmental construct.

It was that time-related historical concept that lay behind both of Lasswell's largest efforts in content analysis: the Library of Congress studies during World War II and the RADIR studies. Both programs made more than a passing effort to contribute to generalizing science, but they were also efforts to contribute to policy by recording and exposing developmental trends in values and ideology in the modern world.[21]

The Library of Congress effort was what Harold Lasswell called a "World Attention Survey."[22] It attempted to plot what changes were taking place in the press of the major nations in their awareness of and attitudes toward other nations and major political symbols. The most basic categories were favorable (plus) and unfavorable (minus) treatment of self and other. These are as fundamental a set of political categories as exist. They can be, and were, elaborated further, but there is a lot to be learned simply from documenting who is becoming more (or less) plus or minus toward whom around the world. These are facts that every diplomat, journalist, and politician intuitively keeps track of. There is much to be gained by compiling systematic, verified knowledge of them.

The Library of Congress study was in substantial part an intelligence effort. It was designed to improve our understanding of the political dynamics of various countries around the world, including the German enemy, third countries, and also ourselves. As an intelligence operation it was not particularly successful. It was operating beyond the state of the art, and as a result it contributed far more to content analysis methodology than to substantive understanding of the enemy at that time. In a parallel effort going on at the same time in the Foreign Broadcast Intelligence Service more intuitive methods of content analysis were being used, with considerable success, to anticipate German actions. These were complementary rather than competing efforts and we have learned a lot from both. The lessons of the FBIS effort have been thoroughly analyzed and evaluated by Alexander George in his book on propaganda analysis for intelligence purposes.[23] George demonstrates that at that time the efforts of the FBIS to use formal quantitative methods were unfruitful. The technology available did not permit flexibility in considering propaganda strategy and in evaluating the varied importance of statements in different contexts if much quantification was to be done. Quantification required rather mechanical simplifications that defeated the intelligence objectives.

It should be added that in 1969 this is no longer necessarily true. The possibility of keypunching text into computer-readable form and of retrieving and regrouping material in an interactive mode might lead to very different conclusions if an effort were made today similar to the 1940s one that George evaluated. The value of the Library of Congress experiment in advancing our understanding of the fundamental problems of statistical analysis of meanings would then be apparent.

The RADIR project (Revolution and the Development of International Relations) undertaken at the Hoover Institution from 1948 to 1953 was also a world attention survey, but this time for a sixty-year period, 1890–1950. The purpose was to document a developmental construct labeled "The World Revolution of Our Time." Newspaper editorials from prestige papers in five countries were examined to ascertain the rise and fall of major political concepts, particularly those pertaining to democracy and authoritarianism, violence and peace, and self and other (i.e., identity).

This time a good deal did emerge that clarified the development of the ideologies of our times. In the democratic powers, the vanishing of the conservative symbols of order and authority was documented and dated. The decline of symbols of Marxist ideology in favor of an ordinary plebeian nationalist symbolism in the Soviet Union continued through the various zigs and zags of the Communist Party line. Everywhere democracy was less often interpreted in terms of rights and freedoms and more often interpreted in terms of mass participation. In America the focus on violence increased. For historians, if they learned to use the new, more precise methods of observation that modern social science permits, the data was rich.

In another of its aspirations, however, the RADIR project did not succeed. The results never became relevant to policy. The designers of the project certainly thought that they were clarifying the central issues of our time, around which the great battles of national policy were being fought. It was no accident that one of the by-products of the RADIR project was a volume called *The Policy Sciences.*[24] It is also no accident that while the volume contained much excellent social science, there was little about policy in it.

As one of those chiefly involved in the RADIR project, I think I may fairly say that however much we were committed to policy relevance, we did not, at that time, understand what that would demand of the research. The policymaker is not satisfied with being told that the total focus of society on violence is increasing, though he might find the fact (if it is a fact) interesting and disturbing. He certainly wants to know things like how to control riots in specific neighborhoods of thirteen cities during three months of the year. Even if we had understood how far our work fell short of policy relevance, however, there was nothing we could have done about it. The technology then available to us precluded anything but a highly generalized, broad-sweep approach to a sixty-year content analysis. This was not obvious at first because the RADIR project generated much data about specific issues, times, and places. We recorded 105,000 instances of occurrence of 416 symbols in some 20,000 editorials from five countries over a sixty-year period. The data were there for very pinpointed analyses. What we lacked was the computational power to make more than a very few analyses of all that data. The data were recorded on manual cards. Nor would it have solved the problem if they had been on IBM cards, for at that time the cards would have had to be analyzed by unit-record equipment As the RADIR reports pointed out, the structure of language does not lend itself to unit-record file organization. Language is above all relational. The important thing about a symbol is the context of other symbols in which it occurs—which symbols precede it and which follow it.

The point may be illustrated by one of the more interesting results of the RADIR studies concerning the symbol "democracy." There is a widespread view that the word has been a fad. Politicians, regardless of their true ideology, so it is said, label their convictions democratic. But in fact we found that, in general, the use of the symbol "democracy" increased as a function of the total set of symbols representing its subject matter. It was not a fad of the word but a genuine shift of attention to the subject matter of democracy that was taking place in the world revolution of our time.

The introduction to the report of the RADIR symbol studies by Lasswell and associates stated the hope that the evolution of the computer, then just appearing on the horizon, would provide the key to the solution of the problem of quantitative analysis of language, and indeed it has done that.[25] Until that happened, after the end of the RADIR project, there was about a ten-year hiatus in the further development of content analysis for the intelligence function. Content analysis continued to be pursued for limited purposes, usually for the testing of well-defined hypotheses. David McClelland's development of a system for scoring need achievement in stories is an example. But the use of content analysis as a broad social indicator had to await the development of the computer.

The situation is now ripe for a revival of the insight that Harold Lasswell had a quarter of a century ago. In the first place, there is a renewed search for social indicators. Raymond Bauer's book on the subject, an outgrowth of a project of the American Academy of Arts and Sciences, illustrates that widening interest.[26] The growth of programs to accomplish stated national social goals, such as the poverty program and the civil rights program, have made us aware of how meager are our tools for observing the state of society and of changes in it (outside the fields of economics and demography, where published series of indicators have been with us for some time). Similar series are needed to tell us where we stand with regard to other social and political values, such as respect and enlightenment. For years Lasswell has been calling for the development of observational devices to provide intelligence about social and political trends. His plea is now being widely taken up. Thus, a receptive audience exists for a revival of attention surveys.

A second emerging condition for the success of such efforts is the development of structural linguistics. Counting the presence or absence of symbols was always recognized as too simple a method of content analysis to tap trends in meaning. Computational requirements, however, led to severe limitations on the recording of context. From the very beginning of his work on content analysis Lasswell insisted on at least coding each symbol with a pro or contra attitudinal indicator.[27] Much more complicated tagging of symbols to take account of the structures that determine their significance is possible with modern computational equipment, once one understands what options are provided by the structure of language. In recent years, the linguists, particularly the psycholinguists, have had to cope with many of the same problems as content analysts. The progress that the linguists have made permits the conduct of much more meaningful content analyses than in the past.[28]

The third and most critical condition for the revival of content analysis for intelligence purposes has been the development of the computer. There are already numerous computer applications for processing text. Computers are used for making concordances and indexes, for example. They are also used extensively in linguistic research. The main technological requirements are (1) that the computer have a large, readily accessible bulk memory in which to store considerable bodies of text; (2) that the analyst have available a list or string language in which to work so that he can readily process the complex relational data of language; and (3) that the system be interactive and on-line so that the analyst can explore the stored text intelligently, step by step, instead of being swamped by data.

The first major program to take advantage of the potential of the computer for content analysis is reported in Philip Stone's *General Inquirer.*[29] In his preface to the recent volume in which Stone describes this program and the work done with it to date, Lasswell notes that the tedium of hand content analysis had driven most practitioners from the field after a try or two. The *General Inquirer* has brought creative scholars back into the field. Almost all the significant work in content analysis in the past five years, such as the work of Robert North and his colleagues at Stanford, has used the *General Inquirer.* As it exists today, this instrument is not yet what is needed for a world attention survey or other intelligence application requiring the rapid processing of very large bodies of text. The *General Inquirer* was designed for use with moderate-sized bodies of text. It takes a fair amount of processing of the natural language text, and it is not optimized for rapid search over very large memories. It was designed for other purposes such as the efficient creation of dictionaries of key symbols and the close analysis of rich textual material. But whatever else it does, or does not do, the *General Inquirer* points out the path and demonstrates the feasibility of computerized content analysis.

What is feasible, however, is not necessarily useful. The standard answer of mountain climbers when asked why they climb high peaks is "because they are there." This is not a good enough reason for engaging in content analysis. The fact that propaganda, editorials, speeches, and political material of all sorts is poured out in the public media does not per se make it useful to subject these materials to quantitative measurement of what is in them and how that changes.

Yet it would be useful. One of the greatest problems facing policy-makers is the vast flow of unprocessed information that pours past them. Every day the State Department receives about 2,000 cables from abroad. Every day the Foreign Broadcast Intelligence Service records and transcribes the news and public affairs programs broadcast by hundreds of radio stations around the world. Every day politicians, intelligence analysts, and public servants comb newspaper columns and editorials from places of interest looking for clues to reactions to events by various wings and parties of opinion.

No doubt computerized processing and analysis of this flood of material is no panacea. Trivial and irrelevant material can be analyzed to no avail. Clumsy and irrelevant systems can easily be produced. Indeed, at this early stage of development of information-processing techniques, numerous examples of poorly designed systems can be found. Yet the future expansion of computerized text-processing systems is certain, for there is so much potential in them for doing what is useful.

Consider, for example, the present techniques of Kremlinologists and others who attempt to decipher Aesopian communication. Normally, they draw their conclusions from spotting sudden anomalies in the flow of statements. How much better off they would be if they had some way of verifying the impression that the formula spotted is new, or, if it is not new, if they had some way of knowing where it had occurred before. Or consider the intelligence analyst trying to assess attitudes in some other country toward the United States. How much better off he would be if he could mechanically scan and summarize all sources on any given topic at several points in time in a matter of minutes rather than being confined to hunches prompted by a dramatic example or two.

The standard book on content analysis for intelligence purposes tends to deny this apparently obvious conclusion. Alexander George examined the wartime analyses of German radio propaganda to ascertain what clues and methods yielded valid inferences about German intentions. His judgment was that systematic quantitative content analysis yielded little. Sensitive human analysts, who looked for little anomalies which they could not have defined in advance and which depended heavily on context, yielded a lot.

However, George was pitting a clumsy and now outmoded content analysis technique against the intuitive skill of the analyst.[30] Note that content analysis as George evaluated it required that the system of analysis and its categories be fixed in advance and carried on uniformly, regardless of the question put by the analyst. It was this lack of flexible adaptability to the needs of a complex inference structure that George identified as the weakness of quantitative content analysis in World War II intelligence. A modern, computerized retrieval and analysis system would, however, have all the texts in bulk memory and would produce rapid scanning and analysis of them *after* the analyst had come up with a question generated by his intuitive processes. The question and the mode of analysis would be specific and pinpointed to the particular phenomenon that had attracted the analyst's attention. For example, if a World War II analyst noted that a highly prestigious newscaster minimized territorial gain one evening, the analyst might conclude that this man, being close to men of power, was reflecting a policy decision not to press for further expensive advances along the front. But to defend this hunch the analyst would first want to validate his impression that this was a new theme for this news-caster and for newscasters in general, and he would want to do so the same day. Full-time analysts who immerse themselves in a particular subject matter are pretty good at such scanning. Aided by a computerized retrieval and analysis system they could be better.

Whether the initial clue is provided by an anomaly in a systematic time series of a social indicator or by the subtle insight of an experienced observer, George is undoubtedly right in saying that the evaluation of this hunch requires subtle inference processes that are too varied and complex to be preplanned. What has changed, however, is that quantitative content analysis no longer needs to have a rigid, preplanned character.

Thus, the future of content analysis lies, as Lasswell realized from the beginning, in very broad uses in the intelligence function, not just in its occasional use by social scientists for testing general propositions.

In a number of articles Lasswell has described the intelligence function.

> The term "intelligence" refers to the stream of fact and comment upon which choices are based. . . . (The term has dropped out of use in recent decades; save in military circles. We revive the word in order to characterize the communications important to policy.)[31]
>
> When we examine the decision process of any body politic . . . it is usually possible to describe the structures specialized to a function. At the Federal level we think at once of the Central Intelligence Agency, the Bureau of the Census, and the like, when we consider the intelligence function.[32]

In closing, let us examine the intelligence function for public policy as it is organized today to determine where content analysis is relevant to it.

There are three main professions which specialize in enlightening the decision maker so that he can act with humanity and judgment. These professions are social scientist, journalist, and government intelligence operative. While mutual recriminations and institutional jealousies may make their allied activities seem remote from each other, these groups actually blend imperceptibly with one another and would gain from bridging their barriers.

What distinguishes social scientists from the other two groups is their interest in the general. Both the reporter and the CIA agent are devoted to the idea that names, dates, and places make news, while the social scientist typically suppresses all such information as raw data. But it is only necessary to state such an ideal-type distinction to recognize how frequently it departs from reality. Political scientists publish case studies. Clearly, these are also journalism. The kind of social scientist who writes for organs like *Foreign Affairs* is very much concerned with names, dates, and places, as is the historical scholar. On the other hand, occasional journalists—such as Walter Lippmann, Harold Isaacs, or Douglas Cater write studies which are outstanding contributions to social science. Walter Lippmann's *Public Opinion,* published in 1922, has yet to be supplanted in the social science literature.

Governmental intelligence operatives are different from the other two groups in that they give their analyses directly to the policy maker rather than publishing them. This too, however, is only an ideal-type distinction, not one which fits reality. The Foreign Broadcast Intelligence Service publishes hundreds of pages a day of transcriptions of political broadcasts from around the world. For the serious student of public affairs these constitute one of the main worldwide sources of public information. On the other hand, social scientists are increasingly employed in staff roles in both business and government, where their analyses and recommendations serve the decision maker directly. Contract research organizations are increasingly commissioned to provide scientific inputs for enlightened decision making in such fields as market research, city planning, strategy, and so on.

There is, of course, an elementary moral issue. The respondent or informant should be told the truth about whether his individual inputs will be identified and published. He is aggrieved if information he gave as confidential appears in the public press, and he is equally aggrieved if information he gave on the assumption that it would be published for the scientific community as a whole ends up in a private report for one party. So long as social scientists adhere to the simple standard of candor with their informants, no useful purpose is served by taboos that attempt to confine artificially, within three highly artificial ideal types, the many ways of putting information to use on behalf of human welfare.

On the contrary, the natural and desirable trend is toward the increasing use of social science in both journalism and governmental intelligence. The great human triumph of our age is science. The power of scientific method has made its impact felt with revolutionary consequences in field after field. The consequences in warfare are horrifying because this great folly of the human species has been made so satanically effective. But the revolution wrought by the application of science has been just as great in more desirable human activities. The healing of the sick has become an art completely dominated by science. Communication has been revolutionized by science. So has construction. Field after held of practical activities that used to be pursued by independent craftsmen can now be pursued only with the guidance of scientifically educated professionals.

The same take-over by science is only beginning in the social field, but it will happen. Consider the trend in journalism. Increasingly, the town-crier function of rapid dissemination of spot news is being taken over from the press by electronic media. More and more the newspaper becomes a reference resource that offers the opportunity of exploring specialized interests in greater depth than the electronic media permit. Three sections of the paper have already become highly technical, namely, the business page, the weather report, and the sports page. These contain large quantities of sophisticated statistics. In the political news, the newspaper reporting of public opinion polls is the first evidence of the likely trend. Social science and psychological research is increasingly used and misused as news. Sooner or later, as social science explanations become more powerful, the regular reporting of significant social indicators may be expected. Content analysis, for example, may provide summary statistics on trends in publicly expressed attitudes and beliefs around the world. Newspapers might report on themselves. Even now some newspapers do run world press roundups which give short quotations from various other newspapers expressing different views. A quantitative summary analysis of the content of the world press based on a representative sample might be a more significant piece of news. Such technical reporting will come, however, only as social science proves its explanatory power. That will happen, but not quickly.

In the same way, the governmental intelligence function is likely to be increasingly infused with social science. Up to now "the intelligence community," as it calls itself, has tended to be negative toward the social sciences other than economics. Collecting economic statistics and making economic projections for foreign countries are part of the standard work of the intelligence agency of any major power. But social research in other fields has never become a recognized portion of the program of intelligence agencies such as the CIA and is relatively trivial in quantity. Intelligence is still the domain of historians whose focus on names and dates and particulars is congenial to the intelligence community. If it could be done, an elite analysis of the CIA might, I suspect, confirm the continued reliance on historians and very minimal use of behavioral scientists. One can hope, however, that this is a passing phase. The growing power of the behavioral sciences will force the intelligence community to modify its archaic image of itself as "old area hands" and to accept behavioral scientists, as it has now accepted economists and electronic engineers.

A central problem for government intelligence agencies is the vast mass of material which they have to process. In addition to the State Department's 2,000 cables a day, the world press runs to thousands of pages. Radio-monitoring reports add to that flow. Systems for retrieval and analysis of this large mass of content can clearly serve to enable the decision maker to act with the judgment and knowledge that this large collection of information makes potentially possible.

There are those in the academic social science community who would like to deny that their activity has anything to do with the process of providing enlightenment to public policymakers. It is hard to understand why any scholar would be unsympathetic to processes of disseminating enlightenment, but scholars too are part of society and are subject to its pressures and hysterias. At the moment of writing the United States is going through one of those periodic waves of anti-intellectual hysteria which plague our society. In each of these waves certain patterns of political behavior recur. One of these is that intellectuals who have purported to be defenders of high moral values are "exposed" by demagogues as really part of a secret conspiracy with satanic forces of evil. The wave of exposure spreads guilt by association to ever larger circles, and the wickedness of the original secret plotters becomes axiomatic. Displaced onto public objects, this fantasy seems to tap very deep feelings in the American man on the street. It relieves his guilt about people who have been urging undesired moral imperatives upon him. It helps him deny his own involvements with movements and organizations that have proved less than perfect. It cuts down the intellectuals to whom he feels inferior. Whether the attacks are directed at anarchosyndicalists as in the 1920s, or communists as in the 1950s, or the CIA as in the 1960s, they provide agitators like Joseph McCarthy and *Ramparts* with a wide and expandable list of targets. It is not surprising that many honest but fearful scholars seek immunity by protesting that they have no contact with or resemblance to the supposed secret conspirators.

Fortunately, these mass neuroses are passing waves, though each leaves its residue of damage behind. There is no reason to doubt that in the long run the process of providing accurate and complete information to government policymakers will be recognized as an honorable role which contributes to peace and the humanity of governance. There is no reason to doubt that social scientists will proudly recognize that one of their great contributions to society is the improvement of the governmental intelligence process.

It is certain that arms races and wars grow out of situations where incomplete knowledge about the plans and preparations of potential opponents cause exaggerated fears and excessive defensive reactions. Secrecy in the modern world is generally a destabilizing factor. Nothing contributes more to peace and stability than those activities of electronic and photographic eavesdropping, of content analysis and textual interpretation, that have at great cost and effort opened up those nations to realistic assessment who for misguided considerations of short-run advantages have tried to place a curtain of secrecy around themselves.

Once it has been conceded that enlightenment of rulers is a good thing, and that excellent intelligence is likely to make governance more humane, the dilemma of privacy presents itself. This is not particularly a problem stemming from international research and intelligence, for there is little justification in a democratic world for protecting the privacy of rulers. The acute dilemma for social scientists is choosing between the social value of disseminating knowledge widely and the personal value of individual privacy. This dilemma appears in much of Lasswell's writing about the intelligence function. In an essay written in 1943 entitled "Legal Education and Public Policy" he wrote:

> The realism of the decisions made by the officers or members of any organization depend in no small measure on the quality of the intelligence that reaches them. . . . One requirement for an adequate stream of intelligence is disclosure of source. . . . Besides the disclosure of source, positive means of obtaining access to the media of communication are essential. . . . Still a third aspect of the intelligence function is access to facts that interested parties try to conceal.[33]

In 1957, after the phenomenon of McCarthy, Lasswell qualified this view in another essay, "The Normative Impact of the Behavioral Sciences": "By this time, however, I think we have accumulated enough experience to recognize that it is wiser to forego some kinds of knowledge, and to bear the resulting cost, than to break down the barriers to privacy under some circumstances."[34]

On the whole, the lesson of the social sciences seems to be that we must all learn to live with a much higher degree of exposure than earlier, less knowledge-oriented societies tolerated. Psychological and psychoanalytic techniques are modes of revealing the innermost recesses of ourselves. Sociological research, political research, the press, personnel systems, are all ways of making us individually and collectively more conscious of each other. Yet there are and must be limits. This is not the place to explore the question of the limitations we must impose on ourselves as scientists out of respect for the humanity of our subjects. They are clearly many and complex. Yet even more important in the long run, in a world in which science is making knowledge increasingly available, is to learn to live with knowledge.

If social science has exposed us all to the glare of new kinds of observation, it has also given us a new appreciation of the foibles of the human condition. If psychology has exposed us all, it has also perhaps made it possible for us to be more tolerant and appreciative of what is exposed. Perhaps much of the answer to the dilemma of privacy posed by the social sciences is the capacity for greater tolerance that the social sciences also teach. These sciences help us live with each other as we really are.

Content analysis poses the dilemma of privacy less acutely than do most social science techniques of observation. One of its advantages is that it is not intrusive. The analysis of texts that are already parts of an established record is less disturbing to the persons who are the sources than those techniques that require face-to-face disclosures. The social sciences will be increasingly asked to provide social indicators that measure unintrusively the normal flow of human behavior. Content analysis is one of the techniques for doing this.

Notes

1. Note such typical titles in the bibliography of Lasswell's writings as: "The normative impact of the behavioral sciences," "Clarifying value judgments: Principals of content and procedure," and "The developing science of democracy: How to integrate science, morals, and politics."
2. *The language of politics* (originally published in 1949), Cambridge: Massachusetts Institute of Technology Press, 1963, p. 51.
3. Ostrogorski traces the modern pressure group to the Wilkes riots and petitions in 1768. The prevalent view at that time, stated by Horace Walpole, was that the formation of committees that arrogate "a right of considering and deciding on questions pending in Parliament and of censuring or approving the part taken by particular members" was a challenge to the authority of the Parliament, the institution set up precisely for the purpose of discussing what public policy ought to be. Voluntary associations were thought to be unconstitutional and to constitute a "dual power," as Lenin accurately designated them. M. Ostrogorski, *Democracy and the organization of political parties.* New York: Macmillan, 1902, pp. 121–22.
4. L. D. White, ed., *The future of government in the United States: Essays in honor of Charles E. Merriam.* Chicago: University of Chicago Press, 1942; reprinted in H. D. Lasswell. *The analysis of political behavior.* New York: Oxford University Press, 1947, p. 1.
5. "The relation of ideological intelligence to public policy." *Ethics,* 53 (1942): 27; reprinted in Lasswell, *Analysis of political behavior.* New York: Oxford University Press, 1947, p. 122.
6. Ibid.
7. Lasswell, *Language of politics,* p. 51.

8. Harold D. Lasswell, *The decision process: Seven categories of functional analysis.* College Park: University of Maryland Press, 1956.
9. Richard L. Merritt, "The representational model in gross-national content analysis." In Joseph L. Bernd, ed., *Mathematical applications in political science II.* Dallas, TX: Southern Methodist University Press, 1966, p. 46.
10. Robert C. North, Ole R. Holsti, M. George Zaninovich, and Dina A. Zinnes, *Content analysis.* Evanston, IL: Northwestern University Press, 1963, p. 28.
11. Harold D. Lasswell, "Clarifying value judgment: Principles of content and procedure" *Inquiry,* I (1958):94–95.
12. Lasswell, "Developing science of democracy," p. 11.
13. Ibid., pp. 11–12.
14. Ibid., p. 32.
15. Ibid., pp. 32–33.
16. Lasswell, "Clarifying value judgment," p. 95.
17. Ibid.
18. *American Journal of Sociology,* 46 (1941):455–68.
19. He starts out by saying only that the purpose of his article is to consider the possibility that we are moving toward a world of "garrison states," but he then goes on to say: "The picture of the garrison state that is offered here is not a dogmatic forecast. Rather it is a picture of the probable."
20. Lasswell, *Analysis of political behavior,* p. 155.
21. There is a passing point to be made of some psychological interest. Timeless generalizing science is a young man's game. (*Vide* the power of the young in physics and mathematics.) Understanding time and development takes a more mature kind of wisdom. In his forties, Lasswell had development concepts very much in mind as he framed the design of both the Library of Congress project and the RADIR project. As a young man associated peripherally with the one and centrally with the other, I found real excitement only in the scientific generalizing aspects of these studies and bent my own contributions in that direction, looking for essentially timeless models of symbol interaction (see my quantitative model of communist reaction to defeats in *Language of politics* and my model of verbal reactions of nations to each other in *Symbols of internationalism.* Stanford. CA: Stanford University Press, 1951). Now, a decade and a half later, Lasswell's strategy has become far more understandable and congenial to me.
22. Harold D. Lasswell, "World attention survey." *Public Opinion Quarterly,* 5 (1941), 456–62.
23. Alexander L. George, *Propaganda analysis.* Evanston, IL: Row Peterson and Co., 1959.
24. Harold Lasswell and Daniel Lerner, eds., *The policy sciences.* Stanford, CA: Stanford University Press, 1951.
25. H. D. Lasswell, D. Lerner, and I. Pool, *The comparative study of symbols: An introduction.* Stanford, CA: Stanford University Press, 1952, p. 63.
26. Raymond A. Bauer, *Social indicators.* Cambridge: Massachusetts Institute of Technology Press, 1966.
27. "A provisional classification of symbol data." *Psychiatry,* 1 (1938): 197–204.
28. The recognition of the possibility of fruitful interaction between content analysis and linguistics stems from the Social Science Research Council's Committee on Psycholinguistics. The results of these deliberations are

reported in I. Pool, ed., *Trends in content analysis.* Urbana: University of Illinois Press, 1959.

29. Philip Stone, *General inquirer.* Cambridge: Massachusetts Institute of Technology Press, 1966.
30. George, *Propaganda analysis.*
31. "Stabilization technique and patterns of expectation." In M.F. Millikan, ed., *Income stabilization for a developing democracy.* New Haven, CT: Yale University Press, 1953, p. 633.
32. Lasswell, *The decision process.*
33. In *Analysis of political behavior,* p. 78.
34. *Ethics,* 67 (1957): 35.

3

Scratches on Social Science: Images, Symbols, and Stereotypes

Occasionally in science different disciplines using different jargons develop equivalent theories unbeknownst to each other. Long periods may pass before their equivalence is recognized.[1] Sigmund Freud on symbols, Walter Lippmann on stereotypes, Robert Abelson on balance theory, and Harold Isaacs on images have, each in their way, covered common ground. Though stemming from different disciplines and documented by different evidence, their findings nonetheless converge. All four writers examine those simplified representations that people use to order their perceptions of the buzzing confusion of empirical reality around them.

Each of the four treatments recognizes that the representations in any individual's head are related by an associative logic which does not meet the test of veridical proof. These representations in an individual's head are acquired by him early and are held tenaciously against empirical challenge.

The representations are essentially visual and descriptive; the words to refer to them are nouns, not verbs; their referents can be seen in the mind's eye with portrayable features or traits. The representations are also emotionally charged and heavily value-laden; there are among them, representations of "the good guys" and "the bad guys." The representations often come in pairs of terms both of which, by any semantic definition, refer to the same thing (e.g., courage and foolhardiness, patriotism and chauvinism, British subject or limey). Such representations of the same referent by a pair of alternative terms allow the pseudo-logic in the subject's head to be maintained.

From *The Mixing of Peoples: Problems of Identity and Ethnicity* (1976), edited by Robert I. Rotberg.

The benign element and the malevolent element can alternatively be elicited when required to represent different feelings about the same semantic meaning.

The representations which a person chooses to use, and also how he values and characterizes them, serve to define his own identity. Many of the most important representations are themselves names of organized groups or unorganized plurals of persons to which an individual may belong or from which he is excluded. Others are associatively linked to such groups or plurals. A person's sense of his identity is expressed by how he positions himself for or against these emotionally charged, group-linked representations.

We have in the above few paragraphs tried to describe the common domain among four writers, and to do so using a fifth jargon, neutral among them. The word "representation" in the last paragraphs, wherever it occurred, could have been replaced by "symbol" or "stereotype" or "image." The paragraphs would then, with other appropriate changes of language, describe at least a part of the theories of some one of the authors whose parallel writings we are describing. Let us take up the parallel theories of these four writers in a chronological sequence.

Freud developed his analysis of symbolism most fully in the *Interpretation of Dreams* (1900). But, as Freud said in 1925: "Many of the things that we study in dreams. . . . have little or nothing to do with the psychological peculiarity of dreams. Thus, for instance, symbolism is not a dream-problem, but a topic connected with our archaic thinking. . . . It dominates myths and religious ritual no less than dreams."[2]

The symbols that Freud dealt with refer mainly to the body, to sex, and to close personal relations. It is such symbols that occupy his interpretation of dreams. Only rarely does he discuss symbols that deal with ideology or national or group identity, but occasionally he does. Thus, where he talks of his own Jewish identity and his youthful reactions to anti-Semitism, he tells us how Hannibal (the Semite) and Rome "symbolized" for him "the tenacity of Jewry and the organization of the Catholic Church."[3] "I began to understand for the first time what it meant to belong to an alien race. . . . The figure of the Semitic general rose still higher in my esteem."

In orthodox Freudian jargon one distinguishes the "symbols" in a dream from other entities in the dream to which the patient associates via his own unique experiences. Symbolism, as Freud used the term, refers to what he believed to be "a fragment of extremely ancient inherited mental equipment."[4] It was part of a common human language, and when a symbol appeared in a dream the patient could usually provide no associations to it. Nonetheless, much of what Freud says about symbolization may help us understand the broader processes of representation by an image, whether that image is a culturally shared one which Freud calls a symbol or an individualized representation that grows out of private experience.

Symbolic thinking, Freudian analysis tells us, is vague and prelogical. It is a method of distortion. The conscious symbol is used to hide an objectionable, unconscious idea. "The censoring ego uses regressive methods. In dreams, symbols appear . . . as a tool of the dream censorship and also as . . . archaic pictorial thinking, as part of visualizing abstract thoughts."[5]

Thus, symbolization is one of the methods of defense by which humans structure their perception of the world into an orderly and acceptable one. Symbolization operates in conjunction with a large family of defense mechanisms which people use to ward off impulses and perceptions that threaten their egos. One of these defense mechanisms is isolation. Aspects of the self which confound each other are separated intellectually to avoid confrontation. The soldier's professional killing or the businessman's professional seeking of gain is isolated as a professional role from the same man's perception of his personal moral character as a loving friend or altruistic philanthropist. One "type of isolation is represented by attempts to solve conflicts around ambivalence—that is, conflicts between love and hatred of the same person—by splitting the contradictory feelings so that one person is only loved, another one only hated. . . . An example is the contrast of the good mother and the wicked stepmother in fairy tales."[6] Thus symbols tend to be pure in their affect. They live in a dream world where the "good guys" do only good and the "bad guys" do only bad. There are no symbols for the moral ambiguity of reality.

Walter Lippmann's *Public Opinion* appeared in 1922, nine years after the first English translation of *The Interpretation of Dreams.* In his closing summation of Part 3, "Stereotypes," Lippmann cites Freud's book:[7]

> Our access to information is obstructed and uncertain and . . . our apprehension is deeply controlled by our stereotypes . . . the evidence available to our reason is subject to illusions of defense, prestige, morality, space, and sampling. . . . In a series of events seen mostly through stereotypes, we readily accept sequence parallelism as equivalent to cause and effect.

> This is most likely to happen when two ideas that come together arouse the same feeling. If they come together they are likely to arouse the same feeling; and even when they do not arrive together a powerful feeling attached to one is likely to suck out of all the corners of memory any idea that feels about the same. Thus everything painful tends to collect into one system of cause and effect, likewise everything pleasant.
>
> In hating one thing violently, we readily associate with it as cause or effect most of the other things we hate or fear violently. They may have no more connection than smallpox and alehouses, or Relativity and Bolshevism, but they are bound together in the same emotion. . . . Emotion is a stream of molten lava which catches and imbeds whatever it touches. When you excavate in it you find, as in a buried city, all sorts of objects ludicrously entangled in each other. Anything can be related to anything else, provided it feels like it. . . . Ancient fears, reinforced by more recent fears, coagulate into a snarl of fears where anything that is dreaded is the cause of anything else that is dreaded.
>
> Generally it all culminates in the fabrication of a system of all evil, and of another which is the system of good. Then our love of the absolute shows itself. For we do not like qualifying adverbs.

Lippmann, the literary American writer, refers to emotions as "a stream of molten lava"; Freud, the philosophical German, talks of them as "the id." The literary American uses the metaphor of digging in a buried city wherein objects are ludicrously entangled. The philosophical German designates the same process by such technical phrases as "free association" and "exploration of the unconscious." Freud coined a jargon; Lippman talks about symbols in symbols.

In some important respects, what Lippmann describes as "stereotypes" are a generalization from, rather than a synonym for, Freudian symbols. They refer to public affairs rather than to intimate ones. Their meaning is only occasionally and marginally hermeneutic. The "Hun" may have been a stereotype of Germans in the era when Lippmann wrote, but there was little mystery to be unveiled in that symbolism. What was meant required no free-association to bring it out; it was mostly on the surface. True, there is an element of inexplicitness. There are connotations of the metaphor that are not spelled out. Huns, we understand, are barbarian, ruthless, and cruel. But then, perhaps they may also be thought of as heathen, strong, ugly, illiterate, or successful. Many of these other traits carried over into some 1920s images of Germans, but which ones did so may differ from speaker to speaker. There is a layer of hidden meaning that only probing can bring out. Nonetheless the hidden meaning in stereotypes is shallow compared with that in the symbols in the Freudian language of dreams. Lippmann applies the shared theory of representations to a language of public discourse in civic affairs not to a hidden language of the unconscious.

Lippmann stresses that stereotypes are crude and inaccurate, short on detail, and dominated by conventional cliches. Sunsets are portrayed as red, which few sunsets are. An Italian dish is noted for garlic, only one of its ingredients. Lippmann is normative about all this. Stereotyping is not only a feature of cognitive processes empirically noted by him, but rather an abuse of thinking that makes the achievement of civic rationality difficult. Stereotypes are not only a necessary element in thought, but also a fault of uninformed, unsophisticated, irrational men. They are found among the ignorant masses more than among the thoughtful intelligentsia.

We have overstated the case. Lippmann understood that in the economy of human thinking the use of simplified images is inevitable. Stereotyping, he recognized, is not confined to prejudiced or thoughtless men. "The attempt to see all things freshly and in detail, rather than as types and generalities, is exhausting, and among busy affairs practically out of the question" (59). Yet in emphasis, Lippmann clearly perceived stereotypes as abuses. The main thesis of *Public Opinion* presumes that. The thesis is that for democracy to work, mass opinion must be raised from its defective ordinary functioning by the rational educative efforts of an intelligent, organized elite of political scientists.

Lippmann belongs to a class of writers, including Alexis de Tocqueville, M. Ostrogorski, Roberto Michels, Vilfredo Pareto, Gaetano Mosca, Max Weber, and Bernard Berelson, who may be called realistic critics of democratic theory. All of them held up Rousseauean democratic ideals against the empirical facts of democratic practice and found the theory wanting. The theory postulated that publicly minded citizens would inform themselves about issues and then vote for what they perceived to be the common good. The empiricists easily showed that most citizens were more self-interested than publicly minded; that most knew what they wanted first, and then sought rationalizations for it; and that only the few participated on most issues. One conclusion, Mosca's, for example, was to dismiss democracy as a pious fraud. Another conclusion, Lippmann's, was to seek a means to bring the reality closer to the ideal. Lippmann's purpose was to find ways to improve the quality of public life, to reduce the stereotypic element in public affairs thinking and to make it more objective, more publicly minded, and more rational.

Stereotypes are thus, for Lippmann, unfortunate simplifications even if to some degree inevitable. They are linked to each other by obscure associations. They provide a handy but inaccurate map of the social world. Furthermore, one of their defects is their fixity. A stereotype, once held, is not readily abandoned. Instead of re-evaluating at each moment the changing facts of the real world, people selectively perceive an event (e.g., the redness of the sunset), shaping the observation to the salient features of a pre-established stereotype.

There is another reason, too, Lippmann argues, "besides economy of effort, why we so often hold to our stereotypes when we might pursue a more disinterested vision. The systems of stereotypes may be the core of our personal tradition, the defenses of our position in society" (63). Stereotypes are what Lasswell called "symbols of identification."[8] Most stereotypes can be positioned in society's ethnic and status structure. The British butler, the hardhat construction worker, the hippie student, the *kolkhoznik* tractor-driving girl, are all stereotypes that belong somewhere in a population of the mind's world. And the self belongs somewhere in that world, too. Where one fits in it is symbolized by hairstyle, the clothes that one wears, the car that one chooses, the accent of one's voice.

In the decades of the 1920s and 1930s, it was in the literature on ethnicity that Lippmann's coinage, "stereotype" took hold as part of the common language. It is now a word that most well-educated high school students know. If you ask one of them to define it, more often than not, he will tell you that stereotyping is a way of talking about ethnic groups; that it refers to the fallacy of assuming that all members of an ethnic group have a common trait—usually a trait that excites derision. Lippmann used the concept more broadly, but that ethnic use of the word as a special case is true to his analysis.

It would be natural, in the context of a discussion of ethnic stereotypes, to turn directly to Harold Isaacs' work, for in recent decades that is what he has written about. However, as we are proceeding chronologically, there is another major treatment of representations which we cannot omit: that found in balance theory.

The formulation of balance theory came from Fritz Heider in 1946.[9] Its outstanding current exponent and elaborator is Robert Abelson. The most basic idea in balance theory is represented by a triangle.

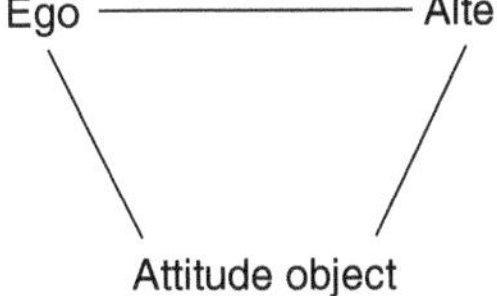

Ego perceives alter as having an attribute.

Each link in the triangle can be given a sign + or –. Thus ego may like or dislike alter. The attitude object may have favorable or unfavorable attributes. Alter may have or reject, may favor or disfavor them. Thus "the great doctor saved my father's life" is plus all around.

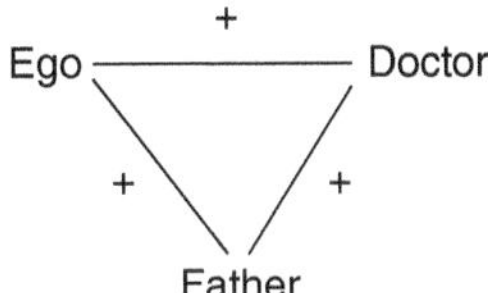

That is a thoroughly balanced statement. But "the great doctor saved the brutal dictator's life" is a different kind of statement. It arouses a certain measure of ambivalence. One is not sure how one feels about it. Such an event certainly could happen; nonetheless it creates a psychological tension in one who thinks it.

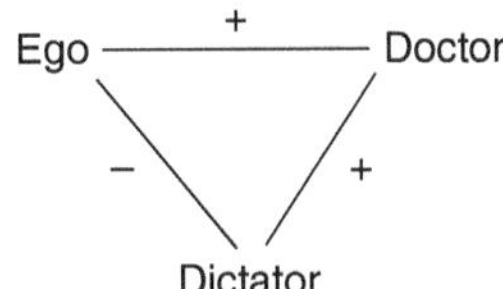

The existence of such tension is, according to balance theory, a condition conducive to attitude change. In that unbalanced situation there may be some inclination to come to think less well of the doctor or to come to think that the bond between the doctor and the dictator was not wholly positive. The doctor as professional may have done his duty, but may also have done it with distaste or been forced to do it. It is easier to accept the picture that way.

Balance theory does not assert a specific predicted outcome. It identifies, rather, a condition under which the relation among cognitive elements will be stable and a condition in which the relation among them will be unstable. (It is unstable if the product sign is negative.)

If it is unstable, the individual may handle the situation by any one of many defense mechanisms including avoidance (i.e., thinking about other things), attitude change regarding the elements, or differentiation. The last is the split that we have met before in the analysis of dreams. The great doctor becomes two symbols: the skillful physician who does his job and the coerced citizen who hates the dictator.

The highly simplified formal model represented by the balance triangle is an analytical step forward in that it provides the basic element for a formal calculus whereby one can model the complex processes of symbolization or stereotyping. The triangle is but the atom with which larger models can be built. It itself is a trivially simple concept, and occasionally people whose reading in balance theory goes no further than learning about this basic atom dismiss the whole thing as trivial. As Abelson's later work illustrates, one can go far, using balance notions, to create sophisticated analyses out of such relatively elementary building blocks.[10]

The first step toward complexity, taken in an article by Abelson and Rosenberg, is to generalize from a set of three to a set of "n" elements.[11] Suppose there is a set of elements in an individual's psyche, each linked to each other by a plus, a minus, or a zero (i.e., unlinked). How can one determine whether the structure as a whole is balanced? If it is not balanced, how much change in the structure would be required in order to eliminate the tension and restore balance? Abelson and Rosenberg work out the mathematics of such n-element matrices. There are rather powerful theorems that can be used in analyzing the psychologic of associated symbols when they are presented in this way.

Abelson's most recent formalization of cognitive processes has pushed further toward Freud, Lippmann, and Isaacs, in seeking to incorporate still more of the complexity of human thinking. We noted above that balance theory incorporates the various defense mechanisms such as forgetting, selective perception, etc., as ways of responding to imbalance. When the mental world does not neatly fit into good guys doing good things and bad guys—bad things, there are various psychic gambits available to avoid the pains of ambivalence. In his most recent work, Abelson has attempted to formalize them into a finite and well defined set of strategies.[12] The particular psyche he has used as a case study is a hypothetical Goldwater Republican thinking about communism and the United States, war and peace, good and evil.

A description of the symbols, associations, stereotypes, *topoi,* scratches on the mind of this prototypic right-wing ideologist is formalized in Abelson's treatment. The goal of the exercise is to produce a computer-manipulable model of the man's cognitive strategies. Indeed, Abelson's point is that stereotypic psycho-logic is simple-minded enough to be successfully simulated by a computer program. The ideologist uses a limited bag of strategies. In content, the strategies which Abelson describes are perhaps most similar to the *topoi,* or standard arguments, in Aristotle's *Rhetoric,* but they also cover the same ground that we have covered before in discussing symbolization, association, psycho-logic, polarization, and splitting of images accordingly. The Goldwaterite true believer is chosen by Abelson as an extreme illustration of such stereotypy, of a man with images formed early in his primary environment and carried rigidly by association into the world of politics, where he holds onto them with strong resistance to change, by means of a series of simple strategies.

Harold Isaacs's treatment of the "scratches on our minds" starts in one respect at the opposite pole from Abelson's. While Abelson stresses the universality and simplicity of the cognitive strategies used in stereotyped thinking, Isaacs delights in savoring the infinite variety of ways in which humans play that game. Abelson is a social psychologist in the mathematical tradition. Isaacs is a former journalist and observer of life. But there is no contradiction. A game—the game of cognition or any other—has formal rules, and one writer may make his mark by the codification and analysis of their logic. Another writer watches the game being played and conveys its excitement, its suspense, its uniqueness as a single event. His is an art form. But he is watching the same game and is also aware of the rules; he, too, by his description of the single case helps us to understand the general rules. Isaacs is that sort of artist.

The psychoanalytic literature, Lippmann, and the literature on ethnic stereotypes (but not balance theory) must certainly have entered quite consciously into Isaacs's thinking as he started in the early 1950s to write on American images of India and China. For a quarter of a century, Isaacs had been writing about Asian politics as a journalist and scholar.[13] In 1953 he joined a new program on international communication that the Ford Foundation had established at MIT This author, Daniel Lerner, Raymond Bauer, Howard Perlmutter, Eric Lenneberg, and Harold Isaacs were its initial staff. We set out to study how foreign information affected political behavior. We were interested in the penetration of modern information into the developing world,[14] and also the penetration of information about the outside world into American public affairs.[15] Isaacs chose for his study the formation of American images of India and China.

His was a study of stereotype formation. That was also the area in which Howard Perlmutter worked at MIT. Their work was in a long tradition going back to Theodore Bagardus's social distance scale in 1925. That instrument asked whom one would be willing to work with, accept as a neighbor, or marry. Such work on ethnic stereotyping peaked in the 1930s and 1940s in response to both Nazi and American racism.

The classic work was by Adorno, Frenkel-Brunswick, et al.[16] Perlmutter used the *F*-scale from that study and found that it correlated positively not only with anti-foreign prejudice, but also with xenophilia, that is, favorable identification with things foreign.[17] He also worked on the process of impression formation regarding foreigners.[18] Ethnicity, he showed, was the strongest dimension governing the formation of an image of a person who belonged to any other nationality than one's own. Ethnicity dominated profession, for example, as a source of images.

It was against this background of extensive social research on ethnic stereotyping that Isaacs undertook his program of interviews with Americans who had played some key role in Far Eastern policy. His interviews were rich in detail and he reported them with all their idiosyncratic drama. His interview technique was open-ended and encouraged free association on the Freudian model, a style of interviewing more congenial to an ex-reporter than the psychometric instruments that Perlmutter, for example, used. Isaacs encouraged his respondents to work back gradually to their earliest associations with the symbols of India and Indians, China and Chinese. What emerged was often a relatively fixed image formed as early, for instance, as when the child put money in his Sunday school mite box for the heathens whom the missionaries went out to save.

What came through the interviews was the same logic of stereotypes that we have been discussing in reviewing Freud, and Lippmann, and Abelson. There were good guys and bad guys. There were respondents who described "lo, the wonderful Chinese" and who held the image of Chinese as a supremely intelligent people, heroic in war and idealistic in peace. Typically such sinophilic Americans found India and Indians dark, dirty, and unpleasant. On the other hand, there was the smaller group of indophilic Americans who saw Indians as spiritual. Those typically saw the Chinese as sly and inscrutable. Reactions to the dirt of Asian cities evoked in sinophiles horror at the filth of Calcutta while indophiles were appalled by the dirt in Shanghai.

Although the India-China polarization provided for most of the respondents a neat hero-villain casting (one way or the other), the scene in their minds could rarely be quite that simple. History has thrown Americans back and forth in shifting alliances in Asia. The Chinese were our heroes against Japanese aggression until 1949. But then the mainland became Communist China beset by madnesses such as the cultural revolution. Japan became a land of delicate art, political democracy, and the postwar economic miracle. More recently, China, since the Nixon visit, once more has become a wonderland in the tales of returning travelers—as one told me, it is a land that had changed his life, for he had seen that a society based on altruism can work. Japan at the same time has become increasingly in American eyes an economic competitor, a land of environmental pollution and of ruthless economic men. Thus the splits in national stereotypes are there, with each half-image available to be used when needed to sustain consistency. There are, Isaacs tells us, the images of the benign and wise Charley Chan and the image of the cruel and mysterious Fu Man Chu. There are the images of the tea ceremony and the kamikaze pilot. These cohabit in our minds. As alliances shift the appropriate image comes forth to explain reality and keep it consistent with a viscous cognitive mass. At each moment there is one country in Asia to represent the good, the extraordinary, and the heroic, and another country to represent the devious, the inscrutable, and the cruel. The plot and symbols remain the same even if the characters trade places from time to time.

In "Scratches" the main interest is in the cognitive processes by which people acquire the images that they hold and in the strategies that they use to defend them. The debt to Freudian notions of symbolism and to Lippmann on stereotypes is clear, and was presumably conscious. The parallelism to social psychological theories of attitude structure such as Abelson's is equally clear, though there is no reason to believe that Isaacs was aware of those theories or subject to any direct influence from them. Those ideas were in the social science environment, however, and could undoubtedly have been communicated, unattributed, by informal conversation in a university environment.

In Isaacs' works since "Scratches" one particular element of the theory of symbols or images, as we have described it above, is particularly stressed, namely the notion of identity. Symbols, as we have seen, often help define the self and the other. The stereotypes that one holds of people and groups position the self as *for* some people and *against* others. All of Isaacs' books since "Scratches" deal with the changing identities of groups in the post war world. Like most people who have used, analyzed, or developed the concept of stereotype, Isaacs has been particularly interested in ethnic identities—American blacks in Africa, American Jews in Israel, Filipinos caught between Spanish, indigenous, and American identities, and ex-untouchables in India released from the age-long fixity of their assigned status have been among the cases that he has dealt with.

There are various ways of talking about people's images of self and other. Harold Lasswell uses the phrase symbols of identification. Erik Erikson, who spent the academic year 1958–59 in a seminar with the social science faculty at MIT, talks of identity. However the notion may be expressed, it involves, first, the assignment of group names; second, the classification of people under those symbols; and, third, the attribution of traits to those groups.

The four writers whom we have discussed, Freud, Lippmann, Abelson, and Isaacs, would see themselves as very different from each other. And in some respects very different they are. But they are all feeling over different parts of the same elephant. The common theory shared by all four writers may be summarized in nine points.

1. Humans organize the buzzing confusion of reality into simplified representations. These universal simplifications, rooted according to his theories in human sexuality, Freud called symbols. Those that had their roots in ideology or adult experience, he discussed little. The other writers were more eclectic and wrote of whatever images or stereotypes they found to occur in the realm of discourse that they were observing. Abelson described what he found in Goldwater Republican ideology. Isaacs is most concerned with the contents of the symbolism as it appeared in the psyches of important actors on the current world scene. He describes them vividly. His motivation is substantive and political rather than psychological or theoretical. The new nationalisms emerging on the world scene fascinate him, particularly where the resulting images reflect strain among conflicting traditions.
2. The simplified representations are not an inchoate list, but relate to each other in a quasi-logic. It is not the logic of veridical truth, but an emotional or psycho-logic. Freud describes it in terms of associations. Abelson examines it most sophisticatedly, and gives it the label

psychologic. The most basic rule is that good people do good things, and bad people bad. Moral ambivalence is the equivalent of illogic.

3. These simplified representations are acquired early. Freud traced those that he deals with farthest back into the childhood experience. Isaacs, too, traces those that he deals with back to the first recalled experience of them. Abelson and Lippmann are not primarily concerned with the date of acquisition.
4. All four writers agree that once acquired, those simplified representations are defended strongly against change. They are clung to tenaciously, often in the face of evidence. Freud and Abelson classify the defense mechanisms used.
5. Simplification and the defense of existing cognitions against new evidence are both deplored and also accepted as inevitable by all of these writers. Lippmann is most moralistic. Stereotypes, he believes, are bad things, to be overcome by educated men. Yet he, too, realizes that they are inevitable characteristics of thinking. The economy of mental effort does not permit each issue to be examined *de novo* every time, nor can every presumption be challenged if the duration of deliberation is to be less than eternity. Thinking is an allocation of scarce mental resources. Freud and Isaacs both seem deeply if not explicitly aware of the inherent agony of the resulting human condition; the impossibility of full rationality is the central object of Freud's analysis. We all think neurotically or irrationally, for to be human is to do so. Yet Freud, a liberal steeped in the tradition of progress and perfectionism, seeks to help men achieve a higher level of consciousness, to become less victimized by the mechanism of their own psyches.
6. The representations that we are discussing are visual, referred to by nouns. They are, in short, "things." Isaacs uses the word "images." Freud is explicit about the visual quality of dreams. Heider deals with attitude objects.
7. The things represented have rather unequivocal values on a good-bad scale. The world of the mind is a low grade Western. There are good guys and bad guys. There is no moral ambiguity there. All four writers are at one about that. The resistance of humans to living with moral tension provides the dynamic in balance theory. Change occurs to restore balance whenever it is departed from.
8. One mechanism to maintain univocal moral balance is the splitting of representations into pairs that are given different names but stand for the same thing. Freud and Abelson describe this process. Isaacs illustrates it in absorbing detail.
9. The representations that people hold serve to affirm their identities. Many of the representations are of groups. Others are held to with fervor because to contradict those hallowed beliefs would be a denial of one's identity. It may not be orthodox Freudian psychology to place emphasis on symbols of group affiliation as against individual gratification, but the notion of identity is certainly present in Freud. It was

> there strongly enough for Erikson to bring it forth as a central notion and for Lasswell to have used it in his application of psychoanalysis to politics. It was natural for Isaacs to move in his writings from dealing with images to dealing with identity as the central focus. They cannot be discussed in isolation from each other.

It is sometimes argued that the social sciences are not cumulative. Unlike the practitioners of modern physics, we can still read Aristotle with profit. But to some degree the social sciences are cumulative; there is progress. There is, for example, a theory of symbols, stereotypes, and images that has progressed visibly in the past half century, elucidated by a variety of authors in a variety of ways. From the cumulation of their different treatments, there has arisen a distinctly higher level of understanding. Abelson's formal models, Freud's insights, Lippmann's applications to politics, and Isaacs's phenomenological perceptiveness have all contributed, each in its way.

Notes

1. For example, Everett Rogers, in *Diffusion of innovations* (New York: Free Press of Glencoe 1962), brought together the work done in the 1940s by rural sociologists on the diffusion of agricultural innovation with the work of sociologists of mass communication led by Paul Lazarsfeld dealing with the two-step flow of communication in politics and marketing. Another instance concerns voting studies and balance theory. In *Candidates, issues and strategies* (Cambridge, MA: MIT Press, 1964) a psychologist recognized the equivalence of the cross-pressure voting theory of Bernard Berelson, Paul Lazarsfeld and William McPhee as presented in *Voting* (Chicago: University of Chicago Press, 1954) with the balance theories of attitude change developed in psychology by Fritz Heider and Abelson.
2. "The occult significance of dreams" in Sigmund Freud (ed. Ernest Jones), *Collected papers* (London: Hogarth Press, 1950), V, p. 158.
3. *The interpretation of dreams,* in *The basic writings of Sigmund Freud,* (tr. and ed. by A.A. Brill) (New York: Modern Library. 1938), p. 196.
4. "Psycho-analysis," 1922 in *Collected papers,* V, 116; also *Interpretation of dreams,* pp. 251–252.
5. Otto Fenichel, *The psychoanalytical theory of neuroses* (New York: W.W. Norton and Co., 1945), p. 48.
6. Ibid., p. 157.
7. Waller Lippmann, *Public opinion* (New York: Free Press, 1965), pp. 99–100. Cf. Freud's discussion of absolutism in dreams. *Interpretation of dreams,* p. 288.
8. Harold D. Lasswell, *World politics and personal insecurity* (New York: McGraw Hill, 1935), pp. 29–51 Lasswell and Abraham Kaplan, *Power and society* (New Haven, CT: Yale University Press, 1950), p. 104.
9. "Attitudes and cognitive organization," *Journal of Psychology,* XXI (1946), 107–112.

10. Cf. "The Structure of Belief Systems," in Roger C. Schank and Kenneth M. Colby *Computer models of thought and language* (San Francisco, CA: W. H. Freeman 1973).
11. Robert P. Abelson and M.J. Rosenberg, "Symbolic Psychologic," *Behavioral Science*, 111 (1958), 1–13.
12. Abelson, "The Structure of Belief Systems."
13. *The Tragedy of the Chinese revolution* (London: Secker and Warburg, 1938; 2nd rev. ed., New York: Atheneum, 1966).
14. Daniel Lerner, *The Passing of traditional society* (Glencoe, IL: Free Press, 1958).
15. Raymond A. Bauer, Ithiel de Sola Pool, and Lewis Dexter, *American business and public policy* (New York: Atherton, 1963).
16. Theodor Adorno, Else Frenkel-Brunswick, et al., *The authoritarian personality* (New York, Harper, 1950).
17. Perlmutter, "Correlates of two types of xenophilic orientation," *Journal of Abnormal and Social Psychology*, LII (1956), 130–135; "Some relationships between xenophilic attitudes and authoritarianism among Americans abroad." *Psychological Reports*, III (1957), 131–137.
18. Howard Perlmutter and Jerome S. Bruner, "Compatriot and foreigner," *Journal of Abnormal and Social Psychology*, LV (1957), 253–260.

Part II

Computer Simulation

Editor's Introduction

> *"We are moving into an era where the limitation on data bank operations will no longer be computer capacity but only the imagination of the researcher and the extent to which raw data is available to him. For survey researchers this new age of rich data covering varieties of groups and long time series promises to bring a revolution in our ability to understand politics."*
>
> —Abelson, Pool, and Popkin [p. 97, below]

> *"By the end of the seven days [the Kaiser and the Tsar] are not looking at the same world, although reality impinges itself of each . . . Even when the same event is in both men's minds, the picture of it differs."*
>
> —Pool and Kessler [p. 114, below]

Computer simulation is a good tool for steady cumulation and integration of social science. Today, thirty-five years after the forecast of Abelson, Pool, and Popkin (above) the elements that can be included, and the complexity of the relationships of elements to one another, are limited more by human imagination and resources than technology itself; and the same is true of the databanks that can bring the simulations to life.[1]

In the beginning, the capacities for data analysis permitted only a small number of variables and the simplest social science that described people by a small set of categories and points on numerical scales: social class, IQ, trust in government (on a 7–point scale), etc. In 1959, Ithiel Pool and Robert Abelson began to explore, at the invitation of the Democratic Party, the capacity of new mainframe computers to include a more complete description of characteristics that might affect voting in the 1960 American Presidential election, and this research is reported in the first two selections:

"The Simulmatics Project"

In response to the invitation they created the first computer simulation of the American electorate based upon public opinion data. They summarized data from 85,000 respondents to public opinion polls during the 1950s and created a simulation with 480 types of voters and, for each type, a profile of 52 opinions and relevant political tendencies (e.g., to vote). Then, assessing the interaction of these 480 types with the defining issues in this campaign, and using census data to recreate the distribution of these types within each of the (simulated) states, they provided campaign advice to the Democratic Presidential candidate, John F. Kennedy, in his campaign against the Republican, Richard M. Nixon.

As the article records, the initial work was a remarkable success. Especially, it helped to predict the effects of openly addressing concerns about Kennedy's Catholicism—effects that were different in the popular vote and (because of different distributions in different states) on the outcome of the election in the Electoral College. An important feature of the simulation was its explicit use of psychological theory to improve empathy and specify how voters dealt with internal crosspressures in weighing such factors, a refinement that could be included rigorously by the simulation method.

"A Postscript on the 1964 Election"

The success in the 1960 exercise was repeated, with improvements, in the 1964 election: The summary report by Abelson, Pool, and Popkin is the second selection in this section. It was a very different Presidential election with different issues (Johnson v. Goldwater). Yet the simulation "engine" (in social science terms) was able, with suitable adjustment of parameters, to represent the American political process in this second election, also to a remarkable degree.

"The Kaiser, the Tsar, and the Computer: Information Processing in a Crisis"

In this third selection, from 1965, Pool and Kessler extend the power of computer simulation to provide a depth analysis of the minds of two decision makers and their interactions across several days of the international crisis that led to the outbreak of World War I. Their initial project incorporates several principles of cognitive psychology that have been observed in laboratory settings and uses the simulation engine to put forward propositions about misperceptions in the crisis.

During the Cold War, research to understand decision making in international crises engaged several leading historians and political scientists. By the time of this study, World War I was widely perceived by historians, in retrospect, to be "a war nobody wanted"—with a terrible human cost paid as a result of misjudgment and misperception during the heat of the crisis. Pool and Kessler, by using the theories of cognitive psychology to design the simulation, are exploring the possibility of drawing broader lessons from diplomatic history: An immediate impetus to the project probably was the Cuban Missile Crisis of 1962, which suggested new urgency to develop this line of inquiry, which might prevent a nuclear war.

Later, the cumulative insights of research concerning crisis decision making were integrated more fully with physiological and psychological studies of behavior under stress by using new indicators of stress provided by content analysis and other methods. It became an important scientific contribution to the study of international relations.[2] It also may have contributed to prevention: Lincoln Bloomfield, Ithiel Pool's colleague at MIT, played an active but an unpublicized role during the Cold War in conducting crisis simulation exercises at senior levels, in Washington and Moscow, to bring such insights and the benefits of training to top decision makers.

These early simulations can be superseded by the computational power, memory, and more powerful programming languages that are available today. Even the ordinary computer simulations of the rise and fall of civilizations, available in any software store, vastly expand the power and visual display capability that was available four decades ago. (The next step—to develop these games into research tools—is to discover what refinements would be needed to provide (for example) a good fit with the actual dynamics of world history.[3])

Notes

1. A passionate and capable advocate of the marriage of humanistic sensibilities and rigorous science through computer simulation is a former MIT colleague of Ithiel Pool, Hayward Alker, Jr., See, for example, his *Rediscoveries and reformulations: Humanistic methodologies for international studies.* Cambridge Studies in International Relations No. 41. (NY: Cambridge University Press, 1996) and references cited therein. For an overview of computer simulation of human behavior see Robert P. Abelson, "Simulation of social behavior" in G. Lindzey and E. Aronson (eds,). *Handbook of social psychology,* 2nd ed. (Reading, MA: Addison Wesley, 1968), vol. 2, pp. 274–356. For current applications of cognitive modeling to international relations, see the work of Ithiel Pool's former student Mathew Bonham, e.g., Mathew

Bonham, Victor Sergeev, and Pavel Parchin, "The Limited Test-Ban Agreement: Emergence of new knowledge structures in international negotiation," *International Studies Quarterly*, 41 (June 1997), pp. 215–240 and Mathew Bonham and Daniel Heradstveit, "Attribution theory and Arab images of the Gulf War," *Political Psychology*, 17:2, (June 1996), pp. 271–292.

2. The late Irving Janis developed this research across several decades—for example in his *Groupthink: Psychological studies of policy decisions and fiascoes* (NY: Houghton Mifflin, 1982), second edition and (with Leon Mann) *Decision making: A psychological analysis of choice, conflict and commitment* (NY: Free Press, 1985). Research into the outbreak of World War I has been fully developed, in the study of crisis decision making, using content analysis methods, by, Ole Holsti, in his *Crisis, escalation, war* (Montreal: McGill/Queens University Press, 1972). See also Margaret Hermann, "Indicators of stress in policymakers during foreign policy crises," *Political Psychology*, 1979, pp. 27–46.
3. See, for example, Isaac Asimov's vision of mathematically-based psychohistory. *Foundation* (Garden City, NY: Doubleday, 1951) and subsequent volumes in the series.

4

The Simulmatics Project

with Robert Abelson

This is the first report on a program of research conducted for the Democratic Party during the 1960 campaign. The research used a new technique for processing poll data and included computer simulation of likely voter behavior. The immediate goal of the project was to estimate rapidly, during the campaign, the probable impact upon the public, and upon small strategically important groups within the public, of different issues which might arise or which might be used by the candidates.

The Data

This study is a "secondary analysis" of old poll results. Students of public opinion are becoming aware that the growing backlog of earlier polls provides a powerful tool to aid in the interpretation of new poll results. Polling has now been routine for three decades, but poll archives are just beginning to be assembled. The main one is the Roper Public Opinion Research Center in Williamstown, the existence of which made feasible the project here described.[1]

The first step in the project was to identify in that archive all polls anticipating the elections of 1952, 1954, 1956, and 1958. (Pre-election polls on the 1960 contest were added later when they became available.) We selected those polls which contained standard identification data on region, city size, sex, race, socio-economic status, party, and religion, the last being the item most often missing. Further, we restricted our attention to those polls which asked about vote intention and also about a substantial number of pre-selected issues such as civil rights, foreign affairs, and social legislation. From 1952 to 1958 we found fifty usable surveys covering 85,000 respondents. Sixteen polls anticipating the 1960 elections were added to this number. The sixty-six surveys represented a total of well over 100,000 interviews.

From *Public Opinion Quarterly* (1961).

Processing the Data

To handle such massive data required substantial innovations in analytic procedures. In essence, the data were reduced to a 480-by-52 matrix. The number 480 represented voter types, each voter type being defined by socio-economic characteristics. A single voter type might be "Eastern, metropolitan, lower-income, white, Catholic, female Democrats." Another might be, "Border state, rural, upper-income, white, Protestant, male Independents." Certain types with small numbers of respondents were reconsolidated, yielding the total of 480 types actually used.

The number 52 represented what we called in our private jargon "issue clusters." Most of these were political issues, such as foreign aid, attitudes toward the United Nations, and McCarthyism. Other so-called "issue clusters" included such familiar indicators of public opinion as "Which party is better for people like you?" vote intention, and nonvoting. In sum, the issue clusters were political characteristics on which the voter type would have a distribution.

One can picture the 480-by-52 matrix as containing four numbers in each cell. The first number stated the total number of persons of that voter type asked about that particular item of information. The other three numbers trichotomized those respondents into the percentages pro, anti, and undecided or confused on the issue.

We assembled such a matrix for each biennial election separately and also a consolidated matrix for all elections together. Thus, it was possible by comparison of the separate matrices to examine trends.

The reduction of the raw data to this matrix form was an arduous task. The first step was to identify in each survey those questions which seemed to bear on any of the fifty-two issue clusters we had listed as relevant to the campaign. One such cluster was attitude toward domestic communism or, as we called it for shorthand, McCarthyism. Over the past decade many questions have been asked on this and related matters in many different polls. One survey might ask, "Are you in favor of permitting a Communist to teach in the school system?" Another would ask, "What do you think of Senator McCarthy?" Another would ask, "Do you think McCarthy has done more good or harm?" The problem was to determine which questions tapped essentially the same attitude, domestic anticommunism. The decision was made by a two-step process. First, questions were grouped together *a priori* on the basis of intuitive judgment, and then this grouping was empirically tested.

The empirical test was conducted as follows: Replies to each questions were separately trichotomized. Typically, the replies had previously been coded in up to thirteen categories. Where more than three replies had been coded, the codes had to be regrouped. On the McCarthyism issue, replies were classified as McCarthyite, anti-McCarthyite, and indeterminate. A reply opposing retention of a Communist in the school system would be classified as McCarthyite. In the case of such a question as "How well do you like McCarthy?" for which a scale had originally been used, cutting points had to be set depending on the distribution.

For each pair of questions in the presumed cluster we then correlated the percentage "pro," and separately the percentage "anti," across voter types yielding two correlation matrices. (The voter types for this operation were 15, a reconsolidation of the 480. Since this operation dealt with percentages on questions from single surveys, consolidation was essential to obtain base numbers in each voter type large enough so that the percentages being correlated would be reasonably stable.) Only those questions which showed high correlations with each other were retained in a cluster. Thus, our assumption that a question about Communist teachers in the schools could be treated as equivalent to a question about McCarthy was subject to empirical validation.

In many instances questions which *a priori* seemed alike had to be discarded from the clusters. Some clusters had to be broken up into two or more. Indeed, in the particular example we have been using here, it turned out that replies to the identically worded question "How well do you like McCarthy" ceased tapping the same attitudes the minute the Senate censured him. Clusters thus represented questions which could be regarded as in some sense equivalent, both on the grounds of political common sense and on the grounds of empirical correlation.[2]

It should be emphasized that empirical correlation was not enough. Such a question as "Which party is better for people like you?" and a question about the image of Adlai Stevenson would correlate strongly because they were both party-linked. However, they were not included in a single issue cluster unless they also seemed politically equivalent.

The final step in the preliminary data processing—the step which gave us our matrices—was to take all cards in any one of the 480 voter types for a particular biennial period and tabulate for each issue cluster the number of replies pro, con, and indeterminate, and the number of cards on which such replies appeared. That last number varied for each cluster since some questions (e.g. turnout) were asked on virtually every survey we used, while other questions were asked only occasionally.

Purposes of the Method

The reader may wonder what purposes were served by reorganizing the data into the standard format just described. That handling of the data lent itself to three main uses: (1) A "data bank" was available from which one might draw the answer to any one of a vast number of questions at a moment's notice. (2) The consolidation of separate surveys made available adequate data on small, yet politically significant, subsegments in the population. For example, we wrote a report on Northern Negro voters based upon 4,050 interviews, including 418 with middle-class Negroes. The typical national sample survey contains no more than 100 interviews with Northern Negroes, a number clearly inadequate for refined analysis. (3) The data format and its transfer to high-speed tape facilitated its use in computer simulation of the effects of hypothetical campaign strategies. This aspect of the project is the most novel and is the one to which we shall return later in this article.

The History of the Project

Before we illustrate those uses of the data, let us detour to examine the history of the project: the fact that it was sponsored and actually used by a partisan group makes the story of its management of some interest to students of public opinion research.

The project was initiated in the early months of 1959 by William McPhee and the authors. Our plan for computer simulation (on a different version of which McPhee had already been working)[3] was presented to Mr. Edward Greenfield, a New York businessman actively engaged in Democratic politics. Through his intervention, a group of New York reform Democrats who had taken major responsibility for raising money for the Democratic Advisory Council became interested.[4] Before this group of private individuals was willing to secure funds, however, they wanted to be sure that the results were likely to be valid and useful. In May of 1959 the project was discussed in Washington at a meeting attended by Mr. Charles Tyroler, Executive Secretary of the Democratic Advisory Council; the members of the Council executive committee; Paul Butler, Chairman of the Democratic National Committee; several other officials of that Committee; Mr. Neil Staebler,

Michigan State Chairman; and a number of social science consultants, including Samuel Eldersveld, Morris Janowitz, and Robert Lane. This group was interested but reserved. It was suggested that the project should be supported for four months initially and at the end of this period a further review should be made.

The Williamstown Public Opinion Research Center agreed to permit the use of polls in their archives on two conditions; First, all basic data tabulated by Simulmatics from their cards were to be made available to the Center so the Republican Party would have an equal opportunity to use such data if they wanted them. We provided a print-out of the data on the computer tape, but not, of course, the programs for simulation nor supplementary data obtained from other sources (e.g. the census) and used in our system. Second, and demanded by both the Roper Public Opinion Research Center and the social scientists engaged in the study, all results could be published for scientific purposes after the election. This article is part of our program to meet that condition.

Given the green light to carry out the project, the principals organized themselves as The Simulmatics Corporation, for although the objective of the project constituted scientific research, it was clear that universities would not and should not accept financing from politically motivated sources or permit a university project to play an active role in supplying campaign advice to one party.

The summer of 1959 was devoted to the data reduction job described above. In October 1959, when the preliminary data processing had been substantially completed, a review meeting in New York was attended by many of the same persons who had been at the Advisory Council meeting in May plus a number of social science consultants, including Harold Lasswell, Paul Lazarsfeld, Morris Janowitz, and John Tukey. Although the degree of confidence in the basic approach ranged from enthusiasm to doubt, a decision to proceed was quickly reached.

The next step was the development of computer programs, some of which will be discussed below. One objective was to make possible rapid incorporation of new data which might, we hoped, become available during the campaign. Our hope, as we shall see, was only slightly fulfilled.

By June of 1960 we were able to prepare a first report as a sample of the kind of thing which might be done by the Simulmatics process. That was the report on the Negro vote in the North.

Our contractual arrangements with our sponsors ended with the preparation of the process and of this report illustrating it, shortly before the 1960 convention. It was understood that actual use of the service in the form of further reports on specific topics would be purchased by appropriate elements of the party in the pre-campaign and campaign period at their discretion. In the immediate pre-convention period, the National Committee felt that it should not make decisions which would shortly be the business of the nominee. After the convention the Kennedy organization, contrary to the image created by the press, did not enter the campaign as a well-oiled machine with well-planned strategy. Except for the registration drive, which had been carefully prepared by Lawrence O'Brien, no strategic or organizational plan existed the day after the nomination. It took until August for the organization to shake down. No campaign research of any significant sort was therefore done in the two months from mid-June to mid-August, either by Simulmatics or by others. In August, a decision was made to ask Louis Harris to make thirty state surveys for the Kennedy campaign. However, because of the late start, data from these surveys would not be available until after Labor Day. On August 11, the National Committee asked The Simulmatics Corporation to prepare three reports: one each on the image of Kennedy, the image of Nixon, and foreign policy as a campaign issue. These three reports were to be delivered in two weeks for use in campaign planning. Along with them we were to conduct a national sample survey which, in the minds of the political decision makers, would serve to bring the Simulmatics data, based as they were on old polls, up to date. (It should be mentioned that one of the most difficult tasks of the Simulmatics project was persuading campaign strategists that data other than current intelligence could be useful to them.) The national survey by telephone was conducted for the project by the Furst Survey Research Center and was indeed extremely useful in guiding the use of the older data. It confirmed the published Gallup finding that Nixon was at that point well in the lead, though we disagreed on the proportion of undecideds (we found 23 per cent). It made us aware that Nixon's lead was due to women. It also persuaded us that voters were largely focusing upon foreign policy at that point in the campaign.

The relationship between the use of such current intelligence and the use of a simulation model developed out of historical data is analogous to the relationship between a climatological model and current weather information. One can predict tomorrow's weather best if one has both historical information about patterns and current information about where one stands in a pattern. While it would be presumptuous to assert that in two weeks of intense activity we approached an effective integration of the two sets of data, that was the ideal we had in mind and which in some limited respects we approximated.

It should be added that the introduction of the national survey data was possible only because of prior preparation for rapid data analysis. The survey was ordered on a Thursday, the field interviewing took place between Saturday and the following Thursday, by Friday morning all cards had been punched, and by Friday night the pre-programmed analysis had been run and preliminary results were given to the National Committee.

The three reports that had been ordered on August 11 were delivered on August 25. The speed of the entire operation is, of course, a testimony to the advantages of a high-speed computer system. Nonetheless, such intense pressure is not an optimum condition for research work, even though rapid analysis was one of our objectives from the start. The reader who suspects that under those circumstances clerical errors inevitably occurred is quite right. It was our good fortune that none of those which we have found since in rechecking have turned out to alter any conclusion, but we do not recommend such limited schedules as a normal mode of work. Nevertheless, with well-prepared computerized analysis, it can be done when necessary.

The reader may ask whether the large preparatory investment was justified in terms of the quantitatively limited use of the project. When we planned the project, we—perhaps unrealistically—anticipated active campaign work from the beginning of the summer until about September 15. (Anything done later than that would hardly be useful.) How far the investment was justified by the two weeks of work actually done is a question which we find impossible to answer. An answer depends on an estimate of how much impact the contents of the reports had on the campaign. The reports received an extremely limited elite circulation. They were seen during the campaign by perhaps a dozen to fifteen key decision makers, but they were read intelligently by these talented and literate men.

Despite the contraction of our effort, our own feeling is one of relative satisfaction that the Simulmatics project was able to provide research on demand concerning the key issues at perhaps the critical moment of the campaign. While campaign strategy, except on a few points, conformed rather closely to the advice in the more than one hundred pages of the three reports, we know full well that this was by no means because of the reports. Others besides ourselves had similar ideas. Yet, if the reports strengthened right decisions on a few critical items, we would consider the investment justified.

Examples of Use of the System

Earlier in this article we listed three uses of the method herein described: providing a "data bank," rapidly available; providing data on small, politically significant groups; permitting computer simulation. The first of these advantages has perhaps already been adequately illustrated. Let us turn to the other two.

Our report on Northern Negro voters did not use a computer simulation but rather illustrated the capability of the process to provide information about small subgroups of the population. Compare here a number of quotations from the report with what we could have said working from a single survey containing responses from perhaps 100 Northern Negroes. The report demonstrated, for example, that between 1954 and 1956

> [A] small but significant shift to the Republicans occurred among Northern Negroes, which cost the Democrats about 1 per cent of the total votes in 8 key states [a shift which continued in 1958]. In those years, the Democratic Party loss to the Republican Party was about 7 per cent of the Northern Negro vote—enough to cause a one half per cent loss in the *total* popular vote in the eight key states. In addition, among Northern Negro Independents, only about one quarter actually voted Republican in 1952, but about half voted Republican in 1956, enough of a shift to cause an additional loss of a little less than one half per cent of the total popular vote in the eight key states.
>
> * * *
>
> The shift against the Democrats is more marked among the opinion leading middle class Negroes than among lower-income Negroes.
>
> * * *
>
> Anti catholicism is less prevalent among Negroes than among Northern, urban, Protestant whites.
>
> * * *

> The most significant point of all is the fact that the shift is not an Ike-shift: it is a Republican Party shift. It affects Congressional votes as much as Presidential votes.

In addition, the report demonstrated that Northern urban Negroes vote as often as whites of comparable socio-economic status, and that "there is no sharp difference between Negroes and comparable whites in their feelings about Nixon."

This report was made available to all the leading Democratic candidates, to the Democratic National Committee, and to the drafters of the Democratic platform. Probably no one can say what influence, if any, it had upon them. Those men themselves would not know which of the many things they read or heard shaped their decisions. As outside observers, we can assert only that the report was placed in the hands of the platform framers in the ten days preceding the drafting of the problem, and was read.

The most dramatic result, however, was, as indicated above, the finding that Eisenhower had not generated among Negroes the kind of personal following that he had among most white voter types. This suggested that the Negro vote presented far more of a problem to the Democratic campaign than appeared at first glance; it could not be assumed that the losses in recent years would be recovered with Eisenhower out of the picture.

Simulations

We turn now to what was perhaps the most novel aspect of the study—the use of computer simulations. We describe, first, how we simulated state-by-state results and, second, how we simulated the impact of the religious issue.

One of the benefits gained from the large number of interviews we used was the possibility of approximating state-by-state results. A national sample survey—even a relatively large one—has too few cases from most states to permit any significant analysis of state politics. The same would have been true, however, even for our voluminous data if we had attempted to do a state-by-state analysis in a simple way. We had an average of about 2,000 interviews per state, but that is a misleading figure. In a small state there might have been no more than 300 or 400 interviews, and on a particular issue cluster that had occurred, for example, in only one-tenth of the surveys, there would be too few cases for effective analysis. We therefore developed a system for creating synthetic, or simulated, states.

By an elaborate analysis of census, poll, and voting data—made more difficult because 1960 census results were not yet available—we developed a set of estimates on the number of persons of each voter type in each state. (Note that since *region* was one of the defining characteristics for the 480 voter types, there were at most only 108 voter types in any given state.) It was assumed that a voter of a given voter type would be identical regardless of the state from which he came. A simulated state therefore consisted of a weighted average of the behaviors of the voter types in that state, the weighting being proportional to the numbers of such persons in that state. For example, we thus assumed that the difference between Maine and New York is not truly a difference between New Yorkers and inhabitants of Maine as such, but a difference in the proportions of different voter types which make up each state. We assumed that an "upper-income Protestant Republican rural white male" was the same in either state, and that a small-city Catholic Democratic lower-income female" was also the same in either. This assumption enabled us to use all cases of a voter type, from a particular region in arriving at a conclusion for a state.

We do not assert that the assumptions on which this simulation is based are true. On the contrary, we can be sure that they are partly false. The interesting question intellectually is how good were the results obtained with these partially true assumptions. The test is, of course, how far state-by-state predictions made on these assumptions turn out to correspond to reality. To the extent that they do, they suggest that the essential differences between states in a region are in distributions of types rather than in geographic differences, even within a voter type.[5]

Upon this simulation of states was built a second and more interesting simulation, one which attempted to assess the impact of the religious issue. Since the one simulation rests upon the other, the effectiveness of the state simulation is simultaneously tested by examination of the religious simulation. The latter, the main simulation actually carried out during the campaign, represented a hypothetical campaign in which the only issues were party and Catholicism. Our report of this simulation was limited to the North because of the peculiar role of party in the South. The outcome was a ranking of thirty-two states ranging from the one in which we estimated Kennedy would do best to the one in which we estimated he would do worst. The ranking was:

1. Rhode Island
2. Massachusetts
3. New Mexico
4. Connecticut
5. New York
6. Illinois
7. New Jersey
8. California
9. Arizona
10. Michigan
11. Wisconsin
12. Colorado
13. Ohio
14. Montana
15. Minnesota
16. Missouri
17. Pennsylvania
18. Nevada
19. Washington
20. New Hampshire
21. Wyoming
22. Oregon
23. North Dakota
24. Nebraska
25. Indiana
26. South Dakota
27. Vermont
28. Iowa
29. Kansas
30. Utah
31. Idaho
32. Maine

The product-moment correlation over states between the Kennedy index on the simulation (not strictly speaking a per cent) and the actual Kennedy vote in the election was .82. It should be emphasized that this satisfying result was based upon political data not a single item of which was later than October 1958. Surveys on the 1960 election were not available soon enough to be incorporated into this analysis.

The basic method in this simulation was a fairly straightforward application of the cross-pressure findings of earlier election studies.[6] These findings enabled us to improve our estimate of how a particular voter will behave if we know the cross-pressures he is under. With such knowledge, an analyst should feel more comfortable making guesses about how voters under particular kinds of cross-pressure will shift in an election than he would about making an over-all intuitive guess at the outcome. The method of this simulation was to make a series of such detailed estimates and then let the computer put them together to give an over-all outcome.

To make these detailed estimates we classified our set of 480 voter types into 9 possible cross-pressure subsets arising from a 3–by-3 breakdown on religion and party: Protestants, Catholics, and others; Republicans, Democrats, and Independents. For each of the nine resulting situations we made a prediction. For example, take the Protestant Republicans. They were not under cross-pressure. Since our data had revealed no substantial dislike of Nixon as an individual among such voters, we saw no reason why their vote in 1960 should differ substantially from their vote in 1956, even though Eisenhower was not running. Thus for them we wrote two equations:

$$V_k = P_{56}\,(1 - P_{35})$$
$$V_n = Q_{56}\,(1 - P_{35})$$

meaning that the predicted Kennedy percentage (V_k) in any voter type of this Protestant-Republican sort would be the percentage of persons in that voter type who had indicated a preference for Stevenson in the 1956 polls (P_{56}), reduced by the nonvoting record of that voter type. $(1 - P_{35})$.[7] The equation for the expected Nixon percentage (V_n) was the same except that it used the 1956 Eisenhower supporters (Q).

The above was the simplest set of equations used. Let us now turn to a more complicated set, that for a group under cross-pressure—Protestant Democrats. First, we decided that, barring the religious issue, 1958 vote intentions would be a better index of the Protestant Democrats' 1960 vote than would their 1956 vote intentions. Too many of them were Eisenhower defectors in 1956 for us to believe that 1956 was a good indicator of normal behavior. On the other hand, 1956 polls would overestimate their Democratic vote, since many of them would defect again against a Catholic. However, it would not suffice merely to subtract the percentage who gave anti-Catholic replies on poll questions, for perhaps those very Democrats who were anti-Catholic were the ones who in practice voted Republican anyway. In short, the question was: Were the bigot defectors right wingers whose vote the Democrats would lose even without a Catholic candidate?. Our system could not give us that information for each respondent incorporated into our data. While one respondent in a voter type might have been polled in a survey in 1958 about his vote intentions, another man of the same voter type, on a different survey, might have been polled on whether he would vote for a Catholic for President. To estimate the correlation between these two variables we had to find one or more surveys on which both questions appeared. We then ran anti-Catholicism by 1958 vote for each of the more numerous

1958 Vote Intentions	Anti-Catholic	Not Anti-Catholic
Democratic	*a*	*b*
Republican	*c*	*d*

Protestant Democrat voter types. We found that among them the ratio *ad/bc* in the following fourfold table averaged about .6. With that information we could estimate how many of the anti-Catholics were hopeless cases anyhow (i.e. had gone Republican even in 1958) and how many would be net losses only in a campaign dominated by the religious issue.

It should be added here that we decided to take poll replies on the religious issue at face value. We were not so naïve as to believe that this was realistic, but since we were not trying to predict absolute percentages, but only relative ones, all that mattered was that the true extent of anti-Catholicism, voter type by voter type, should be linearly related to the percentage overtly expressed. Even this could only be assumed as a promising guess.

Finally, in predicting the vote of the Protestant Democrat voter types, we took account of the established finding that voters under cross-pressure stay home on election day more often than voters whose pressures are consistent. Therefore, for our 1960 estimate we doubled the historically established nonvoting index for these types.

Thus we arrived at equations applied to each Protestant Democratic voter type:

$$V_k = (P_{58} - a)\,(1 - 2P_{35})$$
$$V_n = (Q_{58} + a)\,(1 - 2P_{35})$$

The estimate of anti-Catholic 1958 Democratic voters (i.e. persons in cell *a* in the fourfold table above) was arrived at by the computer, given that

$$a + b = P_{58} \qquad a + c = P_{14}\,(P_{58} + Q_{58})$$

$$P_{14} = \text{percent anti-catholic} \quad \text{and} \quad \frac{ad}{bc} = .6$$

Space precludes a similar examination of each of the other of the nine conditions.[8] Suffice it to say that one other set of serious guesses had to be made, namely what proportion of those Democratic Catholics who had voted Republican in 1958 would switch back to their party to vote for Kennedy and what proportion of Republican Catholics who had voted Republican in 1958 would also switch to Kennedy. After an examination of the trial-heat data from polls which asked about Kennedy vs. Nixon, we decided to use one-third as the proportion in each case, and to use that figure also as an estimate of the proportion of Catholic independents who would be won back by the religious issue.

The simulation required that the computer make 480 separate calculations, each one using the appropriate set of equations from above. During each of the 480 calculations, the computer put into the equations values for turnout record, 1958 vote intention, 1956 vote intention, and anti-Catholicism, derived from the data which had been assembled about that particular voter type. This gave a 1960 vote estimate for each voter type for the particular hypothetical campaign being investigated. Weighted averages of these gave the state-by-state estimates.

These estimates, as we have already noted, turned out to be close to the actual November outcome. They were not intended to be predictions. Or, rather, they were *contingent* predictions only. They were predictions of what would happen *if* the religious issue dominated the campaign. We did not predict that this would happen. We were describing one out of a set of possible types of campaign situation. But by August, when we took our national survey, comparison of our simulation and the survey results showed that this situation was actually beginning to occur. And the closeness of our contingent prediction to the final November result suggests that, indeed, the religious issue was of prime importance.

How close was the religious-issue simulation to the actual outcome compared to alternative bases of prediction? A full exploration of this remains to be made. We must, for example, further vary the parameters used in the simulation to determine which ones affect the results most critically and which values of those give the best prediction. For the present we look only at the one set of values and equations on which we relied during the campaign and which has already been described. (A few variations were tried and dismissed during the campaign, but none that made much difference.) How did this one simulation compare with other predictive data?

An obvious comparison is with the Kennedy-Nixon trial heats on polls taken at the same time as the latest polls used in the simulation. The correlation between the state-by-state result of these polls and the actual outcome is but .53 as compared to .82 for the simulation. The simulation, in short, portrayed trends which actually took place between the time the data were collected and election day. The uncorrected polls two years before the election explained but one-fourth of the variance in the real results, while intelligent use of them taking into account the cross-pressure of voting behavior allowed us to explain nearly two-thirds of the variance.

A more stringent comparison would be with Kennedy-Nixon trial heats run in August 1960, when the simulation was run on the computer. Such a comparison would answer the question of whether the Democratic Party would have gotten as good information at that date by the conventional means of up-to-the-minute field interviewing as it got by reanalysis of old data. Very likely it could have, if it had chosen to invest in a large enough national sample survey to give it state-by-state results, for as far as we can now tell the Catholic issue exerted most of its impact by shortly after the conventions. However, until poll data for that period becomes available we can only speculate. We wish to emphasize, however, that at some point in the history of the campaign, poll data certainly came into close correlation with the November election results and thus with our simulation. The date the raw poll results became as or more predictive than the simulation would be the point in the campaign at which mechanisms of voter behavior anticipated in the simulation became reality.

Besides simulation and polls, what other indices might have forecast long in advance the state-by-state order of voting in 1960? Results of previous elections would be one such index. Perhaps the rank order of the states in a previous election is a good forecast of rank order in future ones, even if the electoral outcome changes. (The whole country could move one way or the other, leaving the order of the states much the same.) But, if one is to use this device, which election should one use? The year 1956 was a presidential election year, as was 1960, but in 1956 the Eisenhower phenomenon was operating. 1958, although more recent and less affected by Eisenhower's idiosyncratic appeal, was a Congressional election year. In our simulation, too, we faced this problem. We resolved it for some voter types one way, for some another. But what happens if one relies on a single simple over-all assumption of continuity between elections? The result is not very good, though slightly better using 1956 than 1958. The product-moment correlation of Northern results between 1956 and 1960 was .39, between 1958 and 1960, .37. The multiple correlation using both earlier years was

.44 with the 1960 election. So far our simulation clearly was superior as a forecast.

Perhaps one might have made a good prediction of the impact of the religious issue by a simple slide-rule method of calculation instead of by an elaborate computer procedure. One could correct the 1956 or 1958 vote by some crude percentage of the Catholic population of each state. That would have worked and worked well if, by some act of intuitive insight, one could have hit on the right percentage correction. One would have had to decide first of all to use 1956, not 1958, as the base, for no simple correction of the 1958 results gives a good correlation with the actual outcome. If one had that correct flash of intuition, one could have surpassed our complex simulation with a correction of exactly 34 per cent of the Catholic percentage of the population added to the Democratic vote. The correlation with the actual outcome achieved by this process is .83. The simulation was better, however, than any correction except 34 per cent. It is better than 33 or 35 per cent. At corrections of 32 and 40 per cent the coefficients of correlation for the simple correction procedure drop below .80.

There was, in other words, a "lucky guess" way of estimating the effect of the religious issue in the campaign which would have given excellent prediction. But even if we had tried to make such an overall estimate and had somehow arrived at the right "lucky guess," we could not have defended it against skeptics. What the simulation did was to allow competent political analysts, operating without inspired guesses, to make sober, scientifically explicable estimates that they were willing to commit to paper before the facts. As the accompanying table shows, the simulation gave results about as good as the very best which *hindsight now* tells us could have been reached by simpler methods if infused by the right lucky guesses.

Correlations with Actual Election Results	
Trial heats with contemporaneous with simulation data	.53
Continuity with 1956	.39
Continuity with 1958	.37
Continuity with 1956 and 1958	.44
1956 results with optimum, or "lucky guess," correction for Catholic vote	.83
Simulation as done during campaign	.82

The essence of the simulation was to treat each voter type separately. Under what conditions should one expect that procedure to obtain a better result than an optimal across-the-board correction applied to the total? Clearly, if the process at work in each voter type was uniform it would make no difference whether we applied correction factors voter type by voter type or to the total. One could add 34 per cent of each Catholic voter type to the Democratic vote for that type or add 34 per cent of total Catholics to the total Democratic vote and come out with the same result. Where there are complex interactions of several variables on a voter type, however, then calculations done the two ways are no longer equal. If, for example, turnout varies between voter types and party voting also varies, then an equation applied to each voter type could not equally well be applied to total voters.

It is clear that we did not use the most predictive values for all parameters in our simulation. Determining what these were with the aid of hindsight is part of our present research program. But before election day we had no way of knowing what they were. (The one-third of 1958 Catholics casting Republican votes likely to go Democratic in 1960 according to our equations should not be confused with the 34 per cent of all 1956 Catholic voters, which turned out to be a good across-the-board correction.) The fact that our result came out on a par with the optimum simple correction which hindsight has enabled us to make is a crude measure of the gain from working voter type by voter type, with account taken of interactions within each type, that is, the gain from the computer operations.

The test of any new method of research is successful use. The outcome of the present study gives reason to hope that computer simulation may indeed open up the possibility of using survey data in ways far more complex than has been customary in the past. The political "pros" who commissioned this abstruse study were daring men to gamble on the use of a new and untried technique in the heat of a campaign. The researchers who undertook this job faced a rigorous test, for they undertook to do both basic and applied research at once. The study relied upon social science theories and data to represent the complexity of actual human behavior to a degree that would permit the explicit presentation of the consequences of policy alternatives.

This kind of research could not have been conducted ten years ago. Three new elements have entered the picture to make it possible: first, a body of sociological and psychological theories about voting and other decisions; second, a vast mine of empirical survey data now for the first time available in an archive; third, the existence of high-speed computers with large memories. The social science theories allow us to specify with some confidence what processes will come to work in a decision situation. The backlog of survey data permits us to estimate the parameters of these processes with fair precision and great detail for each small element of our national population. The computer makes possible the handling of this mine of data. More important still, it makes possible the precise carrying out of long and complex chains of reasoning about the interactions among the different processes. In summary, we believe that conditions now exist for use of survey data in research far more ambitious than social scientists are used to. If it is possible to reproduce, through computer simulation, much of the complexity of a whole society going through processes of change, and to do so rapidly, then the opportunities to put social science to work are vastly increased. It is our belief that this is now possible which was put to a test by the campaign research reported here.

Notes

1. We wish to express our gratitude to that Center, as well as to the MIT Computation Center, and to the men who originally assembled the data, especially George Gallup and Elmo Roper.
2. We should qualify. What has been described is what we started out to do and what we did for most issue clusters. In the end, however, we were forced to compromise on certain foreign-policy clusters. This in itself is an interesting finding. On almost all domestic questions, primarily because they were party-linked or left-right linked, it was possible to validate empirically the equivalence of questions which *a priori* seemed alike. On certain foreign-policy issues this was quite impossible. The political scientist looking at a half-dozen questions about foreign aid or about the UN might conclude that they all should reflect a common underlying attitude toward that matter. However, empirically, in many instances the distribution of replies was highly sensitive to conjunctural influences or shades in wording of the question. Rather than completely abandon the hope of doing any analysis of foreign-policy issues in the campaign, we retained some clusters which failed to meet the correlational test, labeling them *a priori* clusters, not sure of what we would do with them (in fact we did very little), but feeling it better to retain them on the computer tape than to discard the data from the start.
3. William McPhee, *A model for analyzing macro dynamics in voting systems,* Columbia University, Bureau of Applied Social Research, undated.
4. We wish to express our particular thanks to Thomas Finletter, Robert Benjamin, Joseph Baird, and Curtis Roosevelt for encouragement and cooperation.
5. The states where the simulation was most notably off included Arizona, Nevada, New Mexico, Idaho, and Colorado, states mostly of small population,

and states which, in the absence of a "Mountain Region" in our classification, we attempted to treat as Western or Midwestern. Clearly, the assumption of regional uniformity was misleading as applied to them.

6. Bernard R. Berelson, Paul F. Lazarsfeld, William N. McPhee. *Voting: A study of opinion formation in a presidential campaign,* Chicago, University of Chicago Press, 1954.
7. Since we trichotomized results, P56 + Q56 do not add up to 100 per cent. The reader may wonder why a turnout correction is added: are not the residuals the nonvoters? The answer is that a turnout correction is needed because many more persons express a candidate preference on a poll than actually turn out to vote.
8. With the above information, the remaining equations should be decipherable and are reported here for the record:
Protestant Independents, same equations as Protestant Democrats.
Catholic Democrats and Catholic Independents:

$$V_k = (P_{58} + \frac{Q_{58}}{3})(1 - P_{35})$$

$$V_n = \frac{2Q_{58}}{3}(1 - P_{35})$$

Catholic Republicans:

$$V_k = (P_{58} + \frac{Q_{58}}{3})(1 - 2P_{35})$$

$$V_n = \frac{2Q_{58}}{3}(1 - 3P_{35})$$

All others:

$$\frac{ad}{bc} = .6$$

$$a + b = \frac{P_{58} + P_{58}}{2}$$

$$c + d = \frac{Q_{58} + Q_{58}}{2}$$

$$a + c = P_{14}\frac{(P_{58} + Q_{58} + P_{58} + Q_{58})}{2}$$

$$b + d = (1 - P_{14})\frac{(P_{58} + Q_{58} + P_{58} + Q_{58})}{2}$$

$$V_k = \left(\frac{P_{58} + P_{58}}{2} - a\right)\left((1 - 2P_{35})\right)$$

$$V_n = \left(\frac{Q_{58} + Q_{58}}{2} - a\right)\left((1 - 2P_{35})\right)$$

5

A Postscript on the 1964 Election

with Robert P. Abelson and Samuel L. Popkin

No two presidential elections are alike. To the historian every election is a novel rearrangement of persistent elements of national life. To the politician every election is another risky play in a continuing game. To the political scientist every election is a fresh experiment against which to test his theories. The 1964 election campaign, so different from that of 1960—indeed so different from that of any other in American history—was a challenge. How would our methods work in a second election and what would they show about the dynamics of the vote?

As we write this chapter just two weeks after election day, three conclusions stand out.

1. Our basic simulation procedure worked. Once more, with data none of which was newer than two years old, we were able to simulate the outcome on the basis of cross-pressure theory with a degree of accuracy substantially like that in 1960.

2. The dynamics of 1964 were utterly different from those of 1960. In contrast to 1960, when group identification was the main variable in accounting for votes and vote switches, in 1964 it was attitudes on issues that largely accounted for Johnson's landslide triumph over Goldwater. To a degree rare in American politics, policy issues, not personality, dominated the campaign. The three issues that determined votes in 1964 were civil rights, nuclear responsibility, and social welfare legislation.

3. While the methods we have used have proved effective once more, we have also identified certain limits in these two experiences. In any future operation we would now know how to advance the art of election simulation, taking full advantage of the increased capacity of modern computers.

First published in the *American Behavioral Scientist* (1965).

Models of the 1964 Campaign

The 1964 campaign was special in many ways. It was record breaking in the size of President Johnson's victory. Viewed from the future it may turn out to be one of those rare elections that realign the political structure of the country. Such elections are few and far between. With the election of Jefferson in 1800, the Federalist Party disappeared; with the election of 1860, the Whigs disappeared; in the election of 1936, the majority Republican Party became the minority party as it remains to this day. The election of 1964 could turn out to be another such landmark election.

It is premature to assume that after its bruising defeat the Republican Party, captured by an extreme wing, will vanish from the American political scene. More likely the GOP will experience a painful purging and recovery. But whatever happens, it will never be the same party that it was before Barry Goldwater launched his crusade to prove that he would rather be right than president.

Seldom before has a national major party candidate put so high a value on upholding moral and ideological principles rather than representing his people. The standard strategy of candidates in the American two-party system is to seize the well-peopled middle ground. The candidate in some sense holds captive those followers who are extremists of his own wing of opinion; they have little choice but to vote for him even if he is more moderate than they are. To win, however, he must demonstrate to the moderates among the voters that he is squarely in the middle with them. The old European shibboleth that American politics offers the voter no choice since the parties are but Tweedledum and Tweedledee turns the situation on its head. The parties speak like Tweedledum and Tweedledee because each tries to represent that choice that the voters have already made. Far from denying expression to the voter, the two parties are typically so anxious to serve the views of the mass that the job of representing the voters has already occurred well before the candidate presents himself as a spokesman for that middle view in the debate. But not Barry Goldwater. He offered the voters a choice of something it was clear they did not want. The result was a landslide in which millions of voters broke from their traditional party, many for the first time in their lives.

Such broad outlines of the 1964 campaign were visible to any perceptive journalist, politician, or political scientist well before election day. The job in our 1964 pre-election simulation was to represent these dynamics in sufficient detail and with sufficient rigor to make it possible to calculate how different portions of the American electorate would respond to the campaign on election day. We report in the pages to follow three closely related simulations which we shall designate a five-factor, a six-factor, and a seven-factor simulation, and which successively approximate more fully to what happened on election day.

The five-factor simulation was the basic simulation to which the others are but modifications. The five-factor simulation postulated that voters would behave according to the following simple model:

All Democrats except those who were strongly opposed to civil rights would vote for Johnson.

All Republicans would vote for Goldwater except those who supported the Democratic side on at least two out of three issue-clusters, namely, civil rights, nuclear responsibility, and social welfare legislation.

All Independents who expressed a clear view on civil rights would vote accordingly; those without a clear view on civil rights would vote in accordance with their views on the other two clusters. In estimating how Independents might divide we would disregard those Independents who expressed no views or whose views were evenly balanced.

We call this simple model a five-factor model because in addition to the three issue-clusters (civil rights, nuclear responsibility, and social welfare legislation) the outcome is also determined by two other factors: party identification and turnout. We expressed this model mathematically in the following equations.

For Democratic voter-types:

$$Vj = P_{36}(1.0—Q_1 P_2)$$

For Republican voter-types:

$$Vj = P_{36}[P_1P_3 + P_1P_4(1-P_3) + P_3P_4(1-P_1)]$$

For Independent voter-types:

$$+(1 - P_1 - Q_1)P_3(1 - P_4 - Q_4)$$

Where

P_{36} = percent of the voter-type with established voting habits (turn-out factor).

P_1 = percent of the voter-type for civil rights.

Q_1 = percent of the voter-type against civil rights.

P_2 = percent of the voter-type feeling strongly about civil rights.

P_3 = percent of the voter-type for nuclear restraint.
Q_1 = percent of the voter-type against nuclear restraint.
P_4 = percent of the voter-type for social welfare legislation.
Q_4 = percent of the voter-type against social welfare legislation.
Vj = percent of the voter-type predicted to vote Democratic.

The apparent simplicity of the model hides a couple of points of some importance. First of all note that we are assuming statistical independence among the three issues that determine the votes of Republicans and Independents. Unlike what we did in the 1960 simulation we did not assume any individual-by-individual correlation within voter-types between attitudes on civil rights, nuclear responsibility, and social welfare. A quick and admittedly superficial review of the data indicated that we could assume these attitudes to be orthogonal, and so we did.[1]

A second point that does not appear from reading the equations is that the issue-clusters that we used to index the three key issues were not raw survey data accepted at face value. They were modified values of issue-clusters in our data bank. Since each raw issue-cluster was composed from a large number of different questions asked at different times, it could be an arbitrary matter what proportion of the public was listed in the data bank as being for and against each issue. For example, on civil rights, a question on whether the respondent approves the Supreme Court's school decision produces many more answers on the pro side than does a question on whether the respondent favors open occupancy in housing.

In our 1960 simulation we made no allowances for this arbitrariness. We used the P's and Q's from the various issue-clusters just as they came from the data bank. It will be recalled for instance that we decided to use the exact proportion of respondents who indicated that they would hesitate to vote for a Catholic for president as our measure of anti-Catholicism. We noted, however, that if we had had some basis for doubting the relevance of that figure we might have chosen to weight it by a factor, for example, to assume that .8 or 1.1 of those who gave that answer really felt that way. In 1960 we could afford to take the data bank percentage at face value because we were not trying to estimate true vote percentages but only rank orders of states. The absolute level of P or Q in an issue-cluster did not matter. In 1964, our simulation objective was more ambitious. We wanted to hit the right absolute level. That would clearly depend on the levels at which division occurred on three attitudinal issues. We therefore had to give weights to the raw issue-clusters in some instances.

The civil rights clusters—both the cluster on attitudes toward civil rights and the cluster on the saliency of civil rights—were used exactly as they came out of the data bank. On social welfare legislation and on nuclear responsibility the over-all mean of the distribution was at a level that called for modification. Ten percent of those respondents in each voter-type who at the date the question was asked gave replies classified as against social welfare legislation were assumed to have swung over to the pro side by 1964. Similarly, one-third of all those respondents who had given replies against nuclear restraint were assumed to have swung over to a more pacific posture by 1964. In the latter case there was an obvious reason for this large shift. The nuclear test ban treaty had been signed in October, 1963, just a year before the election. The most recent data that we used were from at least a year before that. Many of the questions used in the nuclear responsibility cluster asked about fallout or about the banning of nuclear testing. Many individuals who opposed signing a test ban treaty with the Russians when the treaty was still a starry-eyed dream could be expected to favor it once it had become an accomplished fact, ratified by the Senate and apparently being observed.

Each of these adjustments fixed the mean distribution of views on the issue to about the same 60–40 level of support for the Democratic side that already held in regard to party affiliation and civil rights. It thus weighted the clusters roughly evenly. These parameter settings to a large extent determined the over-all outcome of the simulation. The fact that this five-factor simulation gave Johnson 62 percent of the national vote—he got 61.4 percent—is not in itself a significant confirmation of the simulation procedure. That is largely a matter of good luck and good judgment in estimating the parameters. As in our 1960 simulation the real test is how close the simulation came to the results state by state.[2]

The five-factor simulation yields a result that is only moderate, that is, a correlation with the November results of .52, and a median error of 0.61. The extent of deviation was no surprise. When we ran the five-factor simulation before the election we recognized that it did not represent all the relevant variables in the campaign, but it did serve to represent the action of the most interesting issues in the campaign. For prediction, however, it was obvious that certain other factors had to be considered too.

The obvious deficiency of the five-factor simulation lay in certain regional idiosyncrasies. In 1960 we had been able to represent the North rather well but the South much less well. In 1960 we also had made some serious errors in states that were not well classified within the regions to which they were assigned. Oklahoma, for example, was not a typical Southern state, but we grouped it in the South. In general we had had trouble with the Mountain states for with our system of simulated states we were representing states like Montana and Wyoming with data from such dissimilar places as California, and were representing states like Nebraska and North Dakota with data from such dissimilar states as Ohio and Michigan. The states of the Western plains and the Rocky Mountains with their small population tended to be dominated by the larger population centers of the other parts of their assigned region. We realized, after 1960, that we could have done better had we had a separate Mountain region.

As we looked at the five-factor simulation results before the election it became apparent that the same distortions were operating again in 1964 even more sharply. Attitudes on the three crucial issues of the campaign that prevailed in the Eastern Midwest or on the West Coast were producing simulation results for a region which by universal political judgment was considered likely to be Goldwater country.

It would have been easy to introduce an arbitrary geographic correction factor as we did for the South in 1960 in our best-fit simulation whereby, it will be recalled we moved 10 percent of the white vote in the direction of the Republicans, and 10 percent of the negro vote in the direction of the Democrats. We preferred, however, to find some rational basis if we could for an estimate of such a Mountain and Western Plains state correction. A partly rational basis was provided by the extent to which we had erred in 1960 in estimating the Western Plains vote. We found that then, too, we had made them more Democratic than they should have been. Using the 1960 error as our estimate of the likely error in 1964 and rounding because of the basically arbitrary character of this adjustment, we took 5 percentage points off the estimate of the Western Plains states. Examination of the relationship in 1960 between those states and the Mountain states led to a 10 percentage point correction in the latter. All of this was done in advance of the election.

Thus, our six-factor simulation was exactly as before with a geographic correction for a region that had special characteristics but that we had not singled out as a region in our data bank.

The six-factor simulation correlated with the actual outcome .63, and the median error was 3.6 percent.

The seventh factor was also a geographic correction. In the 1964 campaign Johnson's name did not appear on the Alabama ballot. Voters in that state had no opportunity to cast a vote for him regardless of their preferences. Clearly it was preferences that we were simulating in our five- and six-factor simulations, not forced votes. Goldwater was fated to get 100 percent of the Alabama vote, but we simulated what he would have gotten in a free election. The Mississippi situation was less clear-cut. Johnson electors were on the ballot. However the state Democratic Party unitedly swung to Goldwater. No prominent Democratic politician in the state remained loyal. The bolt was organized and complete. Johnson got 13 percent of the Mississippi vote. We had, however, no basis for estimating that 13 percent within the model we were using, for that represents not the free operation of the three issues on the minds of the voters, but rather the voters rebelling against the organization's decisions.[3] The seventh factor was therefore simply to set Alabama and Mississippi at zero voles for Johnson.

This seven-factor simulation correlates with the election outcome .90, and the median error was 3.4 percent.

All of these factors were known before the election, and our basic simulation was run then. Before the election we distributed to friends and colleagues the six-factor simulation. While the results in Alabama and Mississippi were fully determined in advance of the election and not a surprise, we did not then bother to change their simulated results to zero percent for Johnson for we were reporting the consequences of a model, not an ad hoc prediction.

As in 1960, so in 1964; there were some other deviant simulation results in the South, this time Louisiana, North Carolina, and Arkansas. Before the election we had not concerned ourselves in any detail with the specific relationships among the Southern states because we felt on the basis of the 1960 results that these relations were bound to be quite erratic, based on local political factors, as indeed they were.

Table 5.1 shows the relationship of the six- and seven-factor simulations to the actual results. The interesting thing at this point is to examine the deviations of the actual from the predicted vote. What was going on among the electorate in 1964 that is not already taken into account in our simulation model of the world? What other factors were in operation besides the ones that entered into our model?

Table 5.1. 1964 Simulation Results (7-Factor Simulations Showing Percentage for Johnson).

State	Percent Predicted in 7–Factor Simulation	Actual Percent
Rhode Island	69	81
Massachusetts	68	76
Maine	60	69
New York	69	68
Connecticut	67	68
West Virginia	58	68
Michigan	62	67
Maryland	62	66
Vermont	60	66
New Jersey	67	66
Pennsylvania	64	65
Missouri	61	65
Kentucky	59	64
Minnesota	61	64
Oregon	67	64
New Hampshire	62	64
Texas	53	63
Ohio	61	63
Washington	66	62
Wisconsin	62	62
Iowa	60	62
Colorado	57	61
Delaware	64	61
California	68	60
Illinois	62	60
Montana	59	59
New Mexico	62	59
Nevada	58	58
North Dakota	56	58
Arkansas	46	57
Wyoming	58	56
Indiana	60	56
North Carolina	46	56
Oklahoma	47	56
South Dakota	55	56
Tennessee	61	56
Utah	55	55
Kansas	55	54
Virginia	49	54
Nebraska	55	53

(Continued)

Table 5.1. (Continued)

State	Percent Predicted in 7–Factor Simulation	Actual Percent
Florida	51	51
Idaho	57	51
Arizona	59	50
Georgia	48	46
Louisiana	57	44
South Carolina	48	41
Mississippi	0*	13
Alabama	0*	0

* In 6–factor simulation Mississippi 48, Alabama 49

There was clearly a native son factor. Arizona went for Goldwater more markedly than our issue-based simulation predicted, and Texas more strongly for Johnson.

We find two other highly significant deviations While California did give 60 percent of its vote to President Johnson, it was much more Republican than the balance of party and issue preferences in that state would have led us to expect. Our interpretation is that California was one state where a real backlash developed. In the same election that Johnson won by a wide margin, the voters of California by a two to one margin passed Proposition 14, which amended the state Constitution to bar legislation for open-occupancy housing and simultaneously the California voters defeated liberal Pierre Salinger who opposed Proposition 14 by electing conservative Republican George Murphy who refused to oppose it. Johnson carried California despite a surge of anti-civil rights sentiment, but not by the margin he might have expected. With racial prejudice stirred up, many prejudiced voters resolved their cross pressures by voting for Goldwater.

Finally there was a reverse phenomenon in New England. New England rejected Goldwater in a way that went well beyond what could be explained by the factors in our model. We expected Rhode Island to be the most Democratic state on the continent and it was.[4] Massachusetts was second most Democratic in reality; we had expected it to be third. We gave Vermont and Maine to Johnson by large margins and that is how they voted. Nonetheless, New England went more strongly Democratic than the model accounts for.

Thus through our simulation and through the deviations from it, the dynamics of the election of 1964 become fairly clear. Some special forces were in operation in New England, in California, in Texas and Arizona, in Alabama, and Mississippi; indeed such local variations were more important than they had been four years earlier. These variations modified a powerful surge of ideological voting against Goldwater, the candidate who first injected ideological issues into the campaign. He lost votes on civil rights, nuclear policy, and social issues. Johnson lost only segregationists.

Indeed the most dramatic aspect of the 1964 election was the extent to which it was genuinely dominated by issues rather than by social stratification or by personality. On the surface the reverse was the case. The press commented often that the speeches in this ostensibly ideological campaign failed to pose any issues clearly. There was little high-level discussion of issues. But whatever the contents of campaign output, the voters to an extraordinary extent did cast their votes on issues. That has not been true in all elections. When Lazarsfeld, Berelson, and Gaudet studied the 1940 election, they found that they could predict a man's vote with a high degree of confidence from a few of his social characteristics such as religion, rural-urban residence, and socioeconomic status. Issue stands were not very predictive. In 1960 a man's vote could be predicted quite well on the basis of his party and religion. That was so only to a very limited extent in 1964. True, the negro vote went overwhelmingly for Johnson, as did the Jewish vote. But these were exceptions. Johnson succeeded in creating a truly national coalition. He became, as he said he wanted to be, the candidate of all sorts of Americans. Probably never in recent years has there been so small a spread between the votes of business, professional people, white collar people, on the one hand, and blue collar people on the other. In our simulation only seven percentage points separate the Democratic vote among blue collar voters from that among the A and B SES people. Both gave their majority to Johnson. What determined a person's vote was not his social status as much as how he felt about national issues. One consequence of the serious attention that the public paid to issues was an enormous number of defections from party ties. The opinion pollers can report to us from empirical surveys what number of Democrats voted for Goldwater and what number of Republicans voted for Johnson. Our simulation also provides an estimate. Altogether we find 17 percent of Democrats voting for Goldwater but these include many in the South. In the East and in the whole North we find 10 percent of Democrats defecting to Goldwater. Among Republicans the defections were massive. More than a third of all Republicans voted for Johnson according to our simulation.

In 1960, it will be recalled, we found that of seven million voters one in ten had switched from their expectable vote on the religious issue. In 1964 the number of voters who broke with their normal party vote on issue grounds was one in five or six.

Throughout this discussion we have stressed the vast differences between the election in 1960 and the election in 1964. The simplest evidence of that difference is the fact that the correlation state by state between these two elections actually comes out negative though not significantly, –.16. That testifies to how great the variety of outcomes a single stable attitude system of the American people can provide. Even though the attitudes are stable enough so that with two- to ten-year-old data we can accurately calculate how people will vote, two such different elections can yet emerge.

Lessons from the Past and for the Future

The 1964 simulation project reported here was conducted in a very modest fashion. It was not sponsored research. Unlike the unusual 1960 situation in which the Democratic Party launched the research project a year in advance, the Democratic Party had virtually no systematic research program in 1964. A number of state surveys were done but without much planning or coordination. Whatever was done was done in the very last months of the campaign.

The 1964 simulation was undertaken by the authors for scientific purposes. Its objective was to confirm the procedure we had developed four years earlier. Being unsponsored the 1964 research had to be done on a minimum budget, but also it could be done in a university environment. We conducted the research at MIT where available free computer time made the study possible.[5] To bring our data bank up to date, we obtained from the Roper Public Opinion Research Center 20 surveys conducted in the years 1960–62. These additions to the data bank were particularly important because they brought the civil rights and nuclear responsibility issues into the current context.

For simplicity and economy we adopted the rule that we would not change our basic 1960 system in any way. We used existing computer programs from the 1960 study. We made no changes such as, for example, redefining regions or voter-types. All of these simplifying limitations were adopted in accordance with our narrow purpose of replicating the 1960 study.

By now, however, we know many ways in which to improve such election simulations. If we by any chance repeat such research in 1968, it will be done differently in many respects.

In 1960 we worked with an IBM 704 computer, large and fast in that day but inflexible and slow by present standards. We did not then feel it practical to repeatedly process 130,000 cards so we obliged ourselves to group all responses into distributions within 480 voter-types. The development of modern computers has made this transformation of individuals into summary groups an unnecessary simplification. Today we could store and rapidly retrieve that many or more individual interviews. If we were programming the operation now we could keep the individual interviews available and regroup them at will into varying voter-types according to the character of the issues. We could change the definitions of regions at will (which we would have liked to do), or include age, or ethnicity in the definition of the voter types on some occasions. More accurately we could include ethnicity to the extent that a national origin question was asked of the original survey respondent and the data stored on his card. The one thing that cannot be done in a secondary analysis such as our simulation is to provide raw information that the survey researcher did not originally ask. We are often deprived of information on such politically important matters as national origin because many polls do not ask it. Occasionally, however, the question is there. In a flexible simulation system which permitted the creation of voter-types at will, we could retain all such occasional information to be used whenever it was there and relevant.

By retaining the information from each original survey card in a fashion for rapid retrieval and reuse we could also retain the freedom to modify and remake issue-clusters. By reference to the original information on individuals, we could estimate better any correlation that might exist between variables and regroup them when needed. Our assumption in the 1964 simulation that attitudes on civil rights, nuclear responsibility, and social welfare legislation were largely uncorrelated proved to be a satisfactory one. We would have been better off, however, if we could have tested the relationship among questions on these three topics wherever they co-occurred within our data bank. We could then with much more confidence have calculated the number of Republicans disagreeing with Goldwater on at least two issues.

In short, we are moving into an era where the limitation on data bank operations will no longer be computer capacity but only the imagination of the researcher and the extent to which raw data is available to him. For survey researchers this new age of rich data covering varieties of groups and long time series promises to bring a revolution in our ability to understand politics. For politicians and for citizens it promises the prospect of a more intelligent understanding of the civic process. The tools that we are now developing can handle models of a complexity adequate to the complexity of the political process itself. Not every election will be as intricate as that of 1964, but they will all be different and challenging to understand.

Notes

1. There would, of course, be correlations across voter-types. Negroes and Jews would favor both civil rights and social welfare measures. But within a voter-type there need be no correlation across individuals. Those few negroes who oppose integration are not necessarily the same individuals as those who oppose higher minimum wages, for example.
2. All statements about real November results refer to AP figures as of November 13. They are almost complete but not official. Thanks are due AP for specially providing them to us.
3. With negroes providing nearly half of the Johnson votes, the nationally loyal white Democrats who broke with the state party were remarkably few.
4. Recall that Hawaii and Alaska are not included in our data bank or results.
5. Thanks are due to Project MAC and its timesharing computer system for extraordinary facilities. Project MAC is an MIT research project sponsored by the Advanced Research Projects Agency of the Department of Defense, under the Office of Naval Research, contract #Nonr-4102(01). Mr. Noel Morris conducted the computer operations.

6

The Kaiser, the Tsar, and the Computer: Information Processing in a Crisis*

with Allan Kessler

Summary

Crisiscom is a computer simulation of national decision makers processing information during a crisis. The project has several purposes:

1. It is designed to increase our understanding of the process of deterrence by exploring how far the behavior of political decision makers in crisis can be explained by psychological mechanisms. This is done by comparing the output of the highly simplified computer model based on principles of individual psychology with records of actual political behavior.

2. It is designed to put together a good deal of what we know about the psychology of deterrence into a rigorous and formal system and thus to serve as an integrating device for that body of knowledge.

3. It is designed to be used in human games of the type represented by Bloomfield's DETEX games to provide inputs for teams that cannot be staffed with humans and to represent aspects of the environment that are not played out by the human players.

4. It is designed perhaps ultimately to provide a way of simulating a variety of possible crises. It will be some time before we have enough confidence in the model to use it in such a semi-predictive fashion, but that cannot be ruled out.

In the Crisiscom computer model two human decision makers are represented (the number is easily expansible). Each of them receives a large number of messages which enter into his cognitive system.

First published in the *American Behavioral Scientist* (1965).

The elements of the cognitive system of each simulated decision maker are messages that represent interpersonal relationships among international actors. For example, "President Johnson" (an actor, A_1) "visits with" (a relation, R_x) "The Prime Minister of Great Britain" (an actor, A_2). The set of relations, R, is at present limited to two—affect and salience. Affect refers to the attitude or feelings which an actor, A_i, has toward another actor, A_j, or toward an interpersonal relationship. Salience describes the importance of an actor or interpersonal relationship or another actor. The cognitive system of A_n, (the world he knows) is thus comprised of elements A_1, A_2,, A_m, and affects or saliences which relate them *as perceived by* A_n.

A_n, came to perceive these relationships as a result of receiving messages about the actors and their interpersonal relationships. However, the total information conveyed in these messages is too great for any one human to handle. Not all the information is absorbed by A_n. Psychological mechanisms restrict his input and distort it. As a result each decision maker has an incomplete and imperfect picture of the relationships among all actors. As the simulation has been run recently, both actors have been fed the same set of messages about the world but by the end of a week's crisis they have quite different perceptions.

In the present program the cognitive systems of only two of twenty-four actors are completely represented, namely the cognitive systems of decision makers J and K. J and K receive information about themselves and about the other actors in the form of messages written by a scenario writer. Each message has the format A_n, R_a, A_m. For example: The King of Ethiopia confers with President Nasser of Egypt. These messages are written in natural English and as long as the sentence order is A_n, R_a, A_m, the computer accepts them.

The scenario consists of a large number of messages of the kind just described about interpersonal relationships among the actors. The decision maker does not pay attention to all messages. In accordance with well established psychological principles, he is "selectively exposed" to a subset of them. He pays attention to some, ignores others.

These incoming messages that are selected not only enter into the decision maker's attention space, they also change his basic image of the world with which he started the simulation. This basic image is represented by an affect matrix which tells how each actor feels about each other actor. New messages alter slightly this continuing perception of the relationships in the world.

In our present simulation the following hypotheses about selective perception operate on the messages in the scenario:

1. People pay more attention to news that deals with them.
2. People pay less attention to facts that contradict their previous views.
3. People pay more attention to news from trusted, liked sources.
4. People pay more attention to facts that they will have to act upon or discuss because of attention by others.
5. People pay more attention to facts bearing on actions they are already involved in, that is, action creates commitment.

In its present stage the model is thus a rather simple representation of a number of the major mechanisms that come into play in crisis, but clearly not of all of them. In the future a number of additional mechanisms of decision making will be grafted onto the model. The model is modular permitting continued growth and refinement.

We have been utilizing historical crisis events to test our simulation, even in its present simple form. We have written a scenario of messages representing the week of the outbreak of World War I. This week was chosen because it is extensively written up by historians and has also been replicated by gaming procedures. Thus comparison is possible between what seemed important to national decision makers as described by historians, as played by game players, and as put out by the simulation.

The scenario messages were written by going through historical documents about the week, but most of all from the newspapers of that week. The two key decision makers we have represented are the Kaiser and the Tsar. Appended to this report are a sample of the list of messages they received, a sample of the list of messages that went into the attention space of each one on each day, and part of the final affect matrix (representing their basic picture of the world).

The results are intuitively very satisfactory. The Kaiser and Tsar behave as we think they would. Each pays attention to those events that affect him particularly. They each miss some key cues that if they had been mutually perceived might have prevented war. Instead each sees the overt military acts of the other unmitigated by his moderating intents, while remaining conscious of his own moderate intentions that he must have (wrongly) assumed equally obvious to the other.

Readers not interested in the computer processes can turn to the next to the last section headed, A Test of the Crisiscom Model Against A Real World Crisis. It deals with the World War I experiment.

Purpose of the Project

Crisiscom is a computer simulation of the behavior of national decision makers in international crisis. More specifically it is designed to represent the ways in which psychological mechanisms enter into their processing of the information they receive. It is designed to simulate the process whereby two different decision makers acquire in their own minds quite different pictures of the world in which they are interacting. A flow of messages representing the real world comes to the decision makers. They selectively attend to different messages in this flow leaving each decision maker with a quite different image of the world from that of the other. This in a nutshell is the process simulated by the Crisiscom program.

There were several reasons for developing such a simulation. First among them is the desire to explore how far a limited set of psychological relations can take us in understanding the behavior of national decision makers in a crisis. We are attempting by the simulation to push to the limits the hypothesis that the basic principles of individual psychology which describe how individuals behave in personal crises also account for the behavior of national decision makers in a world political crisis. We do this not because we believe this proposition to be true. On the contrary, it is perfectly clear that individual psychology accounts for only a small part of international politics. However, the best way to ascertain what part, if any, individual psychology plays in the determination of political behavior is to postulate the truth of the extreme proposition and then see what conclusions it leads us to. We can then compare those conclusions with reality. We are, in short, engaged in a kind of experiment—the kind sometimes called a Gedanken experiment—in which we press an idea to see where it breaks down.

Our procedure corresponds to the ideas of the philosopher Hans Vahinger in his book *The Philosophy of As If.* We model a hypothetical world based on certain propositions to ascertain just what the consequences of these propositions would be; we look at the world *as if* they were true.

Various devices have been developed to explore hypothetical futures of which computer simulation is only one. Gaming is at present an increasingly popular and effective tool for answering that what if question. It is effective because it forces each player to specialize on thinking about a particular set of roles and particular aspects of the situation. The same player trying to write an essay predicting how things would be in some specified hypothetical future would miss many of the eventualities which other players force onto his attention as they play out their own required roles.

Human gaming, however, has certain limitations as well as some enormous advantages. One of its limitations is that it is expensive and time consuming. For the results to be useful the players should be experts on the roles they are representing. There are limits to the numbers of experts one can collect and to the periods of time for which one can commandeer them. Furthermore, in the time available it is usually possible to play out only one alternative out of the many branches that history could follow depending on eventualities.

Computer simulation gets around both these disadvantages of human gaming though at its own price. The computer runs fast and can run the same game over many times with minor variations. However, in all candor, it is necessary to recognize that no computer program ever written contains as much expertise as is stored in the heads of a group of specialists.

Thus an intelligent approach to the problem of exploring strategic futures is to use both human gaming and computer simulation and also combinations of them. Computer simulation should be developed to assess how far it can approximate the results achieved in human games. It should be used to play out many variants of situations that one can game with experts only once. Finally, the two procedures can be linked. A computer can be used to produce the results of minor teams or of nature or other factors for which players themselves cannot be provided.

With these considerations in mind, we can now summarize the purposes that the Crisiscom project has set out to achieve. It set out to explore how realistic a simulation could be produced with a relatively constricted and simple model arising entirely from the propositions of social psychology about human behavior in crisis. Secondly, it set out to produce a program that would provide messages that could be used in mixed human-machine games. Thirdly, in the process of achieving these objectives it served to advance our understanding of the psychological system known as deterrence by working out the interactions of various propositions about behavior in a crisis. Finally perhaps it advanced us a few steps toward the point where such computer simulations might have some predictive value.

The Model

We now proceed to describe the Crisiscom model by three successive elaborations, each covering the same ground, but each more fully and accurately than the last.

1. The Crisiscom Model in Sketchy Form

The Crisiscom simulation represents the interaction of national commanders in a crisis in which they confront each other.

a) Each receives information about the world.
b) Each handles this information in ways which are determined by his own background and by the principles of psychology.
c) Each then reacts by originating new messages.

This happens each time period, so the model cycles through those three steps over and over. The messages put out by the commanders become part of the input of messages at the next period.

A skeleton basic flow chart is presented in figure 6.1. The two commanders are designated DM(J) = decision maker J, and DM(K) = decision maker K. In the present version of the model this is a man-machine simulation rather than a pure machine simulation. The decision making portion of the model is done by human simulation; the bias and distortion portion by the computer.

We now describe the model in greater detail.

2. The Crisiscom Model Somewhat Elaborated

In the real world decision makers receive information about their world from various sources and through various media. In most cases the volume of information they receive is too large for them to attend to, so they use a variety of techniques of selective attention, forgetting and distortion, in order to limit this information to proportions they can handle.

Let us consider the selective attention and distortion processes. Two decision makers, J (let's say for Mr. Johnson) and K (let's say for Mr. Kosygin) receive messages from a human scenario writer as to the events and relationships occurring among 24 countries or country blocks. For example, associated with the recent Guantanamo affair, messages of the following nature would come to J and K.

Guantanamo affair. USA arrests Cuba's fishermen. Each message is a statement related to some event having two actors and a relationship

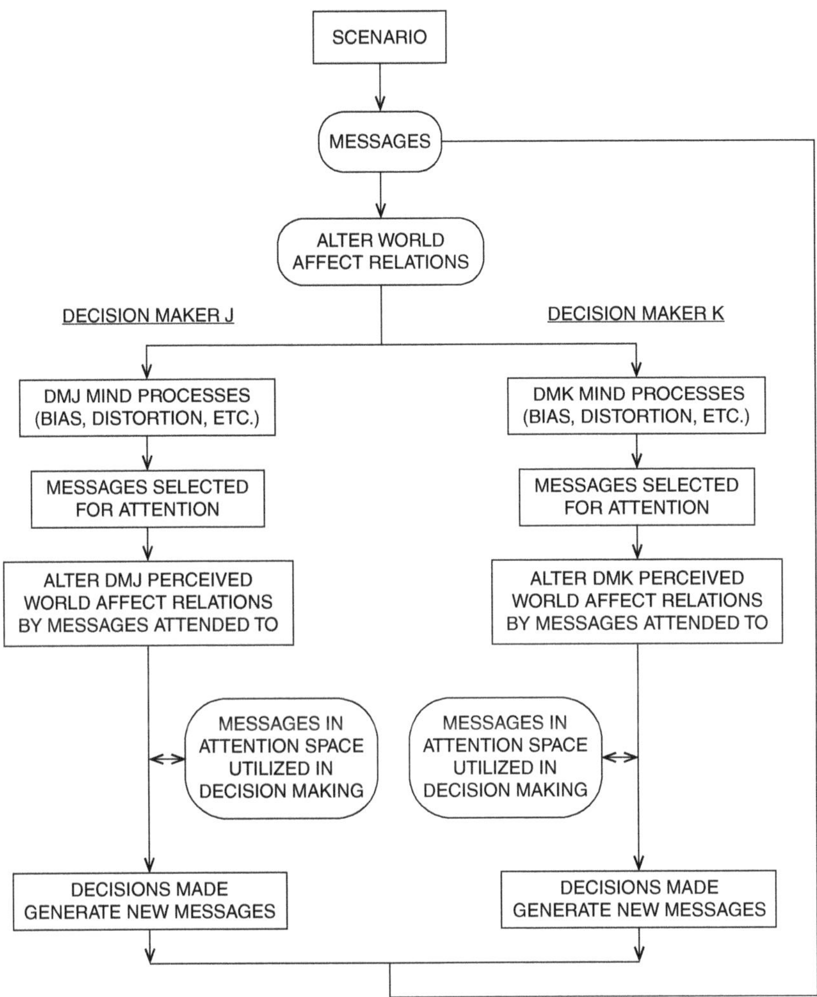

Figure 6.1. Crisiscom General Flow Chart.

between them. Another message related to Guantanamo would be: *Cuba cuts water supply to USA military base.*

The importance of the message to each decision maker, their feelings about the reliability of the source of the message, their attitudes toward the particular countries' relationship, and the importance of the relationship to the countries involved all are important in determining the probable nature and extent of distortion of the message before it reaches J or K.

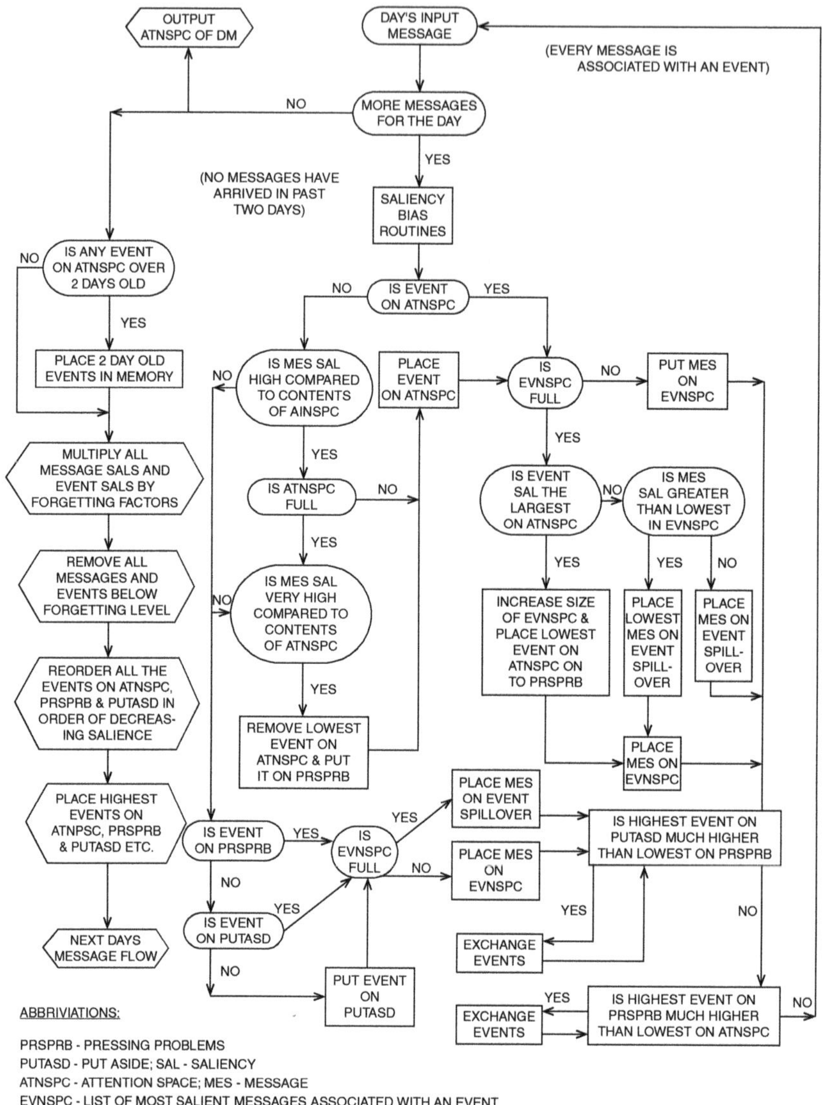

Figure 6.2. Message Input Flow for a Decision Maker on a Decision Day (Third Approximation).

Underlying the distortion processes is the decision maker's perception of the world, his perception of the attitudes and feelings—or affect—existing between each pair of countries. For example, J may perceive that the Soviet Union has negative feelings toward Communist

China while France has a more positive affect toward Communist China. A decision maker's perceptions tend to remain stable and change significantly only when new information about countries' relationships is greatly at variance with his present perception. Similarly, a decision maker will pay less attention to messages that differ from his present perception of the relationship between the countries involved. However, relationships *that do come to his attention*, and that differ from his present perception, will alter that perception. (Emphasis has been placed on "relationships that do come to his attention" because, on a given day, the decision maker cannot attend to all messages: some must be put aside as pressing problems, some are ignored and some forgotten. The most important events are attended to, that is, are placed in the decision maker's attention space. On some days, a decision maker who is concerned with very important events may put aside events that would have come into attention space if they occurred on another day. What the decision maker attends to is a function of the importance of the messages in his present attention space and this importance, or salience, is itself altered by the distortion processes. Thus, what J attends to may differ from what K attends to. In turn, the information to which K and J attend differentially alters their perception of the world. Once events have been attended to they are placed in the decision maker's memory where they are subject to forgetting. This classification and ordering of messages and events is illustrated in detail in figure 6.2.

At present, decisions based on the information in J's and K's attention spaces are made by humans who receive this information at the end of a decision day. Later, this output will be the input to simulated decision processes which will generate messages to be placed in the environment.

3. The Crisiscom Model More Fully Elaborated

Figure 6.2 is a flow chart of the computerized portion of the simulation for a single time period.

Crisiscom Input

Messages from a scenario writer are the input for Crisiscom. Every message is a combination of two countries and a relationship between them.

Messages are associated with a unique event. At present the scenario writer must specify the following values for each message.

AFFT — The affect (–1 to +1) of the (REL) between CONE and CTWO

SLCONE — The salience (0 to +1) of (REL) for CONE

SLCTWO — The salience (0 to +1) of (REL) for CTWO

SALJ — The salience (0 to +1) of the message for DM(K)'s Public Opinion

SALK — The salience (0 to +1) of the message for DM(J)'s Public Opinion

SALPOJ — The salience (0 to +1) of the message for DM(K)

SALPOK — The salience (0 to +1) of the message for DM(J)

ASOURJ — J's affect (–1 to +1) toward the message source

ASOURK — K's affect (–1 to +1) toward the message source

Examples of messages can be found in the appendix.

Every message received by a decision maker, DM, is distorted according to the following saliency bias routines.

1. People pay more attention to news that deals with them.
   For example, IPI studies show a tendency of foreign news selection to focus on those things that deal with self. Indian news in American paper concerns American aid to India.
2. People pay less attention to facts that contradict their views.
   This is in accord with cognitive balance theory and cognitive dissonance theory. It is emphasized by Robert Abelson and Alex Bernstein, however, that this is a relatively weak proposition, since "experience both in the experimental laboratory and in the field suggests considerable latitude for muzziness in the operation of cognitive consistency forces."
3. People pay more attention to news from trusted, liked sources. Hovland, Irving Janis, and H. H. Kelley, *Communication and Persuasion.*
4. People pay more attention to facts that they will have to act on or discuss because of attention by others.

This proposition is generalized from several studies, none of which test the proposition directly. Among the relevant studies is that by John and Matilda Riley which showed that children tend to select programs on television according to whether the information in the program is relevant to conversation in their reference group or not.

Decision makers are concerned with events that occur in their world. George Miller has hypothesized that a person can attend to

762 things at a time. Decision makers can attend to 762 events, that is, his attention space has 762 events in it. Associated with each event the decision maker can attend to 762 messages. An event space has these 762 messages in it. Other associated messages are placed on the event spillover. The selection of input events and messages for attention is a function of the number and importance of the events and messages presently in the decision maker's attention space. In the long run the decision maker will attempt to attend to the messages and events he perceives as most salient to him. However, in the short run this may not be feasible as there is a certain amount of inertia which tends to give precedence to the events the decision maker is presently attending to over the new events that arrive.

The decision maker keeps his attention space and event spaces as full as possible, and continually seeks information to keep them full. He may attend to few very important events, many unimportant events, or some number in between these extremes depending on the salience of the messages he is receiving as he perceives them. If an event is very important to him, he will seek as many messages as he can attend to. If an event is unimportant to him, he will not attend to a large number of messages. A decision maker's attention space holds up to 9 unimportant events. Unimportant events have up to 5 messages in their event spaces. The decision maker will attend up to 5 very important events. Normally an important event may hold up to 9 messages. However, very important events may hold many more messages at the expense of attending to fewer events. It is possible for the decision maker to attend to only one extremely important event having a large number of messages in its event space. Therefore a continuum of few events with many messages, to many events (9) with few messages is specified for the selection of information for the attention space.

Events not attended to immediately are placed aside as pressing problems or put aside according to their importance.

When a very important message compared to the contents of attention space arrives, and its event is not in attention space, the event associated with this message may displace an event in attention space.

At the end of the day the attention space of each decision maker is made available to the programmer.

To bypass the decision processes, any event which has its most recent message over two days old is placed in memory. The salience of an event is exponentially reduced over time until it is below the forgetting level at which time it is deleted.

Each day the mind spaces are reorganized by placing the events and messages in the hierarchy of the mind spaces in order of importance ignoring all inertia factors.

A Consideration of the Psychological Principles

The decision maker's "mind" represented in the Crisiscom simulation consists of two main parts: one representing the kind of stable backlog of experience that each person carries with him into any new situation; the other representing the flow of new messages and information which the decision maker processes. The first of these is represented by the affect matrix (and in principle in later versions of the model in the matrices representing other relationships besides affect). The affect matrix is part of the initial condition of the simulation at t_0. It states how the decision maker perceives each actor (in the present runs actors are countries) in relation to each other actor. Not all cells in the affect matrix need be filled out. In some instances the decision maker may have no idea how two actors feel about each other. The matrix is not symmetric. Actor One may have an affect of 2.3 toward Actor Two while Actor Two has an affect of 1.1 to Actor One. Such sharp differences are, of course, unusual. The affect matrix summarizes the way in which each decision maker views the world. It thus provides the base line against which he tests incoming messages.

The other part of the decision maker's mind is a hierarchical set of list structures, the items on the lists being messages. This hierarchy is composed of: (1) an attention space, (2) a pressing problems list, (3) a put-aside list, and (4) memory. The put-aside list acts as a buffer for the memory. Onto it go the messages that are hardly considered and it is from the bottom of memory that forgetting deletions occur. The pressing problems list is used for important messages that could not be considered on the day of their arrival, important things that have to be put off until tomorrow. At the beginning of the day some pressing problems may go immediately into the attention space. The attention space is for those things being considered on the given day.

In memory are stored all messages that have been considered and have managed to avoid being deleted by the forgetting deletion operations.

It is in this framework that the selective process of retention takes place and in which in turn the affect matrix gets modified by the flow of new information.

This model conforms rather closely to what we know about the actual characteristics of human information handling. It has to be a rather complex model to do so. Powerful as the pleasure principle may be in guiding human behavior, the algorithm people use in conforming to it is a complex one.

The simple algorithm, that people pay attention to what they like to hear and disregard what they do not like to hear, does not work. There are contradictory experimental results as to whether people are more likely to see good news or bad news. Sometimes it is one; sometimes it is the other. So this is *not* one of the determinants of bias in our model. The process is a more purposeful one. The determinant seems to be an unconscious pleasure maximizing calculation that takes into account the consequences of inattention. An unpleasant story that has no action consequences for the hearer may be disregarded because that way pain is minimized. But a "danger, live wire" sign will get high attention because, by taking note of that unpleasant fact, the pain can be minimized. Experiments show that most people do not read newspaper stories that contradict their political views, but debaters read carefully statements that disagree with their stand because they thereby increase the probability of a pleasant outcome, winning the debate.

Our model handles information in ways that conform to this complexity of human rationality. It does pay less attention to facts that contradict prior views, but more attention to action relevant facts.

A Test of the Crisiscom Model Against a Real World Crisis

We have run the seven days from 25 July through 31 July, 1914, through the Crisiscom simulation. A seven-day crisis will do very little to the basic image of the world that a decision maker holds. The affect matrix which represents that image of the world should remain quite stable. When the events are as world shaking as those of 1914 there may indeed be deeper effects drastically changing his views in the future, that is, a sleeper effect. That could be the case even if nothing else happened, but it takes time for such attitude changes to occur. Nonetheless in a crisis of any intensity some perceptible shift in the image of who is good and who is bad and who loves whom should be visible, even if not large. That is what happens if one compares the affect matrices from beginning to end of the week.

The place where big changes may be expected in a short period is in what the decision maker is attending to.

Both the changes in attention and the changes in the affect matrices are recorded in the computer output describing our major test of the Crisiscom simulation so far. That test is a replication of the minds of the Kaiser and the Tsar in the seven days of the outbreak of World War I. We picked that crisis because it has been widely used in other kinds of gaming and other kinds of research. It has been the subject of a Project Michelson study by Professor Robert North of Stanford University and of human gaming using the device of Harold Guetzkow's internation simulation. At the end of this article the reader will find a sample of the messages that were fed into and the calculations performed by the computer. There are approximately 1,400 of them, 200 per each day of the crisis. To the reader of ordinary history books what is fascinating is the amount of chaff in the communications channel which the historians forget. We collected our messages from the daily newspapers of that time plus the North collection of documents which includes later revelations that at that time were secret to the public. (About one percent of the message input was secret.) These were the messages that might normally have come to the attention of the decision maker as he lived and worked in that particular week. They included vast numbers of casual events in the sporting world, in the business world, progress in the development of airplanes, crime, etc. A volcano erupted in the USA, the English bought a Rembrandt, suffragettes pawned their jewels for funds, there were riots in Russia, strikes in the USA, a mutiny in Mexico, etc. The historian filters out these irrelevancies before he reports to the reader on the subject of his essay. But in the real decision process competition for attention is an important fact. It is handled in our computer simulation. With its speed and large memory a computer can do what an essay writer cannot, that is, it can analyze the interaction between the crisis that interests us and the rest of what was going on. This is a unique advantage the full significance of which we did not realize until we actually became involved in this sample simulation.

But needless to say as war is breaking out the Tsar and the Kaiser did not give much of their energies to the trial run through the Panama Canal or terrorism in Ireland. They selected a few events to which they gave attention. The attention space, it will be recalled, contains material on 762 events with each having the capability of having 762 messages considered. However, it will also be recalled that terribly important events reduce the number of things to which attention is paid (a psychological proposition that is well confirmed). That is what happened in the period with which we are concerned. It was normally the case that less than 49 messages were in the heart of the attention space.

The computer also has stored other messages on a pressing problems list, a set-aside list and memory. We save the reader the tedium of reproducing this vast mass of data.

It is clear that the computer has selected for the attention space a reasonable set of the most important messages. The reader should recognize that this is partly but not wholly a reflection of the initial coding of saliency. That coding is subsequently modified by reactions to the salience of the message to the other side; by its salience to public opinion; and by the passage of time. The reasonableness of the output is therefore by no means guaranteed. In our simulation we sent each decision maker J and K almost the same set of messages. This need not have been done but we chose to do it that way for experimental purposes.

The way in which the psychological processes in our model work may be well illustrated by looking at the difference in the messages accorded attention in the course of Day One. Both the Tsar and the Kaiser gave more attention to Austria's ultimatum to Serbia. The fact of the ultimatum was the primary message for both men. For the Kaiser, however, almost as important was the fact that Germany's mobs rallied for war. For the Kaiser, Serbian reaction was the *third* ranking message closely followed by Germany's fears that Austria's ultimatum was too harsh. The Tsar ranked the messages in a somewhat different order. Behind the bald fact of the ultimatum, the *second* most significant fact for him was the reaction to the ultimatum in Serbia. That Germany's mobs rallied for war was also important although *third,* but that Germany feared that Austria's ultimatum was too harsh was a much less credible and therefore less salient news event. The fourth most important event was Russia's own reaction.

The event of the Austrian ultimatum to Serbia was one that both men could not dismiss from attention, but much of the rest of what they saw in the world was quite different. The Tsar preoccupied himself with the visit of the French President to Russia and with Russia's alliance with France. He worried about England's possible noncommitment to what later became the Allied cause and requested a show of England's support.

The Kaiser did not concern himself with the Tsar's alliance problems but rather with some of his own. He attempted to localize the Serbian conflict and paid a lot of attention to that. He concerned himself with Belgian neutrality and also with a purely domestic financial matter, ordering banks to hold 10 percent of their assets.

By the end of the seven days J and K are not looking at the same world although reality impinges itself on each. Three events, Russia's mobilization, Germany's mobilization and the secret treaties, are in the attention space of both men. But two events, the collapse of Europe's stock markets and Germany's military precautions, are also in the attention of the Kaiser, while two other events, Serbia's Balkan allies and the Russian press, are in the attention of the Tsar.

Even when the same event is in both men's mind, the picture of it differs. Let us look at Russia's mobilization. The Kaiser is primarily concerned with the facts: "Russia orders complete mobilization," "Russia's Tsar declares war is inevitable," "Russia calls up reserve troops," "Russia's troops are near Germany's border." The Tsar, on the other hand, who has administrative responsibility for the mobilization is, in addition, concerned with various political aspects of it. Most notably included in his list is the message "England confers with Russia on mobilization measures." Also included is that "France advises Russians to speed up military preparations" and that he as "Tsar orders general mobilization." The last is a different message from the fact that Russia as a country had ordered complete mobilization. It identifies the Tsar's personal role.) The relation to France is particularly interesting. The Kaiser reflecting wishful thinking pays attention to the message that "France asks Russia to cut down mobilization." He neglects the message which the Tsar retains that "France asks Russia to speed up preparations." Here is the kind of reversed perceptions that causes the breakdown of international discourse.

The differences in the material in attention space devoted to German mobilization is in some respects a mirror image of that just noted for the Russians. Here we find the Russians paying attention merely to the bald fact "Germany mobilizes." (Note that this is repeated as three different messages. The program permits this for messages of truly extraordinary importance; they thus fill much of the attention space.) The Kaiser, on the other hand, also pays attention to such administrative aspects as "Germany's war chiefs confer on mobilization" and "Germany's officers press for mobilization." The Kaiser also thinks about his justification that Germany has threatened to mobilize if Russia continues arming. Here again we find the expectable psychological aspects of the situation well represented in the simulation. The Tsar gives no thought to the process which justifies German mobilization in the mind of the Kaiser, only to the fact.

Further Development of the Crisiscom Simulation

The Crisiscom simulation is now a working model. It has been used on the gaming of one crisis and can be used on others, but it is not at the end of development. We would like to see it further developed, further tested, and further used.

The development of a model of this sort is partly an open-ended matter. More and more aspects of reality can be built into it. Right now we have a very small model representing a limited range of the psychological mechanisms that are relevant to crisis. Specifically, we represent the processes of selective attention and very little more.

There are a number of obvious next steps. One of them is to introduce distortion processes. Right now a message that is received can be rejected or accepted. It cannot be changed by the receiver. We know that receivers do distort messages. We wish to introduce balancing processes whereby, though the message sent to J and K might be the same, the message that appeared in attention space could be different.

Another important direction of development is to introduce more relations than just affect. Some specific relations of military and naval reference would be useful, that is, mobilizing forces. A relatively small dictionary of relational terms would give the model greatly enhanced flexibility and perhaps some predictive power.

Another important development permits J and K themselves to generate messages as well as receiving them. In the process of generating messages they would be programmed to reflect the character of their countries and perspectives. These messages would then become part of the message flow, making Crisiscom a truly dynamic model whose ultimate play of a game would be hard to predict *a priori.*

Finally, we plan to replace much of the initial coding of saliency now done by a human with computer operations based on Robert Abelson's Hot Cognition model.

Note

This work was supported by the Naval Research Laboratory under a contract to the Simulmatics Corporation and by the Advanced Research Projects Agency of the Department of Defense under Contract 920F-9717 with the Center for International Studies, MIT. This contract is monitored by the Air Force Office of Scientific Research. We have made use of the computer time sharing system of Project MAC, an MIT research project sponsored by the Advanced Research Project Agency, Department of Defense, under of Office of Naval Research, contract Nonr. –4102(01).

Appendix

Explanatory Notes

1. DM means decision maker.
2. Decision Maker 1 is the Kaiser. Decision Maker 2 is the Tsar. They are not considered as individuals but as symbolizing two nations' top decision maker.
3. ATNSPC means Attention Space.
4. In the Affect Matrix the row label is the country which feels a certain way about the country named in the column label.
5. In the listing of messages in Attention Space:

The First number under each message is a current saliency measurement.

The second number under each message is an affective significance measure relating to the subject's treatment of the object.

The third number under each message indicates the day the message first appeared.

Lines without numbers label an event. The messages about that event follow it.

The Attention Space of the Kaiser at the End of Day 1.

The ATNSPC OF DM 1 AT THE END OF DAY 1

LOCALIZATION HOPES.

GERMANY ASSERTS NEED FOR LOCALIZATION OF SERBIA'S CONFLICT.
(0.67195 0.24999 1$)
ENGLAND REQUESTS LOCALIZATION OF CONFLICT IN SERBIA.
(0.42719 0.27999 1$)

AUSTRIA'S ULTIMATUM TO SERBIA.

AUSTRIA SENDS ULTIMATUM TO SERBIA.
(0.66989 0.67999 1$)
GERMANY'S MOBS RALLY FOR WAR.
(0.66759 0$ 1$)
ULTIMATUM AROUSES ALARM IN SERBIA'S CAPITAL.
(0.58053 0S 1$)
GERMANY FEARS AUSTRIA'S ULTIMATUM TOO HARSH.
(0.35165 –0.10999 1$)
RUSSIA'S COUNCIL MEETS TO DISCUSS AUSTRIA'S ULTIMATUM.
(0.34117 –0.12999 1$)
FRANCE DENDUNCES SEVERITY OF AUSTRIA'S ULTIMATUM.
(0.34065 –0.41999 1$)
RUSSIA DENDUNCES SEVERITY OF AUSTRIA'S ULTIMATUM.
(0.33717 –0.42999 1$)
ENGLAND DENDUNCES SEVERITY OF AUSTRIA'S ULTIMATUM.
(0.26801 –0.37999 1$)
RUSSIA ACCUSES AUSTRIA OF PLOTTING INTERNATIONAL WAR.
(0.021981 –0.50999 1$)
GERMANY DENIES FOREKNOWLEDGE OF AUS'S ULTIMATUM.
(0.20505 –0.26999 1$)
USA FEARS WAR IMMINENT IN SERBIA.
(0.13231 –0.09999 1$)

BELGIUM'S NEUTRALITY.

BELGIUM REASSERTS NEUTRALITY STATUS.
(0.65695 0$ 1$)

GERMANY'S BANKS.

GERMANY ORDERS BANKS TO HOLD TEN PERCENT OF ASSETS.
(0.65637 0$ 1$)

RUSSIA'S ALLIANCE WITH SERBIA.

RUSSIA'S ASSURES SERBIA FULL SUPPORT.
(0.63795 0.71999 1$)
SERBIA ASKS RUSSIA FOR FULL SUPPORT.
(0.58353 0.31999 1$)

A partial List of Messages Inputted to the Kaiser and the Tsar on Day 1.

```
DATE JULY 25 1914 ..
(1$)
ENGLAND'S MUSEUP .. ENGLAND OPENS NEW MEMORIAL MUSEUM ..
(.OC .1B .OC .05 .C3 .04 .03 .75 .68 .0)
USA TREATY WITH JAPAN .. USA SENATE DELAYS SIGNING JAPAN LAND TREATY ..
(-.18 .18 .25 .11 .18 .06 .08 .57 .65 0)
CANADA'S RAILROAD .. CANACA MEETS WITH USA TO DISCUSS RAILROAD LOANS ..
(.31 .35 .21 .09 .08 .07 .06 .71 .48 0)
USA HYDROPLANE .. USA HYDROPLANE PREPRESS FOR TRIAL RUN ..
(.00 .21 .00 .13 .13 .15 .15 .82 .64 0)
HAITI'S REVOLUTION .. USA SENCS WARSHIPS TO HAITI ..
(-.61 .48 .52 .28 .20 .23 .18 .76 .72 0)
AUSTRIA'S ULTIMATUM TC SERBIA .. AUSTRIA SENDS ULTIMATUM TO SERBIA ..
(-.68 .73 .75 .68 .70 .58 .58 .91 .88 0)
RUSSIA'S ALLIANCE WITH FRANCE .. FRANCE'S MINISTER GOES TO RUSSIA TO STR
ENGTHEN ALLIANCE ..
(.57 .53 .68 .49 .68 .24 .39 .59 .81 0)
CRISIS IN IRELAND .. ENGLAND FEARS CIVIL WAR IN IRELAND ..
(-.48 .67 .63 .23 .22 .20 .19 .48 .36 0)
PROHIBITION .. USA WITNESSES MORE PROHIBITION DEMONSTRATIONS ..
(.00 .29 .00 .09 .07 .06 .06 .43 .45 0)
DEATH OF LORD MEMYSS .. ENGLAND'S LORD MEMYSS DIES ..
(.00 .37 .00 .12 .10 .08 .08 .81 .89 0)
AUSTRLA'S ULTIMATUM TO SERBIA .. ENGLAND DENDUNCES SEVERITY OF AUSTRIA'S
ULTIMATUM ..
(-.38 -.36 .40 .31 .42 .24 .21 .63 71 0)
RUSSIA'S ALLIANCE WITH FRANCE .. FRANCE GIVES RUSSIA FULL DIPLOMATIC SUP
PORT ..
(-.63 -.51 .61 .41 .61 .28 .45 .61 .90 0)
PRINCE OF WALES .. ENGLAND'S PRINCE IMMERITS FOUR MILLION POUNDS ..
(.00 -.19 .00 .05 .04 .07 .08 .56 .58 0)
BICYCLE RACES .. ITALY BEATS USA IN BICYCLE RACE ..
(.08 .11 .08 .04 .03 .06 .07 .41 .31 0)
USA IMMIGRATION .. USA RAISES QUOTA FOR RUSSIA'S IMMIGRANTS ..
(.39 .21 .32 .12 .32 .25 .34 .32 .75 0)
MEXICO'S CIVIL WAR .. PEASANT MDBS SIOBM MEXICO'S CAPITAL ..
(.00 .63 .00 .26 .20 .21 .14 .51 -.20 0)
AUSTRIA'S ULTIMATUM TO SERBIA .. GERMANY DENCES ECREKNOWLEDGE OF AUS
'S ULTIMATUM ..
(-.27 .45 .36 .45 .31 .41 .25 .73 -.56 0)
AUSTRIA'S ULTIMATUM TO SERBIA .. RUSSIA ACCUSES AUSTRIA OF PLOTTING INTE
RNATIONAL WAR ..
(-.51 .46 .48 .36 .46 .40 .32 -.14 .42 0)
RUSSIA'S ALLIANCE WITH SERBIA .. SERBIA ASKS RUSSIA FOR FULL SUPPORT ..
(.32 .62 .53 .49 .53 .55 .39 .43 .82 0)
SERBIA'S REPLY .. AUSTRIA ALLOWS TWO-DAY TIME LIMIT FOR SERBIA'S REPLY.
-

(-.29 .44 .51 .42 .48 .28 .31 .73 .75 0)
AUSTRIA'S ULTIMATUM TC SERBIA .. FRANCE DENDUNCES SEVERITY OF AUSTRIA'S
ULTIMATUM ..
(-.42 .39 .41 .40 .43 .32 .38 .55 .51 0)
MEXICO'S CIVIL WAR .. MEXICO'S LEADERS SIGN ARMISTICE ..
(.00 .73 .00 .28 .22 .23 .21-.31 .42 0)
HAITI'S REVOLUTION .. NEW VIOLENCE BREAKS IN HAITI'S CAPITAL ..
(.00 .68 .00 .31 .30 .26 .26 .66 .43 0)
JEWEL ROBBERY .. THIEVES STEAL JEWELS FROM GERMANY'S DUTCHESS ..
(.00 .11 .00 .11 .06 .27 .09 .81 .35 0)
GERMANY'S STEAMSHIP LINES .. GERMANY'S STEAMSHIP LINES RAISE PRICES TO U
SA ..
```

A Partial List of the Final Affect Matrix of the Kaiser.

THE AFFECT MATRIX OF DECISION MAKER I AT THE START OF DAY 7

	ALASKA	AUSTRA	AUSTRI	BELGIU	CANADA	COLOMB	DENMAR	ENGLAN
ALASKA	0.	0.220	0.140	0.160	0.480	0.	0.210	0.330
AUSTRA	0.190	0.	0.100	0.210	0.370	0.	0.220	0.620
AUSTRI	0.100	0.060	0.	0.130	−0.200	0.	0.130	−0.329
BELGIU	0.200	0.210	−0.210	0.	0.230	0.	0.470	0.580
CANADA	0.370	0.380	0.230	0.160	0.	0.140	0.230	0.520
COLOMB	0.	0.130	0.	0.	0.230	0.	0.190	0.210
BENMAR	0.130	0.200	0.310	0.430	0.200	0.	0.	0.460
ENGLAN	0.180	0.480	−0.264	0.590	0.610	0.140	0.390	0.
FRANCE	0.110	0.200	−0.504	0.380	0.360	0.210	0.280	0.657
GERMAN	0.150	−0.120	0.682	−0.310	0.240	0.	0.290	0.395
GREECE	0.	0.160	0.380	0.240	0.	0.	0.128	−0.140
HAITI	0.120	−0.130	0.	0.	0.230	0.330	0.	0.310
IRELAN	0.140	0.210	0.210	0.410	0.160	0.	0.360	0.490
ITALY	0.	0.310	−0.170	0.230	0.130	0.	0.280	−0.310
JAPAN	0.150	0.120	0.130	0.200	0.270	0.	0.130	0.310
LUXEMB	0.	0.140	0.210	0.480	0.130	0.	0.410	0.400
MEXICO	−0.100	0.	0.	0.	0.210	0.380	0.080	−0.210
MONTEN	0.	0.	−0.450	0.210	0.	0.	0.270	0.210
PERU	0.	0.140	0.120	0.180	0.230	0.560	0.	0.210
RUSSIA	0.380	−0.100	−0.839	0.130	0.310	0.	0.240	0.426
SERBIA	0.	0.	−0.738	0.130	0.	0.	0.210	0.130
TURKEY	−0.140	0.100	0.390	−0.100	0.110	0.	−0.140	−0.380
USA	0.610	0.300	−0.140	0.310	0.680	0.320	0.200	0.540
VENEZU	0.140	0.	0.	0.	0.210	0.410	0.	0.270

	FRANCE	GERMAN	GREECE	HAITI	IRELAN	ITALY	JAPAN	LUXEMB
ALASKA	0.310	−0.100	0.	0.130	0.	0.100	0.200	0.
AUSTRA	0.280	0.170	0.110	0.	−0.160	0.190	0.210	0.080
AUSTRI	−0.399	0.670	−0.300	0.	−0.070	−0.235	−0.090	−0.120
BELGIU	0.550	−0.290	0.	0.	−0.130	0.120	0.	0.390
CANADA	0.370	−0.260	0.110	−0.160	−0.130	0.060	0.	0.230
COLOMB	0.130	−0.130	0.	−0.320	0.	0.100	0.	0.
DENMAR	0.460	0.320	0.110	0.	0.230	0.260	0.080	0.530
ENGLAN	0.630	0.321	0.210	−0.130	−0.360	−0.280	0.260	0.290
FRANCE	0.	0.380	0.260	0.	−0.190	0.290	0.110	0.430
GERMAN	−0.330	0.	−0.220	−0.300	0.	0.400	0.310	−0.280
GREECE	0.240	0.380	0.	0.	0.	0.380	0.	0.200
MAITI	0.150	−0.310	0.	0.	0.	0.120	0.	0.
IRELAN	0.220	0.160	0.100	0.	0.	0.190	0.	0.240
ITALY	0.260	0.320	−0.280	0.	0.	0.	0.230	0.310
JAPAN	0.210	0.340	0.100	0.	0.	0.170	0.	0.
LUXEMB	0.510	0.230	0.210	0.	0.	0.130	0.	0.
MEXICO	0.100	−0.290	0.	0.340	0.	0.120	0.	0.
MONTEN	0.310	−0.330	0.400	0.	0.	0.100	0.	0.200
PERU	0.160	−0.180	0.	0.380	0.	0.	0.	0.
RUSSIA	0.690	−0.615	0.310	0.120	−0.110	−0.200	−0.260	0.240
SERBIA	0.310	−0.460	0.431	0.	0.	−0.330	0.	0.200
TURKEY	−0.400	0.370	−0.280	0.	0.	−0.400	0.	0.110
USA	0.500	0.530	0.140	−0.400	−0.130	0.120	0.270	0.
VENEZU	0.130	0.180	0.	0.230	0.	0.	0.	0.

Part III

Forecasting

Editor's Introduction

"Those of us whose profession is the search for understanding, however, must learn to live with self-exposure. Just as understanding is gained by unrelenting exposure of one's unconscious, so also can understanding be aided by exposure of one's conscious assumptions."

—Ithiel Pool, p. 127, below

"Every road sign that says, 'Caution, dangerous intersection' is hopefully a self-defeating forecast."

—Ithiel Pool, p. 151, below

"The International System in the Next Half-Century" and "The Art of the Social Science Soothsayer"

In the mid-1960s Ithiel Pool was invited to participate in an exercise to forecast the future of the international political system during the next fifty years. The invitation resulted in the first selection, "The International System in the Next Half-Century." In the next decade his MIT colleague, Nazli Choucri, co-edited a book about forecasting in international relations, followed-up the initial article, and invited Ithiel to contribute the second selection, with reflections about how his predictions were turning-out and the enterprise of social science forecasting.[1]

Pool's publication of his forecasts was unusual: outside of economics, the prospect of tying one's professional reputation, in print, to predictions—that could be widely seen to be wrong—can engender immediate caution among social scientists, and at least a passing protestation of professional modesty. Pool was right—such exercises are good intellectual discipline, to be forthrightly recommended. (But in the past 35 years, almost no senior political scientist has done it again.)

Ithiel Pool's early death prevented further essays in later decades to review his initial assumptions about the forces that would shape world politics and what he had learned. Several of the original predictions that raised eyebrows at the time—e.g., the breakup of the Soviet Union, the dissolution of Russia's hold on Eastern Europe, and the weakening of Communist ideology in China—have come to pass, and it would be instructive to know whether Ithiel had deeper insight (and how!), or was just lucky.

The reader may find it an interesting exercise to infer Ithiel's conscious assumptions and causal theories as a basis for his or her own predictions for the next fifty years after reading this essay. For example:

- At the time, he obviously believed that deeper historical forces produce long-term trends and that individual leaders—even great men have less importance. The passing of DeGaulle and Mao, he forecast, would make a noticeable difference, but system-level theories and processes would explain the future of their countries in the long run.
- The prediction of political instability and violence in sub-Sahara Africa could be inferred as a straightforward prediction from the record of earlier decades and the continuation of local factors that political scientists had identified as contributing to past instability and violence. It is the application of a research-based "tomorrow will be like yesterday" method.
- He perceives a genuine, although slow, capacity to learn in the international political system, e.g., a growing use of UN forces for interventions in Africa.
- His predictions reflect a judgment that Communism could not survive in the long-run given the limitations of state planning for economic prosperity, a desire for freedom, and a preference for older national and ethnic/sectional loyalties.[2]

The follow-up essay, a decade later, becomes more reflective about forecasting. It begins to discuss new dimensions, especially the importance of self-fulfilling prophecies and self-defeating prophecies, that were emerging from Pool's new research to forecast the social and political impacts of new telecommunications technology. For example, at the conclusion of the third selection (below), "Foresight and Hindsight: Forecasting the Telephone." there is an early visionary memorandum from Alexander Graham Bell to his investors. It hopes to become—and did become!—a self-fulfilling prophecy—foreseeing a possible future (currently unfeasible and impossible) that *could* be created by assembling the necessary pieces (e.g., capital investments, further inventions) that discussion of the vision could help to call forth.

At the time, Pool also was writing his book, *Technologies of Freedom,* that was designed to influence the future by making a forecast that he wanted to become self-defeating. Pool's book argued that the legal doctrines that justified earlier regulation of telecommunications technology could produce an extraordinary restriction of freedom if they were—as he predicted could happen—extended thoughtlessly to cover new, digital forms of electronic communication (e.g., including the Internet, but also more traditional methods such as newspapers that would rely upon digital technology). His book defined thinking about these issues (I.e., that freedom of speech was the key issue) and he proposed new policy guidelines that would, if adopted, make the forecast wrong. He seems to have succeeded in defeating his own prophecy, which he had hoped to do (an issue that is discussed in my contribution to this volume, "What's Next?," below).

"Foresight and Hindsight: The Case of the Telephone"

This third selection presents a retrospective technology assessment, an innovative method to use historical cases to improve social science. In this study, Ithiel Pool and a team of his graduate students returned to the early years of the telephone to determine which methods, used by prognosticators and business investors at the time, successfully predicted its social and economic impacts. (Today, it seems obvious that the telephone would spread and be used for voice communications, but this future was not obvious to most people at the time of Bell's invention.) The story is too good to substitute my brief summary. At this point, I will simply recommend that the reader can apply a retrospective assessment to the development and spread of personal computers, the Internet, or success of new types of software, as these were forecast at any time during the past decades. Who—if anybody—got the developments and their social and political impacts right? How did they know?

Notes

1. Choucri, Nazli and Robinson, Thomas W, (eds.), *Forecasting in international relations: Theory, methods, problems, prospects.* (San Francisco: W. H. Freeman, 1978). For an overview of the development of forecasting methods, see this volume and William Ascher, *Forecasting: An appraisal for policy-makers and planners.* (Baltimore, MD: Johns Hopkins University Press, 1978).
2. Ithiel Pool was a consultant to Radio Free Europe/Radio Liberty and Voice of America during the Cold War. Their short-wave radio broadcasts emphasized such issues to build a case, among their listeners, for such steps. Whether Pool had access to classified knowledge about trends, or was making a prediction that he hoped would contribute to a self-fulfilling prophecy, or both, is unclear.

7

The International System in the Next Half-Century

Since the day when the earliest oracle prophesied darkly, every gypsy fortuneteller and every pundit in the press has known a few elementary devices for avoiding disconfirmation. One can, for instance, predict without hours or date. "It is going to rain" is a prophecy that will eventually be confirmed. One can predict in ambiguous terms, or predict that which one knows to be planned already or under way; this way one may pass for wise.

In the arena of public affairs such vagueness has its uses. He who would influence people or events need not expose his inexorable fallibility to public ridicule. Those of us whose profession is the search for understanding, however, must learn to live with self-exposure. Just as understanding is gained by unrelenting exposure of one's unconscious, so also can understanding be aided by exposure of one's conscious assumptions.

That conviction shapes the form of this essay. We seek to anticipate the character of the international system of the year 2000. It is projected with as much specificity as a historian will use in the year 2000, writing retrospectively.

The predictions are not stated in arrogant confidence, for the results are certain to be proved wrong. The only thing of which one can be confident is that reality will depart radically from these predictions. Such predictions may be taken to be the modal items on subjective probability distributions. If forced to bet between each prediction and alternatives to it of comparable detail, the predictions chosen are those on which the author would prefer to bet. This is not to say that the predictions made are probable. It is highly unlikely, for example, that Okinawa will be part of the fifty-second state of the USA. But if

First published in *Daedalus* (1967).

forced to predict whether there will or will not be a fifty-second state by the year 2000, I would bet on the side of there being one. If we further assume that there will be a fifty-second state after Puerto Rico becomes the fifty-first and are asked to bet on any one piece of real estate being part of it, the Pacific string of islands would be my guess as the single most likely option. This is the way I played the game.

That game was played in 1965. Today, over a year later, the predictions then made are already partly disconfirmed; they stand as stated to be measured against the cold test of reality. China, for example, is moving much faster than I would have believed possible two years ago. At the moment of this writing, still in Mao's lifetime, the beginnings of guerrilla warfare are visible. Perhaps we shall not have to wait for 1985 to see a struggle out of which a more moderate though allegedly Communist regime will emerge or the break-off of certain border areas by the Soviet Union.

The events in the passing year clearly make what was written in 1985 seem a bit antique. And insofar as any one prediction is awry, other predictions will become so too. The world is a tightly linked system. The choice to write a history in reverse was, in part, an expression of a sense of incapacity to conceive in any other way of what 2000 will be like.

What life will be like in 2000 is a function of what life will be like in 1990, and that in turn of 1980, and so on back. The path of history is a branching road with many forks. The picture we have of 1970 shapes our picture of 2000, and the errors we make in anticipating 1970 spread their effects to our predictions of 2000. Only by imagining the steps along the road can we effectively imagine where the road will lead us.

Let us, therefore, state as clearly as we can an hypothesis about the course of world events from 1985 to the early twenty-first century. Such a statement is a precondition to fruitful debate among prophets and provides a template against which historians can measure where their assumptions have turned out to be wrong.

The Prediction

There will be no nuclear war within the next fifty years.

1965–1970

In the period 1965–1970, Mao Tse-tung and De Gaulle will die. Within two years after De Gaulle's death, presidential power in France, while not abolished, will largely have atrophied, giving way to a wide coalition government strongly committed to European economic cooperation and integration, but just as non-cooperative with NATO as De Gaulle was. The non-cooperation will be on economic and pacifist grounds, rather than on nationalistic ones.

Major fighting in Vietnam will peter out about 1967; and most objective observers will regard it as a substantial American victory. Sporadic terrorism will, however, remain endemic not only in Vietnam, but throughout former Indochina and Thailand as the Communists try to prove that this is only a defeat in a particular battle within a widening combat. The result of continuing instability will be economic distress in the area. There may be several reversals of government so that, for example, by 1970 a pro-American military dictatorship might exist in Cambodia, while a reformist coalition might have overthrown the regime in Thailand. These are not specific predictions. The prediction is that there will be a pattern of varied, nationalist, religious, reformist, and military regimes in the area changing fairly continuously.

In the United States Lyndon Johnson will have been reelected in 1968. The rate of economic growth will have not only continued, but accelerated, creating a chronic problem of inflationary pressure and labor shortage. Substantial immigration will be taking place, though not by 1920s standards. Just beginning by 1970, it will not be recognized at that time as a continuing trend. It will still be viewed as an exception. Negro voting in 1968 will have come up to white levels, except in five states. By 1970 the central civil rights issues will be the introduction into the South of certain federally financed, special-opportunity programs in education and small-business loans. The major areas around which social protest movements will be organized will be matters of personal self-expression—for example, demands for sexual freedom or for less conformity in school systems. In regard to international relations, the protesters will begin to be more explicitly antinationalistic and in favor of less emphasis on sovereignty.

In Latin America, there will begin to be much greater differences between rich countries and poor countries with a few countries experiencing economic booms.

In Africa, there will have been sporadic famines, general chaos, and predominantly military dictatorships.

In the Soviet Union, though economic growth will have continued, there will be even greater discontent with the functioning of the economic system than there is now. There will be much Aesopian discussion of such possibilities as the abolition of the *kolkhoz* and the Party, of firms' investing independently, and so forth. There will be noticeable problems of unemployment. The major changes will, however, not have occurred by 1970. In Eastern Europe at least one country will have experimented with the abolition of central planning in everything but name. Within Europe, East-West travel will have risen to flood levels. Communism will be pretty much of a dead issue in some East European countries, though none will have overtly rejected it.

The death of Mao Tse-tung will not have led to significant change in the Chinese government or policies.

Throughout the world, the Communist movement will seem to be a declining force, but miscellaneous forms of anarchy and disorder will be just as strong as ever.

1970–2000

The trends that I have predicted for the first five years are the beginnings of trends I expect to continue for the most part for the subsequent twenty years. There will, however, be some discontinuities that should be noted. In about 1977, a major war will break out in Africa among the nations there. When it has continued for some months, there will be a massive U.N. military intervention requiring the continuing stationing of troops there for a protracted period. In China, a protracted famine in one portion of the country will lead to the outbreak of guerrilla warfare around 1985. There will be a seesaw struggle for about five years during which the Soviet Union will seize certain border areas, particularly Manchuria (1990). A so-called moderate regime will ultimately come in whose line will be that the attempt to establish Communism in China was premature, and that what China needs is massive foreign aid regardless of ideology. It will continue to be a one-party military dictatorship, asserting itself to be Communist.

Around 1980, there will be a major political crisis in the Soviet Union, marked by large-scale strikes, the publication of dissident periodicals, a temporary disruption of central control over some regions, and an open clash between the major sectors of the bureaucracy over questions of military policy and consumer goods. This will stop just short of revolution, though it will result in the effectual abolition of the Communist Party or its splitting up into more than one organization, the abolition of the *kolkhoz,* and so forth. During these events, the Soviet hold over Eastern Europe will be completely broken. An unconsummated attempt at East German-West German unification will occur. This will stop the revolution in the Soviet Union from going full course. In the last analysis, German unification will be aborted by diplomatic pressure from Western Europe and the United States. This will create a kind of U.S.-Polish-Hungarian alliance with guarantees against Germany and, implicitly, against the Soviet Union. The result will be the further disintegration of NATO; a close relationship will, however, emerge between the United States and France, rather than Germany. From this point on, it will be generally recognized that Communism is a moribund ideology. The rates of economic growth in the capitalist world will be steadily outstripping those in the rest of the world.

At the same time, the widening gap between the developed and underdeveloped countries will be softened only by the extraordinary growth of a few of the latter—two or three countries in Latin America, Taiwan, one or two spots in North Africa and the Middle East. In response to this situation, the decade 1990–2000 will see the beginning of the breakdown of the nation-state system. Africa will establish some form of regional federation with a large-scale international force of foreign troops present. There will be a mixture of local autonomy and regional controls. There will also be a foreign-aid program with many strings attached. It will be hard to define what constitutes the nations of Africa in the classic sense of nation.

The United States will admit its fifty-first state, Puerto Rico, and its fifty-second state, a string of Pacific Islands including Okinawa.

A European parliament will be established including most, but not all of the present European countries from England to Rumania. The nations will not be abolished, but will enter into a loose confederation. Some patchwork of East and Southeast Asian states will also enter into a confederation including most of Indonesia, which will have broken up in 1980. Around the year 2000 the Soviet Union will be forced to loosen its grip on Manchuria, turning it into some semi-independent state with ad hoc relations with both China and Russia.

During this period, there will have been some, but relatively little, nuclear proliferation. Several states will have acquired token nuclear capability: India in 1975; Pakistan in 1980; Egypt and Israel simultaneously in 1983; Germany with some sharing of controls in 1985; Japan in 1990; and Algeria in 1995. Much more important than the proliferation of these token capabilities will be the emergence around 1990 of a new family of even more dangerous weapons. It will be generally recognized that means exist for a sneak attack by a poor country upon any nation in the world with results verging on total destruction. No country will, however, have built the system yet. The decade 1990 to 2000 will see massive increases in expenditures by the major powers for reconnaissance, intelligence, and covert influence in places where such weapons might secretly be developed.

2000–2015

This large-scale increase in reconnaissance, intelligence, and infiltration will, in the decade 2000–2010, have further major effects in modifying the nation-state system. There will, for example, be federations of political parties—comparable to the federation of Catholic parties today or the Communist movement—cutting across national lines. Millions of people will be trained for overseas assignments and sent to work abroad. International corruption will be carried out on a vast scale by powerful nations seeking to assure their security against dangerous developments. In the latter years of the half century (circa 2010) there will be attempts to use the U.N. as a reform instrument, substituting serious international supervision for the unilateral devices of intelligence, infiltration, and corruption to maintain security. An open-frontiers treaty will be signed by many countries establishing an absolute right of travel and conversation by nationals of any country.

The amount of actual violence in the world will have started to decline about 1990, particularly after the model of the international African intervention suggests that local wars will no longer be tolerated. From 1970 to 1990, there will have been two or three local wars in Asia which will not have been allowed to go to the point of conquest.

In the fifteen years after 2000, there will also be for the first time rather rapid rises in the living standards of the people of Asia and Africa as population control becomes fairly complete and new technologies of food and industrial production begin to make massive differences. In that decade and a half, the trend will no longer be a widening gap between the developed and underdeveloped areas. The developed areas will be putting sums on the order of $100 or $200 billion a year into the economies of the developing areas in one form or another. A major problem that the United States will face at the end of the half century is a widespread ideology around the world that equality is a right and, as such, imposes an obligation on the rich to help the poor. The right of the United States to decide for itself what it will do in that direction will be very widely challenged.

8

The Art of the Social Science Soothsayer

Forecasting as Sophism

Around 1951 when the Rand Corporation was first being formed, Abraham Girshick and Abraham Kaplan launched as one of the first activities of that organization a study on what makes a good forecaster in international relations. The new organization was to help policymakers understand better what was going on in the world. What could be more important than to determine whose recorded forecasts had proved reliable and why? They collected past forecasts with an eye to scoring them. But the study had to be abandoned. It turned out that even after the passage of some time, there were practically no forecasts that they could score as having proved right or wrong. Social scientists, journalists, and statesmen alike talked with such equivocation that no one could say with certainty whether their forecasts had been right or wrong.

Now, social science is not forecasting, and forecasting is not necessarily specific prediction; we shall develop these points below. But the ability to make a specific prediction under some appropriate circumstances is a legitimate test of the power of a science. It is also true that society often views social scientists as soothsayers, from whom it expects anticipations of the future. Such soothsayers use many devices to avoid the hard test of empirical confirmation:

1. There are predictions without date. "It's going to rain" is a prototype of such predictions. Implicitly that means it's going to rain "soon," but what is soon? Sooner or later it will certainly rain. So it is with any cyclical or periodic phenomenon. All wars must end, so those who predict the end of a war are eventually proven right. In the American

From *Forecasting in International Relations* (1978) edited by Nazli Choucri and Thomas W. Robinson.

political system one may predict that the public will become dissatisfied with the performance of the incumbent party and will vote it out of office. Some day it will. One can predict the end of the bull market or the end of the bear market, but without a date such a prediction will not make one rich. Nor are such predictions a contribution to knowledge.

2. There are forecasts that are really statements of intent. The teacher who grades on a curve "predicts" that there will be 15 percent A's, if that is his norm. He is really announcing his intent. He is forecasting that which is within his power. Such statements, however, do contain an element of forecast; it is not the forecast of the grades, for about that he is making a current statement of intent. The forecast is: "I will not change my mind." That is indeed a legitimate forecast about one man's psyche, but one for which the relevant evidence and prior probabilities are different than a forecast about grades on a curve.

So, too, in politics and world affairs, when a statesman forecasts that colony X will be freed next year, or that there will be continuing terrorism in some disputed area, only to a small degree is he making a forecast. Rather he may be saying something about his present intentions regarding something within his power.

Of course there are mixed cases. When the president of the United States says that South Vietnam will not be overrun, and when Hanoi says the imperialists will be driven out of South Vietnam, each is making a statement about its present intent. But since the outcome is not fully under either's control, each is also making a genuine forecast that his side will in fact succeed in doing what it intends to do. At the same time, the outcome rests, to a substantial degree, on the intensity of the intent. If the president of the United States were to say he will use any weapon in his arsenal to achieve his goal in Vietnam, he would presumably no longer be making a prediction, but rather a threat, for he did have it in his physical power to impose his will. If, however, his intent is limited to achieve what he can achieve only with more moderate means, then to that degree he is making a prediction if he forecasts success. No wonder that Girshick and Kaplan, reading texts of past statements, found it impossible to extricate unambiguous predictions in the mass of forecasting statements. When statesmen talk it is a matter of exegesis to sort out how much is prediction and how much is intent.

3. There are apparent forecasts that are really scoops. A columnist writes that cabinet minister John Doe will resign next week. That is again a prediction only of the fact that the decision already made about which the journalist got a leak will not be changed in the next week.

The statement is primarily an assertion of a current but secret fact. It differs from above-discussed statements of intent in that here we are dealing with statements made by third parties who *report* the intent of a decision maker rather than with statements of intent by the decision maker himself. But the statements still report current facts more than it forecasts. Most forecasts in the news media are of that character. They may start as a trial balloon, a deliberate leak, or an investigative discovery, but they are reporting rather than forecasting.

4. There are "either-or" forecasts. Either there will be detente or the strain between the great powers will be exhausting. That example says very little more than that there will either be detente or there won't be. It is a particularly vapid example, because the "either" and the "or" between them cover the whole possibility space. Quite different would be the statement that either X or Y will be the next president of the General Assembly. That is a significant forecast, for presumably there are many other possible presidents, and the forecast that it will be one of only two people narrows the possibility space considerably.

Thus, "either-or" statements found in the literature cannot casually be dismissed as illegitimate or vapid. Many of them may be significant conveyors of large amounts of information. However, the very fact that they may be sensible makes them attractive camouflage for vacuity. The "either-or" statements that appear in public print are often nearly, if not totally, vapid.

5. There are "if . . . then . . ." forecasts, which, to the extent that they are assertions of functional relations, are really propositions rather than predictions. Nonetheless, they are another kind of forecast, in some instances directly translatable into "either-or" forecasts, but also sometimes different.

For instance, those cases where the "if" statement does not come true leave it indeterminate whether the prediction is confirmed or not. Consider the prediction "If China and the Soviet Union reconcile their differences, then Japan will draw closer to the United States." It is ambiguous whether the converse is also being asserted, namely that if China and the Soviet Union remain at odds, then Japan will draw away from the United States. Since it is this latter situation that actually emerged as the reality, the original prediction must be regarded as untested.

For soothsayers, such ambiguity provides an easy gambit. There are many forecasts in which the "if" condition is almost certain not to happen leaving the soothsayer's ability as a pundit virtually untested. The assertion that "if nuclear war occurs, then civilization will be destroyed" is a highly plausible piece of punditry that hopefully and probably will never be tested. Another example in the large class of disaster forecasts are those of catastrophe from continued exponential growth: "If we don't do something about it, the population explosion will make the world unlivable." Perhaps so, but it is virtually certain that we will do something about it, perhaps not before there are painful consequences to motivate us, but well before the world becomes unlivable.

Clearly, the disaster forecasts are not nonsense. On the contrary, the two examples given are both plausible and wise statements. But those of us who believe such statements must do so not on the basis of empirical tests, for the test situation will probably never occur, but on the basis of theoretical inference. Often, however, sheer faith rather than rigorous theory constitutes the basis for such forecasts.

6. There are forecasts where confirmation may well be pure chance. A particularly troublesome case is the unique event forecast. Religions have been founded because a prophet predicted correctly that a war would start or a plague break out at a particular time, and then it happened as foretold. The forecast was right no doubt, and the forecaster deserves whatever kudos go with being right. But was it luck or inspiration? That is clearly what underlies the debate between true believers and skeptics.

Even where a forecaster maintains a record of repeated success over time, it is sometimes obscure, in the absence of careful analysis, whether his performance is better than chance. Where an outcome is highly probable, the forecaster who consistently sticks to predicting that outcome will succeed more often than he will fail. Medicine men have practiced that from time eternal. Most illnesses are not fatal, so if the doctor promises you recovery if you do what he prescribes, he will be proven right more often than not, regardless of whether his treatment was causal. Most international crises do not lead to war. A soothsayer who practiced optimism would have a pretty good batting average. Almost any politician could defend the wisdom of his government's foreign policy or the effectiveness of the United Nations by such an argument; they have avoided a myriad of potential wars. Currently, for example, detente can be defended by asserting that it will assure continued avoidance of war between the great powers. Perhaps that is so, but the mere continuation of the most probable state, no war, is hardly proof.

Of the various high probability outcomes that soothsayers forecast, the most common one is the condition of no change. If one predicts that tomorrow's weather will be the same as today's, more often than not you will be right. Slightly more subtle, but just as arbitrary as the prediction of no change is the prediction of no change in trend. Some years ago it was found that one could have done as well on the stock market as the average of the advisory services if one simply assumed that whichever way the market had moved today it would move tomorrow. Swings tend to last for several days, so on most days the trend continues. Of course, that is no panacea for making money, since the few days when the market reverses its trend can wipe out profits made on most previous days. But if the moral satisfaction of being right more often than wrong is what is wanted there is an easy way to have it: predict the continuation of a trend.

In the literature on international relations, predictions of continuity are the most common of all. Pundits make their reputations by repeatedly prognosticating that developing countries will suffer the toils of underdevelopment, that the Third World nations will object to great power policies, that the Soviet Union will resist tendencies toward decomposition of its bloc, that movements of dissent and for cultural openness will be repressed there, that the United States will resist growth in communist power, and that Europe will object to withdrawal of American support. Like trend predictions on the stock market, such predictions are safe day after day, and indeed in this instance year after year. But how much wisdom do they really show on the part of the pundit? The risk takers are the pundits who forecast the rare revolutionary breaks in these continuities. Any pundit who makes many specific forecasts of such very low-probability turns of events is almost sure to be wrong much more often than the pseudo-prophet who simply predicts continuity each time. Predicting low-probability events may be more important, but it is more difficult and riskier than predicting continuity.

7. Finally, the most common gambit of all for making predictions untestable is the use of vagueness. Examples abound: "The international system is becoming decreasingly viable"; "the nationalist spirit will not be quenched"; "the conflict between the classes will grow ever more intense." None of these statements is meaningless, yet all are vague enough so that even after the fact observers will continue to disagree as to whether the event forecast happened or not.

Vagueness in forecast need not depend on the kind of literary flourishes in the above examples. There were forecasts before the 1972 United States elections that the Republicans would win and forecasts that the Democrats would win. Which occurred? The Republican president won in a landslide, but the Democrats carried the Congress. Many predictions had been vague as to the indicators of party victory. Or consider the American military intervention in Vietnam. For years, if not forever, there will be debate as to whether it was a victory or defeat. If the criterion chosen is the formal statements of purpose of the Johnson and Nixon administrations, the American intervention was successful, for the goal was never stated to be anything more than permitting the survival of the regime in the South for an unspecified time period. If the goal is taken as establishing the credibility among anticommunist regimes of American guarantees, or encouraging the development of stable, noncommunist regimes in Asia, the question is clearly unresolved. If price is entered into the equation, the war can easily be argued to have been a failure for the United States. But neither those who were forecasting victory at various times over the years nor those who kept calling the conflict an "unwinnable" war specified their predictions well enough so that in retrospect one can make them admit to error.

In "if . . . then . . ." forecasts, either term or both may be vague. "If the underprivileged are not given a sense of stake in the system, then there will be civil war." Civil war is presumably a recognizable state, and perhaps one can expect some intersubjective agreement among judges as to whether it occurred or not. But is there likely to be any agreement on the evidence as to whether the underprivileged (whoever they are) had or had not acquired a sense of stake in the system? Perhaps even civil war is not a clear term. Certainly a prediction that one side or another will break a cease fire is predictably obscure. There are violations to any cease fire. How many violations breaks it?

In short, the language in which public affairs is discussed and in which international relations predictions are made is so inadequately specified that one can rarely say that a forecast has been confirmed or disconfirmed. That was the disconcerting finding of Girshick and Kaplan.

Prediction and Forecasting: A Digression on Word Usage

Forecasting, it is often argued, is not prediction. Even if we are quite unable to predict future outcomes, it may well be possible to exercise intelligence in regard to their future. If we call the latter forecasting, then inability to predict may be no indictment of forecasting. Part of the exercise of intelligence in regard to the future is the identification of dangers to be avoided. A forecaster, for example, might analyze the proposal for a multiethnic Palestine. He would do so in the light of events in other areas where attempts have been made to include very disparate hostile populations within the same borders. The Indian subcontinent, Canada, South Africa, Ireland, and Cyprus are cases in point. A forecast of the consequences need not include a prediction that such a national unit would actually be set up, the date of it, or its form. The forecast might well be so negative that the predicted event would never be tried.

Forecasting, in short, can be defined as the identification of alternatives in a stochastic world, the estimation of their probabilities, the tracing out of the consequences (e.g., payoff) of each, and the giving of policy guidance about how to realize a chosen alternative.

Various writers use the terms "prediction" and "forecasting" in different ways but if one accepts that formulation of forecasting, then prediction might seem no part of it, and the failures of public figures, journalists, and social scientists when they try to act as soothsayers is irrelevant. It would be testimony to their sophistication, not their sophism, that one rarely finds specific predictions in their writings. It would only mean that they were not attempting the impossible as they applied their intelligence to the future.

I cannot accept that view. It is in part valid, but in part false. What is valid is that the exercise of intelligence about the future is not *just* prediction. Identification of possibilities, if-then statements, either-or statements, or advocacy of policy choices are all valid and meaningful ways of thinking. What is invalid in the separation of forecasting from prediction is the argument that prediction is not even part of forecasting. Indeed, I would argue that forecasting is impossible if one cannot to some degree predict. In every forecast there are hidden predictions. They can be glossed over, as we have illustrated above. But the forecast is not improved by that. On the contrary, understanding requires that we force the predictions out into the glaring light of day.

A forecast that does not imply a prediction that under some specified circumstances some specified outcome will happen, at least probabilistically, is meaningless. There may be all sorts of qualifications about uncertainty, *ceteris paribus,* etc., but however deeply embedded, a vague or qualified prediction is part of every forecast.

Forecasting as Interpretation

There are good reasons for the vagueness with which historical trends in society are forecast. Nonconfirmable forecasts are not merely the result of sloppiness or deliberate sophistry. The scholar who is careful enough to make his language precise enough for testing, who attaches dates to his forecasts, who specifies the turning points when trends will reverse themselves, would almost certainly be wrong so often as to amuse his colleagues. I have tried such an exercise in precision and I know.

In 1965 I decided to experiment with violating all the Girshick-Kaplan gambits. The American Academy of Arts and Sciences issued a volume of forecasting papers (Bell, 1968) [see pp. 127–33 above—Ed.]. I decided to make the predictions in mine specific and testable. I knew perfectly well that that would make them wrong. I said:

> Those of us whose profession is the search for understanding, however, must learn to live with self-exposure. Just as understanding is gained by unrelenting exposure of one's unconscious, so also can understanding be aided by exposure of one's unconscious assumptions.
>
> The predictions are not stated in arrogant confidence, for the results are certain to be proved wrong. The only thing of which one can be confident is that reality will depart radically from these predictions. Such predictions may be taken to be the modal items on subjective probability distributions. If forced to bet between each prediction and alternatives to it of comparable detail, the predictions chosen are those on which the author would prefer to bet. This is not to say that the predictions made are probable. (Bell, p. 318)

Since I presented what I believed to be the modal probabilities, but ones below 0.5, most of them turned out wrong—as I predicted they would. My first forecast, for example, was that by 1970 both DeGaulle and Mao would be dead. Given their ages, the probability in each case was substantial that in a five-year period they would pass on. In point of fact, of course, one died and one survived. It would be sheer pedantry to argue that one forecast proved "better" than the other. It would be far more sensible to say that chance made one right and one wrong between essentially equally valid forecasts. What happened after that in France and China was conditioned by that chance, and thus the contingencies of history built upon each other. Clearly, picking the most probable path along a tree with many branches, no one of which approaches 0.5, is a route to a large number of errors, whatever uses the procedure may have.

Even though the limitations on the forecasts and the inevitability of error in them were flagged in the introduction to the essay, various authors have written about them since, holding them up to satire because reality diverged from the course laid out in my essay. William Thompson devoted considerable space in his book, *At the Edge of History,* to picking the predictions apart (1971). So did a Soviet author.

My point is not to protest a critic's barbs. Ideologues have the right to pick a rhetorically convenient target, which my piece was, because of its specificity. The point I prefer to make is to show how difficult it is, even afterwards, to evaluate forecasts. In detail the 1965 forecasts were clearly wrong—as it was forecasted they would be. But how far they were wrong in their basic perspective remains a subtle issue into which point of view enters almost as strongly now as it would have in 1965.

Take, for example, the statement:

> By 1970 the central civil rights issues will be the introduction into the South of certain federally-financed, special opportunity programs in education and small-business loans. The major areas around which social protest movements will be organized will be matters of personal self-expression—for example, demands for sexual freedom or for less conformity in school systems. (Bell, p. 320)

Was that a good forecast? I don't know. Certainly the statement about civil rights is a good description of the Nixon program of 1970, but did that make his programmatic choices "the central civil rights issues"? I do not think so, but even with hindsight that is not a matter of simple perceptual fact about which any objective observer could agree. What the central issues were is a matter of evaluative interpretation.

The statement about the character of protest in the schools I would call a bull's-eye hit, but was I right in calling these "the major areas" of social protest movements? No mention is made in that passage of protests against the Vietnam War, since on that I had made a blooper by expecting major fighting to fade out in 1967, not 1973. But even in retrospect, was the dominant feature of the worldwide protest movement of 1970 its pacifism (certainly a significant factor in the United States) or was it personal self-expression? I do not know the answer with any better certainty now than I did when I made the forecast in 1965. It remains in aftcast, as well as forecast, a matter of arguable opinion. It is a muddy and unsatisfactory state of affairs when, even with hindsight and even with regard to unusually specific predictions, the evaluation of the predictions is not an obvious or self-evident fact, but a matter of point of view, emphasis, ideology, and judgment.

To recognize that fact is the beginning of wisdom about forecasting of social trends. We must abandon the overly simple notion that the only reason that forecasts are hard to evaluate is that demagogic writers use those tricks that Girshick and Kaplan identified to fuzz up their texts and make them invulnerable to testing. They often do that, but, in addition, there are profound problems in matching even carefully made statements with reality. These problems are much the same whether the statement is made at a date earlier than the observation (i.e., forecasting) or whether the statement is about current affairs, or whether the statement is made at a date later than the reality referred to (i.e., history). The logical problems of empirical confirmation or disconfirmation of interpretive statements about the world are substantially the same in all of these time frames.

In principle, "postdiction" is just as hard as "prediction"; "aftcasts" are as hard as "forecasts." Consider the "what if . . ." questions of history (Vaihinger, 1925). What if Oswald's bullet had missed? In that event, would America have become involved in land warfare in Vietnam in 1965? If that question had been raised in 1964, the answer would have been a prediction. To answer it now is a postdiction, but logically there is no difference. Very little of what we have learned since 1965 has much bearing on the question of what would have happened if history had taken a different turn on November 22, 1963. The "what if . . ." questions about the counterfactual past are usually just as uncertain as the "what if" questions we ask today about the future.

The fact of uncertainty is a fact of the human condition, in the face of which we still must act. Even if incapable of firm validation, both forecasting and aftcasting are legitimate activities. The historian who attempts to interpret the significance of an event in the past, the news commentator talking about today, or the forecaster looking to the future all suffer from limitations on knowledge. If the forecaster has any greater problem it is only that a wider range of relevant items are as yet unknown. The historian starts with a few more contemporaneous givens that for the forecaster are still unknowns. The unknowns of the forecaster and the aftcaster are, however, not logically different.

Consider an historian trying to explain the outcome of the Cuban missile crisis. He can take it as given that the Soviets tried to place missiles in Cuba, but it is a pure act of aftcasting for him to speculate about *what* would have happened *if* Kennedy's reaction to that move had been to bomb the missile sites. An historian could not write intelligently about what actually happened without taking note of what might have happened under that counterfactual alternative. For someone writing before the crisis, it would have a quite similar act of interpretation to forecast what would happen if the Soviets put missiles into Cuba and Kennedy reacted by bombing them. Logically it is hard to see any difference in the logic of speculation involved in the predictive or the historical statement, even though one more fact would be a given for the historian.

Let us now formalize the points we have been making. Descriptive statements about the world may either describe an alleged counterfactual condition or a condition alleged to have actually occurred. These two classes of statements are validated in different ways.

Statements about conditions that have actually occurred can be tested in the same way and in addition can be tested by empirical observation of the real world. The statement that is compared with data about the real world may have been made before the condition came into being (in a prediction), contemporaneously with the condition, or after the condition had passed (in historical assertions).

Since observations and statements are different orders of things, however, there is always an intuitive leap of inference whenever we say that what is observed is like (or is different from) what is described in the statement. The uncertainty involved in the leap varies in degree as between highly theoretical statements (e. g., "This society is anomic.") and highly empirical statements (e.g., "That is a dog."), but it is always there Even a category as concrete as a dog has fuzzy margins. Is a dead dog a dog? Is a cross between wolf and dog a dog? Was what was seen a coyote or a dog? Or is it an optical illusion or hallucination? So the mere fact that the statement is about an empirical and present fact does not eliminate uncertainty in testing its descriptive validity. The criteria we use in international relations are very fuzzy; when is fighting describable as a war?

Social interpretation consists only in part of statements about the alleged actual facts in the real world. Social interpretation is very largely the comparison of such facts with counterfactual alternatives: What would happen or what will happen if different alternative courses are followed. Thus, forecasts that are interpretations of society cannot be evaluated by just holding them up to the facts. The notion that with the passage of time we will know by looking at hard facts whether the forecast was right or wrong turns out to be a myth. The forecast can be evaluated only in a context of theory that takes into account the counterfactual alternatives.

The recognition of the ambiguity of forecasts is not to denigrate the effort to forecast, any more than asserting that historical interpretations are like forecasts is an attempt to denigrate history. Forecasting, aftcasting, and concurrent interpretation of alternatives other than the actual one are all important activities. When well done they help us to understand the branching tree of history.

Forecasts as Experiments

So far we have examined forecasting and prediction as they occur in the mass media and in public affairs, often sophistically and sometimes as serious interpretation. We turn now to a use of prediction and forecasting in science. Scientists, just as other scholars, interpret reality by theoretical evaluation of counterfactual alternatives. But empirical scientists also engage in the more hard-headed but difficult task of inventing predictions that can be tested by matching them to actual events. That is what the scientist does when he works in a rigorous hypothesis-testing mode. He uses ingenuity to design a prediction so well defined that there will be agreement in calling it confirmed or disconfirmed. That is a hard thing to do. The great scientist is clever in inventing such testable predictions that bear on important matters.

The basic empirical activity of science is controlled observation. The scientist systematically manipulates the objects that he observes so as to be able to say with some confidence whether the resulting data confirm or disconfirm some statement about the empirical world. The name we give to that kind of controlled observation is "experiment" although sometimes the word "experiment" is reserved for a special subclass of extremely controlled observations that we can usually conduct only in a laboratory. Experimentation in a narrow sense is a manipulation that allows us at will to vary one variable while physically holding others constant. But in the broader sense we may also call it an experiment if we merely control the observation—for example, measuring rainfall under a fixed, well defined procedure, even if we cannot physically control the environment that brings the rain. Forecasting outside the laboratory is much like forecasting the out-come of a laboratory experiment except that one waits for nature to produce the desired conditions for observation rather than producing them by manipulation.

Forecasting, done with careful, replicable, explicit procedures, is thus one kind of scientific experimentation, at least in the broad sense of the word "experiment."

In the most rigorous, most definitive experiments the forecast that is tested is a single-point prediction, but in much of science one settles for a looser forecast. When the astronauts brought rocks back from the moon, there was no single prediction as to what the rocks would be. On the moon, as on earth, rocks are mixes that vary from spot to spot. Yet the distribution of the moon rocks, when interpreted through statistical models, fits one alternative forecast better than another. The experimental scientist tries to make as explicit as he can the predictions implicit in his forecasts, but one should not exaggerate the extent to which he can normally do so.

There are many ways of manipulating the environment so as to increase our confidence in the meaning of the data produced. One way is to systematize the sample of observations. When we draw a scientific sample we gain confidence that the observed pattern of results is a valid representation of the world.[1] When we use reliable instruments of observation, we are also increasing our confidence in the interpretation of the world. When, in a laboratory, we apply systematic variation of the conditions of observation and use controls to prevent unintended variations, we are again increasing our confidence in what we are observing.

Another control device used by scientists to increase their confidence in a statement about a process in the real world is to put a prediction on record before observing. The point is to avoid peeking. The complex and inferential statement that 'as Sino-Soviet tensions grow China *will* become more friendly to the United States" may *ex post facto* prove as difficult to confirm or disconfirm with certainty as the statement that "as Sino-Soviet tensions grew, China became more friendly to the United States," but the social scientist who makes the former statement has less chance for fudging. If one makes an empirical observation first, and then interprets it, there are generally a myriad of alternative interpretations that can account for the facts. If one chooses one's hypothesis first without peeking, it is generally far less likely that the observation that is later made will correspond to it. Therefore, predicting an observation in advance is a rigorous control.

Note that scientific forecasting is the forecasting of observations. Often, the world itself may already have been in the forecast state at the time that the forecast was made. In that case, the forecast is not a forecast about the world but about the act of observing. An analyst may forecast, for example, where a reconnaissance satellite will find a missile site. He is not forecasting that it will be put there after his forecast; it is already there. He is forecasting the result of the observation.

A scientific forecast of an observation of something that has not yet transpired at the moment of the forecast can also be made. One may forecast, for example, that the population of China will be 1 billion by 1990. As a scientific testing operation, there is no significant difference between that prediction and a prediction that a contemporary world census would show a population of 800 million. They are both forecasts of an observation as to what one will find, whether or not the condition has as yet come into existence. From a scientific point of view, one important thing about a prediction is that it be a rigorous test that prevents peeking and *post hoc* interpretations. The forecast that deals with something not yet in existence does indeed have a rhetorical or aesthetic merit in that peeking is impossible, so the audience may be more easily satisfied that the test was a valid one, but that is all. In either case one is predicting an observation not yet made. For the scientist then, predicting is just one of a series of available devices for subjecting observation to control. It goes along with many other devices, such as the rigorous use of language, the specification of the extensional limits of the generalization, and the adding of detail. The vague forecast (in 1971) that 1972 would be a Republican year is a less good scientific test than the prediction that the Republicans would sweep the presidency and the Democrats the Congress, or than the prediction that the Republicans would carry twenty-nine states. And since controls can be applied to many dimensions of an observation, there is no simple preference to be expressed between the vague forecast that 1972 would be a Republican year (nude without peeking) and the *post hoc* explanation that an analyst might give of the reasons for the difference in the presidential and congressional results. One of these interpretive procedures has the merit of a control against peeking, and the other has the merit of specificity and detail. As an intellectual operation each has its strengths and weaknesses on different dimensions. Best of all would be a test that would apply controls on both dimensions.

What the scientist tries to do, with all possible ingenuity, is to formulate a prediction that is both testable, specific, detailed, and that (either by the scientist's own manipulations or naturally) has a chance to become the factual state of affairs. Forecasts that can be tested do not just happen. They have to be designed for the purpose.

Forecasting in Policy Science

In the last two sections we considered uses of forecasting where, at least proximately, the knowledge was an end in itself. Now we consider forecasting in applied policy sciences. The politician or the analyst who makes a formal or implicit cost/benefit analysis of policy alternatives is forecasting. He asks such questions as: Will expenditure on education promote equality? Will deployment of more missiles deter an opponent? Will a negotiatory offer be accepted?

Forecasting in the policy sciences involves all of the dilemmas already discussed. The politician deliberating about alternatives is likely to indulge in all the sophisticated devices of futuristic rhetoric that we find in any public debate. He raises "what if . . ." questions about the counterfactual alternatives that could be chosen. Unless there is a chance to try different policies in different times and places, history is going to allow only one choice to be realized and evaluated empirically. Whether other choices would have worked better or worse will remain a matter of interpretation. And even the one branch of the tree of historical alternatives that actually gets tried may be hard to assess empirically because of all of the problems of matching empirical facts to verbal statements.

There is one more difficulty that is particularly harassing to the predictor of policy consequences: the forecaster, by his forecast, himself changes the future about which he is forecasting. That is the classic observer/observed problem in the social sciences.[2]

Consider the case of a defense planner predicting that failure to install some border defenses will result in aggressive action by an unfriendly neighbor. Suppose no special action is taken and border clashes do occur, and then ten years later he returns to do an evaluation study. He will have all of the analytic problems listed previously plus this last one. He will not know what would have happened if defenses had been built; perhaps border clashes would have gone up just as much. He may have trouble evaluating whether aggressive action has in fact gone up, for aggression is not an unambiguous concept. Finally, there is the new difficulty that we are now considering. Did the prediction, rather than lack of defenses as such, produce the increase in border clashes? The prediction was perhaps read in the neighboring country and interpreted as a threat. In short, the prediction could have been a self-fulfilling one.

The world of social behavior is full of self-fulfilling and self-defeating prophecies. Optimism and self-confidence are often keys to success, and pessimism and defeatism the sources of failure. Thus, the belief that one will succeed is a self-fulfilling prophecy of success and the expectation that there is no use trying because one cannot succeed is a self-fulfilling prophecy of failure. In international affairs a prevailing belief that one country is stronger than another is an important element in its being stronger. So, too, in the stock market, when most speculators believe that prices will go up, they do go up.

There are also self-defeating prophecies in the stock market. No one could invent a successful, but public scheme for predicting the market. Suppose that some super-economist of the future proposed a scheme for precisely predicting what the market would do the day after tomorrow. And suppose that his theory was proved by success over a period of time. Soon, if he predicted that the market would go up the day after tomorrow, people would buy tomorrow and the market would rise before the day he forecast. His predictions would be defeated by the fact that he made them.

That phenomenon of self-defeating prophecies is one reason why we should not expect that the social sciences will ever get to forecast as well as the natural sciences. A certain amount of naive literature on the social sciences argues that they are young sciences that have not yet had the time to reach the predictive excellence of such sciences as physics or even meteorology. Some day, according to this thesis, the Newton of the social sciences will come along and give us better theories that will enable us to forecast with accuracy. This is probably fantasy. In the first place, the social sciences are no younger than the natural sciences. They both had early foreshadowings in Aristotle, and then a spurt of original thought in the Renaissance (e.g., Galileo and Machiavelli), new great writings in the period of Newton and Hobbes, and the institutionalization of empirical research in the nineteenth and twentieth centuries. If the social sciences have not succeeded as rapidly as the natural sciences, it is because of the inherently greater difficulty of their subject matter. The strength of the observer/observed problem is one aspect of that difficulty. The problem exists in the natural sciences, too. A thermometer affects the temperature of the object it touches, whose temperature it is trying to measure. But the problem is of enormously greater intensity in the social sciences. One of the features of the social sciences is that they predict the behavior of entities, that is, humans, one of whose most salient features is their ability and interest in hearing the forecasts.

Above we noted a very important class of self-defeating forecasts—the forecasts of catastrophe. Every road sign that says "Caution, dangerous intersection" is hopefully a self-defeating forecast. With the sign, the intersection may become no more dangerous than the average one. We noted above the forecast that a nuclear war will destroy civilization. If statesmen believe this then there will be no nuclear war.

Indeed, one of the reasons why the social sciences seem to be poor in prediction is the prevalence in the social world of self-defeating forecasts of catastrophe. Consider how poor we are as forecasters on urban problems. Why do we seem so incapable of designing programs that will work in reducing crime or in maintaining the quality of life? One reason why we seem to be poor at such forecasts, although we are in fact rather good at them, is that whenever we are able to make good forecasts of undesired results we act on our knowledge and defeat these forecasts. Sometime in the evolution of modern cities we realized that unless fire departments were organized in a certain way, cities would burn down. We realized, too, that unless refuse was removed, we would be consumed in contagion. Unless police and courts were organized, violence would be out of control. Society acted on these and many other forecasts, and made the life of the modern city possible. What remained after the easy problems were solved were the hard problems. If we do not know how to solve the residue of crime that remains after police and courts have been created, it is because there are no simple and obvious predictions about how to control the high tail of the criminal distribution without imposing excessive restraints and costs on the rest of the population. In short, it is not that the social sciences do not forecast well. They forecast all of the time and most of their forecasts are so persuasive that people act to defeat them. The situation in which people do not act to defeat the forecast is likely to be that in which there is considerable uncertainty. The forecasts on which social scientists are judged are the ones that are most likely to be wrong.

These considerations apply strongly to forecasting in international relations. Why are we so poor at forecasting the outcome of wars? One reason is that wars whose outcome is easily predictable seldom occur, since the weaker side sees that fighting would be futile. Wars typically occur in those impasses in negotiations when each side believes it can perhaps successfully insist on its views. Analysts on both sides can easily forecast what the outcome would be if a country in Eastern Europe went to war against the Soviet Union or if Cuba went to war against the United States. Such a war will not occur, even though the felt grievances in each case are adequate. It is thus only the crises where the forces are relatively evenly balanced that flare up and come to the center of attention of the social scientist. In those situations his forecasts will be in demand; however, in those situations his forecasts may not be very good.

Some of the above examples of self-defeating forecasts have an important trait in common—namely, that the forecast fails by becoming known. It is sometimes mistakenly assumed that if social forecasts were not revealed, they could be objectively tested and would not run into the observer/observed problem. That is true for a large class of forecasts but not for all. It is true that if one neglected to put up a "dangerous intersection" sign, and merely predicted that there would be a high accident rate at the crossing, one could test one's forecast over time. However, there is also a large class of cases in which the success of social science forecasts depend upon the forecast being known. Examples are game theory and the classical economics of the free market. In those theories, the forecast takes the form of asserting that if people have full knowledge they will act in a certain way. Most theories of rational behavior are of that character. They assert the existence of a Pareto optimum condition from which no player will want to deviate if all players know that that is the nature of the condition and know what will happen if they move away from the point of stability. The forecast that Cuba and the United States will not go to war depends on both nations knowing and understanding that forecast and the reasons for it.

Thus, in one way or another, in forecasting the consequences of public policy actions, one's analysis must take account of the iterative feedback loop between the forecast and the external world about which the forecast is made. That loop may take a variety of forms, either reinforcing and thus helping to fulfill the predicted outcome, or inhibiting and perhaps defeating it.

Summary

The general tenor of this chapter has been to emphasize the limitations on the possibility of forecasting but not on its usefulness. The social sciences do have contributions to make in improving our ability to forecast. They are, first of all, substantive social science propositions and theories that we can use in our forecasts—theories, for example, such as those on the causes of war. There are, in the second place, social science insights into the conditions of our own knowledge—insights in the sociology and psychology of science. Awareness of such matters as group influences, pressure toward conformity, wish fulfillment, distortions of judgment that occur under stress, and cognitive processes of concept formation can help us to evaluate the conditions that make for or restrict objective judgment. In the third place, there are models of human decision that the social sciences have developed. Models of rationality, "satisficing," utility, bargaining, and information processing help us to predict what people will do in decision situations. Nonetheless the possibilities of forecasting are limited.

We have considered some difficulties of forecasting in four different kinds of social and political discourse. First, we considered how forecasting is done in ordinary political discussion; we noted the hopeless ambiguity of such forecasts. But when we turned to examining the problems of forecasting in more serious and careful political and historical interpretation, we found that the difficulties in evaluating forecasts did not go away; they were much the same. The third kind of discourse we examined was that of rigorous science that could be described as a systematic attempt to make the predictions testable both by applying rigid canons to the formulation of the forecasts and by controlling the conditions of observation. In this way validation of predictions becomes possible, but even here deep logical problems remain. Finally, we considered forecasts as used in deliberations about policy alternatives, and we noted the added dilemma that the forecast itself affects the outcome.

All of this suggests a certain reserve about a naive view that exists as an ideal type, even though no intelligent social scientist defends the view. That naive view affirms that the measure of success of the social sciences is their ability to predict. They may not predict very well right now, but, that view asserts, the time will come when social scientists will be able to anticipate what will happen in society. For the present (it asserts) we should measure how good different social sciences and social scientists are by their batting averages in forecasts. The argument of this paper is that those views are wrong on all points. We argue, to the contrary, that there are inherent limitations on the ability to forecast, that uncertainty is inherent in the nature of knowledge, and that forecasting and aftcasting share that uncertainty in the same way. Useful as forecasting may be, it is not the measure of the quality of social science.

Notes

1. That is, it has "external validity" in the language of Donald T. Campbell and Julian C. Stanley, *Experimental and quasi-experimental designs for research* (Boston: Houghton Mifflin, 1963).
2. Cf. Henshel and Kennedy (1973), pp. 119–126.

9

Foresight and Hindsight: The Case of the Telephone

with Craig Decker, Stephen Lizard, Kay Israel, Pamela Rubin, and Barry Weinstein

Let us try to go back to the period from 1876 until World War II, to ascertain how people perceived and foresaw the social effects of the telephone. By taking advantage of hindsight in 1976, we can ask which forecasts were good, which went askew, and why.

Forecasters: Good and Bad

Some sensationally good forecasts were made. In 1878, a letter from Alexander Graham Bell in London to the organizers of the new Electronic Telephone Company outlines his thoughts on the orientation of the company; it is such a remarkable letter that we quote it in full in an appendix to this chapter. The letter describes a universal point-to-point service connecting everyone through a central office in each community, to in turn be connected by long-distance lines. Aronson noted in chapter 1 that when the telephone was first invented, it was not obvious that it would be used in that way. Bell briefly considered a path that others were to pursue after he had given up—using the device for broadcasting in a mode like that of the modern radio. The reader can refer to Aronson's interesting analysis of why Bell originally pondered that alternative and why he instead came to a clear perception of the telephone as a conversational rather than broadcasting device. The result was a prevision of the phone system as it exists today, a century later. The technology that existed then did not permit universal, switched, long-distance service; Bell's description of such a system was a prescient forecast.

The small group of men who created the telephone system did share Bell's vision. Theodore N. Vail and Gardiner Greene Hubbard,

From *The Social Impact of the Telephone* (1977) edited by Ithiel de Sola Pool.

in particular, worked to implement "the grand system" they had in their minds—a system in which the monopoly telephone company would provide service in virtually every home and office, linking local systems throughout the nation and the civilized world. They visualized the device as one that everyone could afford and saw it organized as a common carrier eventually surpassing telegraph usage.

Their optimism was not shared by all. In 1879, Sir William Preece, the chief engineer of the British Post Office, testified to a special committee of the House of Commons that the telephone had little future in Britain:

> I fancy the descriptions we get of its use in America are a little exaggerated, though there are conditions in America which necessitate the use of such instruments more than here. Here we have a superabundance of messengers, errand boys and things of that kind. . . . The absence of servants has compelled Americans to adopt communication systems for domestic purposes. Few have worked at the telephone much more than I have. I have one in my office, but more for show. If I want to send a message—I use a sounder or employ a boy to take it.[1]

In 1878, Theodore Vail, then a young railroad mail superintendent, quit the U.S. Post Office to join the newly organized Bell Telephone Company. "Uncle" Joe Cannon, a young Congressman, expressed surprise and regret that the company had "got a hold of a nice fellow like Vail":

> The Assistant Postmaster General could scarcely believe that a man of Vail's sound judgment, one who holds an honorable and far more responsible position than any man under the Postmaster General, should throw it up for a d—d old Yankee notion (a piece of wire with two Texas steer horns attached to the ends with an arrangement to make the concern bleat like a calf) called a telephone.[2]

Not all the forecasting errors were on the side of stodgy conservatism. There were also wild dreams of the wide blue yonder. General Carty, chief engineer of AT&T since 1907, predicted there would be international telephony one day, and also forecast that it would bring peace on earth:

> Some day we will build up a world telephone system making necessary to all peoples the use of a common language, or common understanding of languages, which will join all the people of the earth into one

> brotherhood. . . . When by the aid of science and philosophy and religion, man has prepared himself to receive a message, we can all believe there will be heard, throughout the earth, a great voice coming out of the ether, which will proclaim, "Peace on earth, good will towards men."[3]

There is a striking contrast in the quality of forecasting and analysis between the small group of initial developers of the telephone and other commentators. Is it because the founders were particularly intelligent men? Perhaps the same mental powers that made them succeed as inventors and entrepreneurs were at work in their forecasts. Or, second, is it because they were living with the subject, eighteen hours a day, year after year? Should we expect the same insight in a congressman's or journalist's quick comments? Third, the telephone pioneers brought together a combination of scientific knowledge and business motivation; Bell was not just a scientist nor Vail only a businessman. They belonged to that remarkable American species of practical technologists, including Morse, Edison, Ford, and Land, who were both inventors and capitalists. They were interested not only in what might be theoretically possible but also in what would sell; the optimism of their speculations was controlled by a profound concern for the balance sheet.[4] Perhaps such concerns are among the crucial ingredients for good technological forecasting.

The activism of the early developers suggests a fourth possible reason for their success as forecasters: they fulfilled their own prophesies. They had the inventions, a vision of how the inventions could be used, and they controlled the businesses that implemented those visions. This theory does not exclude other propositions. The self-fulfilling prophesy of planners can work if, and only if, it accounts for technical and economic realities. Yet the weight we attach to each of the possible reasons for successful prediction and the conditions under which they apply make a great deal of difference to how we would make a technology assessment.

Some Forecasts

We shall offer further speculation about the factors contributing to accurate forecasts, but first we shall examine closely a few predictions, who made them, and how they look in retrospect.

Universal Service

The telephone was an expensive device in its early years; a subscriber paid a flat amount for unlimited service. Furthermore, the combinatorial nature of a network meant that linkage complexity increased faster than the number of nodes. Until fully automated switching, the company's cost of serving each subscriber was greater the larger the number of other subscribers.[5]

With switchboards, the problem was partially solved. Still, as the number of subscribers grew, the operator's job in making the connection grew more than proportionally; a manual switchboard could only be of a certain size. Bell understood this; in *Financial Notes* in 1905, he is quoted as arguing that as the number of people in an exchange increased, the operator's work increased exponentially; hence, the exchanges would eventually all have to be automated:

> In the telephone of the future I look for all this business to be done automatically. . . . If this can be accomplished, it will do away with the cast army of telephone operators, and so reduce the expense that the poorest man cannot afford to be without this telephone.

One early telephone manager commented that "so far as he could see, all he had to do was get enough subscribers and the company would go broke."[6] Telephone service in large communities was therefore very expensive.[7] In 1896, the fee for service in New York was $20 a month. The average income of a workman in that year was $38.50 a month, a six-room tenement in New York rented for about $10 a month, and a quart of milk sold for 5¢. The first subscribers to the telephone were business offices, not ordinary homes. Residential phones in the AT&T National Telephone Directory of 1896 were almost 30 percent in Chicago, one in six or seven in Boston and Washington, and only about one in twenty in New York and Philadelphia.

Yet Bell's letter of 1878 mentioned connecting "private dwellings, counting houses, shops, manufacturies, etc. etc.," in that order; he was not thinking of the phone as just a business device. He talks of "establishing direct connection between any two places in the city." not just a system limited to industrial or affluent neighborhoods. Perhaps it was too early for him to assert categorically, as he did slightly later, that the telephone could even become an instrument for the poor. But the goal of universality, which became one of the watchwords of the Bell System, was there from the beginning.

Though in its first two decades the telephone's growth had largely been in business or among the rich, by 1896 several factors led to a rapid expansion of service. There was the continued acceleration of an ongoing exponential process of growth, and (with the expansion of the initial Bell patents in 1893) competitors sought to discover and occupy parts of the market not yet served—for example, the fast growing Midwest and rural areas. Perhaps the most critical change, however, was the introduction of message charges. The problem was to reduce the price of phone service for the small user, while still collecting adequate amounts from businesses and larger users.[8] In 1896, the New York phone company abandoned flat rate charges and introduced charges by the message.

Between 1896 and 1899, the number of subscribers doubles; in six years it quadrupled; in ten years it increased eight times. By 1914, there were 10 million phones in the United States, 70 percent of the phones in the world. As Burton Hendrick's October 1914 article in *McClure's Magazine* stated:

> Until that time (1900) the telephone was a luxury—the privilege of a social and commercial aristocracy. About 1900, however, the Bell Company started a campaign, unparalleled in its energy, persistence and success, to democratize this instrument—to make it part of the daily life of every man, woman, and child.

In AT&T's annual report of 1901, President Frederick P. Fish expressed its ethos of growth:

> That the system can be completed and of the greatest utility, it is necessary that as many persons as possible should be connected to it as to be able to talk or be talked to by telephone. . . . [The user's] advantage as a telephone subscriber is largely measured by the number of persons with whom he may be put in communication.

At the turn of the century the telephone was clearly still a luxury, but the leaders of the industry in the United States foresaw its becoming a mass product, and their forecast was at least partially self-fulfilling: they had planned for growth. In 1912, AT&T published a manual of the urban planning process of telephone systems. It prescribed and explained how to do a "development study" for a city; the result would be a document known as the "Fundamental Plan." Since the average life of materials entering a telephone system was estimated to be fifteen years, the plan was to provide adequate capacity for that period,[9] with a planning goal for an ordinary city of at least one telephone for every eight inhabitants.[10] Typically, ducts were only half filled to allow adequate room for growth.

Among the four hypotheses about why the telephone pioneers' forecasts succeeded, the self-fulfilling prophecy seems most apposite to explaining the success of the forecast of growth. Vail and his colleagues had a dream and they made it happen. It was, as it had to be, a realistic dream or it would have failed. But abroad, where the same technology and equally talented men existed, governments and phone companies were structured differently, they followed a different perspective, and growth was slower.[11] The movement of the telephone system to rapidly become a universal low-cost service was more an entrepreneurial decision than a foregone outcome of social processes.

Long-Distance Service

The original telephones of the 1870s could only operate over a range of about twenty miles. Yet Bell in his 1878 letter had already declared "I believe in the future wires will unite the head offices of the Telephone Company in different cities, and a man in one part of the country may communicate by word of mouth with another in a different place."

Even earlier, long-range communication was assumed by Sir William Thompson (later Lord Kelvin), when judging the technical exhibits at the Philadelphia Exposition in 1876, though most of his report covers which words he had been able to understand and which not, on the primitive device at hand.[12]

Vail also anticipated a far-flung global telephone network and saw that strategic control would lie with the company running the long-line interconnections. "Tell our agents," he wrote to one of his staff in 1879, "that we have a proposition on foot to connect the different cities for personal communication, and in other ways to organize a grand telephone system."[13] Yet he daringly forecast: "We may confidently expect that Mr. Bell will give us the means of making voice and spoken words audible through the electric wire to an ear hundreds of miles distant."

Burlingame described his perception:

> As general manager of the American Bell Telephone Company formed in 1880 (for extension of the telephone outside of New England), Theodore Newton Vail saw with an extraordinary prophetic clarity the development of a nationwide telephone system. This prophecy was expressed in the certificate of incorporation of the American Telephone and Telegraph Company formed in 1885 which certified that "the general route of lines of this association . . . will connect one or more points in each and every city, town or place in the State of New York with one or more points in each and every other city, town or place in said state, and in each and every other of the United

> States, and in Canada and Mexico; and each and every other city, town or place in said states and countries, and also by cable and other appropriate means with the rest of the known world.[14]

The first long-distance line was built between Boston and Lowell in 1880 with Vail's encouragement:

> This success cheered Vail on to a master effort. He resolved to build a line from Boston to Providence, and was so stubbornly bent upon doing this that, when the Bell Company refused to act, he organized a company and built the line (1881). It was a failure at first and went by the name of "Vail's Folly." But one of the experts, by a happy thought, doubled the wire. . . . At once the Bell Company came over to Vail's point of view, bought this new line, and launched out upon what seemed to be the foolhardy enterprise of stringing a double wire from Boston to New York. This was to be a line deluxe, built of glistening red copper, not iron. Its cost was to be $70,000, which was an enormous sum in those hard-scrabble days. There was much opposition to such extravagance and much ridicule. But when the last coil of wire was stretched into place, and the first "Hello" leaped from Boston to New York, the new line was a success.[15]

By 1892, there were lines from New York to Chicago; by 1911, from New York to Denver; and by 1915, from New York to San Francisco. Experiments with overseas radio telephony took place in 1915, but the first transatlantic commercial service began only in 1927.[16] While long-distance telephony grew rapidly, Bell's and Vail's predictions preceded its reality. There were many technical difficulties, and not everyone anticipated (as did Bell and Vail) that they would be overcome.

Much of the effort to make long-distance telephony work focused on repeaters, devices that rebuilt the deteriorating and fading signals as they passed through long lengths of wire. Berliner developed one. When Vail was out of the company (before 1907), Hayes—the director of the Mechanical Department—decided that the company could most economically abandon its own fundamental research and instead rely on "the collaboration with the students of the Institute of Technology [MIT] and probably of Harvard College." On research concerned with lone lines, however, Hayes made an exception. He employed George A. Campbell, who had been educated at MIT and Harvard, to study the essentially mathematical problem of maintaining transmission constants over long lines of cable. By 1899, Campbell had outlined the nature of discretely loaded electrical lines and had developed the basic theory of the wave filter.

Around 1900, Pupin at Columbia University developed the loading coil which greatly improved the capabilities of long-distance cable. Before 1900, long-distance lines demanded wire about an eighth of an inch thick; the New York-Chicago line consumed 870,000 pounds of copper wire. Underground wires in particular had to be very thick. One fourth of all the capital invested in the telephone system before 1900 had been spent on copper. With the Pupin coil, the diameter of the wire could be cut in half. Then, still later, the vacuum tube and other developments in repeaters made long-distance communication increasingly economical.[17]

Vail wrote in the 1908 annual report (p. 22):

> It took courage to build the first toll line—short as it was—and it look more to build the first long-distance line to Chicago. If in the early days the immediate individual profit of the long-distance toll lines had been considered, it is doubtful if any would have been built.

One obvious speculation as to why the forecast of long-distance communication was so successfully made by Bell and Vail is that the telegraph shaped their thinking; the telephone's invention, after all, had been a by-product of telegraphy. Bell had been employed to create a harmonic telegraph which would carry messages at different pitches simultaneously, and the telegraph's great achievement had been the contraction of distance. It was not surprising, therefore, that when a way was found to make voice travel over wires, a realizable goal seemed to be its transmission over distances. Quite rightly, telephone enthusiasts saw the technical problems as temporary difficulties.[18]

Video

Experiments on transmission of pictures over wires go back long before Bell's telephone.[19] After that invention, many people felt that since a voice could be captured and sent over wires, transmission of pictures was an obvious next step. The difficulties in going from conception to realization were frequently underestimated by non-technical people. The more naive and less scientifically sophisticated the writer, the more immediate the extrapolation from telephone to television seemed.

Kate Field, a British reporter associated with Bell, projected in 1878 that eventually, "while two persons, hundreds of miles apart, are talking together, they will actually *see* each other!"[20] That belongs in a class of journalistic whimsy along with the *Chicago Journal* suggestion:

> Now that the telephone makes it possible for sounds to be canned the same as beef or milk, missionary sermons can be bottled and sent to the South Sea Islands, ready for the table instead of the missionary himself.[21]

In 1910, Casson made a passing comment in "The Future of the Telephone" to the effect that "there may come in the future an interpreter who will put it before your eyes in the form of a moving-picture."[22] A more serious discussion, *The Future Home Theater*, by S.C. Gilfillan, appeared in 1912.[23] In some respects it is a remarkable forecast, in others a dismaying one:

> There are two mechanical contrivances . . . each of which bears in itself the power to revolutionize entertainment, doing for it what the printing press did for books. They are the talking motion picture and the electric vision apparatus with telephone. Either one will enable millions of people to see and hear the same performance simultaneously . . . or successively from kinescope and phonographic records. . . . These inventions will become cheap enough to be . . . in every home. . . . You will have the home theater of 1930, oh ye of little faith.

Gilfillan believed that both the "CATV" and over-the-air broadcast form of video would coexist by 1930, and also that there would be a television abundance with libraries of material from which one could choose. He thought great art would drive out bad; he described an evening program of Tchaikovsky, ballet, Shakespeare, education lectures, and a speech by a presidential candidate on "The Management of Monopolies"; he thought the moral tone of the home theater would be excellent. And he pointed out that the difficulties in having all this were not technical but human. Let the reader draw his own conclusions!

In 1938, when the Walker investigation of the telephone industry published its report, television already existed but had not yet reached the general public. The Walker Report projected two ways it could develop:

> Television offers the possibility of a nation-wide visual and auditory communication service, and this service might be developed under either two broad methods. The first is by the eventual establishment of a series of local television broadcasting stations similar to the present local radio broadcasting stations . . . or conceivable it may develop

> into some form of wire plant transmission utilizing the present basic distributing network of the Bell System, with the addition of coaxial cable or carrier techniques now available or likely to be developed out of the Bell System's present research on new methods of broad band wire transmission.[24]

The one forecast the report did not make, and which now seems the most plausible, is that over time television would be delivered first one way and then the other. With time unspecified both forecasts may be realized.

Crime

From these forecasts—all of which concerned the telephone system's development—we turn now to forecasts regarding its impact on society. From the first decade of the century, there has been much discussion of the telephone's relationship to crime with diametrically opposite predictions. The telephone is portrayed as both the promoter and the conqueror of crime. A villainous anarchist in a 1902 *Chicago Tribune* short story wires a bomb to a phone to be detonated by his call. But in the happy ending, the bomb is detached seconds before he rings; the police trace his call and catch him.

The telephone is portrayed as part of a process of urbanization with decay of traditional moral values and social controls. The "call girl" was the new form of prostitute; obscene callers took advantage of the replacement of operators by dial phones. The phone company was repeatedly berated by reformers for not policing the uses to which the phone was put. As early as 1907, *Cosmopolitan Magazine* had a muckraking story by Josiah Flynt entitled "The Telegraph and Telephone Companies as Allies of the Criminal Pool-Rooms."[25] Flynt charges:

> Because they are among the country's great "business interests," because the stock in them is owned by eminent respectables in business, and because they can hide behind the impersonality of their corporate existence, they have not been compelled to bear their just share of the terrific burden of guilt. But they have been drawing from five to ten million dollars a year as their "rakeoff" from the pool rooms. . . . Every one of the estimated four thousand pool rooms throughout the United Stated is equipped with telephones used for gambling purposes and for nothing else.

Flynt charges that 2 percent of the New York Telephone company revenues, or a million dollars a year, was derived from gambling in pool rooms. He rejects the argument that the phone company should not attend to what subscribers say on their lines; the company, he says, knows full well who the criminal users are but simply does not wish to forgo the profits of sin.

Prohibition coincided with the telephone system's years of growth to a national network and total penetration. The bootleggers and the rackets made full use of whatever was available to run their operations; it is hard, however, to take seriously the argument of causality—that somehow there would have been less crime without the telephone.

Side by side with that accusation, one can also find in the 1920s and 1930s the reverse argument. The telephone, it was said, gives the police such an enormous advantage over criminals that law and security will come to prevail in American cities:

> When a girl operator in the exchange hears a cry for help—"Quick!" "The Police!"—she seldom waits to hear the number. She knows it. She is trained to save half seconds. And it is at such moments, if ever, that the users of a telephone can appreciate its insurance value.[26]

There were forecasts that crime would decrease, for the criminal would have little chance of escape once telephones were everywhere and the police could be notified ahead about the fleeing culprit. "Police officials feel that the scarcity of dramatic crimes may be due somewhat to the preventive factor present in modern police communication systems."[27]

In fact, enforcement agencies gradually adopted new communications technologies, but usually only slowly and after their usefulness was well demonstrated. Telegraphy was first used in law enforcement to connect police stations and headquarters, but it was not of great importance until encouraged by the International Association of Chiefs of Police, formed in 1893. Recognition of the need for a complex communication system for crime prevention followed civil service reform and the recognition of police work as a specialized profession.[28]

The problem of communication between the police station and the patrolman on the beat received little attention until the 1880s. Before the telephone, the technology available was that used since 1851 for fire alarms. (Between 1852 and 1881, 106 electric fire alarm systems were installed in American cities.)

> The first electric police-communication system of record was installed in 1867. Between 1867 and 1882 only seven more systems were put in operation. . . . 56 systems were installed from 1882 to 1891, 76 systems in the decade, and 84 . . . from 1892 to 1902.[29]

A survey in 1902 found that of 148 systems, 125 were telegraphic, 19 telephonic, and 3 mixed. Although police departments had subscribed to telephones ever since the Washington department took fifteen in 1878, they did not deploy them to the beats. In 1886, the *New York Tribune* in an editorial criticized the New York police for not connecting the stations with the central office by telephone as the Brooklyn police had. The *Tribune* remarked that "doubtless the time may come when every patrolman's beat will be furnished with one of these instruments."[30]

The Chicago department had been the first to move in that direction. Between 1880 and 1893, over 1,000 street boxes were installed. The popularity of such systems received a boost in 1889 when a murderer was caught at the railroad station a few hours after all police in the city had been notified of his description by the phone network. Telephone boxes began replacing signal boxes; yet by 1917 there were only 8,094 telephone boxes to 86,759 of the latter in police and fire service. In short, ideas for police use of communications technology were prevalent but their adoption came slowly. One idea which was never adopted, but was discussed by 1910, was that each individual should have a number by which he could be reached telephonically wherever he might be.[31]

Hindsight induces a jaundiced view of the forecasts that saw the telephone defeating crime. Such prognoses, we should note, were not made by developers of the telephone system, nor by law enforcement experts, but rather by journalists and reformers. Yet let us not be too complacent about our hindsight. Why were these forecasts wrong? Even with all the advantages of hindsight, it is hard to say. A priori it seems sensible that an instrument permitting well-organized, dispersed police agents to contact and warn each other about suspects much faster than the suspects could move should make things harder for lawbreakers. Yet crime increased in the same years the telephone became available to the authorities; this tells something about the limits of social forecasting based on assessment of one isolated technology. To understand the anomaly of growing crime in the same period as improved technologies of law enforcement, one must understand such matters as the public's attitude toward minor crime, the judges' behavior in sentencing, the organizational incentives in the legal process, the social structure of migrant and ethnic groups in the society, and the nature and reliability of crime statistics.

We do not understand those matters very well, even with hindsight. The forecast that the telephone would help the police was not wrong;

it has helped them. The impact on the amount of crime, however, depended primarily on what people wanted to do.

There is substantial evidence that whatever the net trend in criminal activity, the telephone has added to the citizen's sense of security. Alan Wurtzel's and Colin Turner's study in Chapter 11 on how people were affected by the New York City exchange fire in 1975 supports this. The ability to call for help is an important security, yet the relationship of communications to law enforcement is many-sided and complex.

The telephone became part of the pattern of both crime and law enforcement, affecting both. Criminals and policemen alike came to use the telephone, and it changed the way they did things. There even came to be special telephone crimes and telephone methods of enforcement; tapping is an example of both. Yet it is hard to argue that the level of crime or the overall success or failure of law enforcement had any obvious or single valued relationship with the development of the telephone network.

The Structure of Cities

One of our working hypotheses as we began this study was that the automobile and the telephone—between them—were responsible for the vast growth of American suburbia and exurbia, and for the phenomenon of urban sprawl. There is some truth to that, but there is also truth to the reverse proposition that the telephone made possible the skyscraper and increased the congestion downtown.

The movement out to residential suburbs began in the decade before the telephone and long before the automobile. As Alan Moyer describes in Chapter 16, the streetcar was the key at the beginning. Today streetcars have vanished, and the automobile and the telephone do help make it possible for metropolitan regions to spread over thousands of square miles. But the impact of the phone today and its net impact seventy years ago are almost reverse. As John J. Carty tells it:

> It may sound ridiculous to say that Bell and his successors were the fathers of modern commercial architecture—of the skyscraper. But wait a minute. Take the Singer Building, the Flatiron, the Broad Exchange, the Trinity, or any of the giant office buildings. How many messages do you suppose go in and out of those buildings every day? Suppose there was no telephone and every message had to be carried by a personal messenger. How much room do you think the necessary elevators would leave for offices? Such structures would be an economic impossibility."[32]

The prehistory of the skyscraper begins with the elevator in the 1850s; the first Otis elevator was installed in a New York City store in 1857, and with adaptation to electric power in the 1880s, it came into general use.[33] "The need to rebuild Chicago after the 1871 fire, rapid growth, and rising land values encouraged experimentation in construction." In 1884, Jenney erected a ten-story building with a steel skeleton as a frame. The Woolworth Building with fifty-seven stories opened in 1913. "By 1929 American cities had 377 skyscrapers of more than twenty stories."[34]

The telephone contributed to that development in several ways. We have already noted that human messengers would have required too many elevators at the core of the building to make it economic. Furthermore, telephones were useful in skyscraper construction; phones allowed the superintendent on the ground to keep in touch with the workers on the scaffolding. As the building went up, a line was dropped from the upper gliders to the ground.

As the telephone broke down old business and neighborhoods and made it possible to move to cheaper quarters, the telephone/tall building combination offered an option of moving up instead of out. Before the telephone, businessmen needed to locate close to their business contacts. Every city had a furrier's neighborhood, a hatter's neighborhood, a wool neighborhood, a fishmarket, an egg market, a financial district, a shipper's district, and many others. Businessmen would pay mightily for an office within the few blocks of their trade center; they did business by walking up and down the block and dropping in on the places where they might buy or sell. For lunch or coffee, they might stop by the corner restaurant or tavern where their colleagues congregated.

Once the telephone was available, business could move to cheaper quarters and still keep in touch. A firm could move outward, as many businesses did, or move up to the tenth or twentieth story of one of the new tall buildings. Being up there without a telephone would have put an intolerable burden on communication.

The option of moving out from the core city and the resulting urban sprawl has been much discussed, but most observers have lost sight of the duality of the movement; the skyscraper slowed the spread. It helped keep many people downtown and intensified the downtown congestion. Contemporary observers noted this, but in recent decades we have tended to forget it. Burlingame, for example, said:

> It is evident that the skyscraper and all the vertical congestion of city business centers would have been impossible without the telephone.

> Whether, in the future, with its new capacities, it will move to destroy the city it helped to build is a question for prophets rather than historians.[35]

Burlingame, before World War II, already sensed that things were changing. The flight from downtown was already perceptible enough to be noted as a qualification to his description of the process of concentration; both processes have taken place at once throughout the era of the telephone. The telephone is a facilitator used by people with opposite purposes; so we saw it with crime, and so it is here, too. It served communication needs despite either the obstacle of congested verticality or the obstacle of distance; the magnitude of the opposed effects may differ from time to time, and with it the net effect. At an early stage the telephone helped dissolve the solid knots of traditional business neighborhoods and helped create the great new downtowns; but at a later stage, it helped disperse those downtowns to new suburban business and shopping centers.

The telephone contributed in some further ways to downtown concentration in the early years—we have forgotten how bad urban mail service was. The interurban mails worked reasonably well, but a letter across town might take a week to arrive. Given the miserable state of intracity communication, the telephone met a genuine need for those who conducted business within the city.[36]

The telephone also contributed to urban concentration in the early days because the company was a supporter of zoning. The reasons were similar to ones motivating cablecasters today. Cablecasters are inclined to string CATV through comfortable middle-class neighborhoods where houses are fairly close together but in which utility lines do not have to go underground; they get their highest rate of penetration at the lowest price that way. Only under the impact of regulation do they cover a city completely.

The situation of early telephone systems was in some ways similar, though in some ways different. The Bell System strongly adheres to universal service as the goal, yet economics also favored first pushing into neighborhoods where there would be most businesses. At the beginning, when telephone systems first graduated from the renting of private lines between a factory and its office into providing a community system on a switchboard, many persons in a particular business or profession tended to be signed up fairly simultaneously. In some of the New England towns, the physicians made up a large proportion of early subscribers. In London, there were few physicians but many solicitors. Eventually the subscribers became more diversified, yet there was still a tendency for customers to be drawn from certain segments of the population until penetration became more or less universal. Telephone companies, therefore, found it in their interest to have stable, well-defined neighborhoods in cities in which they were laying trunks and locating central offices. Shifting and deteriorating neighborhoods were not good for business.

Zoning of a city helped in planning for future services, so the phone companies (along with other utilities) became supporters of the zoning movement.[37] The Department of Commerce's zoning primer of 1923 stated that "expensive public services are maintained at great waste in order to get through the blighted districts to the more distant and fashionable locations." In the initial development of phone service it was economic to avoid blighted neighborhoods. With a bluntness that reflects the times and would be unthinkable today, Smith and Campbell said:

> It should not be taken for granted that this satisfies the requirements unless there is at least one telephone for every eight inhabitants in an average American city, in which practically everyone is white. Where a large portion of the population belongs to the Negro race, or a considerable portion of the population is made up of very poor workers in factories, the requirements will be less. In some cities one telephone to fifteen inhabitants is all that can be expected.[38]

Zoning, along with other efforts at urban planning, became popular around the turn of the century. After the Chicago fire in 1871, building codes were enacted (around 1890) with explicit provisions for fire-proofing.[39] Codes dealt with allowable building heights and the location of tall buildings in the city. The idea of a planned city was contained in such books as Robinson's *Town and City* (1901) and Ebenezer Howard's *The Garden City*; zoning actually began in New York in 1916. In the intervening years the phone companies were one of the main sources of information fed into the new urban plans. We have already noted that AT&T urged each local phone company to do a developmental study to arrive at a fundamental plan. To do this they collected large amounts of neighborhood data on the population trends in the city, its businesses, and its neighborhoods; the telephone was used as a device for conducting the research. "The most direct means of approaching citizens on the planning issue was reported in Los Angeles where a battery of phone girls calls everyone in the city to secure reactions, while mailing an explanatory folder."[40]

Part of a telephone development study was a "house count" in which the classes of buildings and their uses were determined.[41] In general, the urban reformers and zoning planners received good cooperation from the phone companies and derived much of their data from phone company research.

On a few points, however, city authorities and telephone interests were sometimes at odds. Zoning was often used to prevent the construction of the tall buildings that were heavy users of telephones. Cities also tried to prevent the growth of suburbs outside their boundaries by prohibiting utilities from extending their services beyond city limits. That, if enforceable, would have been a particularly severe restriction on the telephone system because its whole function required that it be interconnected.[42] Robinson noted in 1901 the connection between telephone communications and family cohesion when a family moves to the suburbs.

Thus we find many relationships between the development of the telephone system and the quality of urban life; strikingly, the relationships change with time and with the level of telephone penetration. The same device at one stage contributed to the growth of the great downtowns and at a later stage to suburban migration. The same device, when it was scarce, served to accentuate the structure of differentiated neighborhoods. When it became a facility available to all, however, it reduced the role of the geographic neighborhood. A technology assessment of the device would be misleading unless it included an assessment of the device available in specified numbers.

The Record of Foresight and Hindsight

We may distinguish between those who made technical or business predictions and those who made predictions about the telephone's social impact. Some men did both (Gilfillan, for example), but a separation according to principle emphasis will be useful.

Technical and Business Forecasters

In our research we have looked at the business predictions of Bell, Vail, Western Electric, Elisha Grey, Edison, Hammond Hayes, chief engineer after 1907, J.E. Otterson, general commercial manager of Western Electric and later president of ERPI, AT&T's motion picture subsidiary, and S.C. Gilfillan, a sociologist and historian of technology.

Bell's excellent predictions about the evolution of the switchboard and central office, automatic switching, the development of long-distance service, underground cables, and universal penetration have already been noted. Vail, too, was remarkably prescient. While Bell made his predictions through either scientific logic or visionary insight, Vail predicted goals to be fulfilled and made his dream of universality happen. While on most issues his sense of strategy was keen, he made some errors, as we judge with benefit of hindsight. When Vail and Carty took over in 1907, they shelved the handset (or French phone) which the company had begun to install. In addition, AT&T moved slowly on the automatic exchange because of its massive investment in manual systems. Independents, such as the Home Telephone Company, and European systems (because they were growing more slowly) could adopt automatic switching more easily and earlier. Finally, Vail underestimated the potential of wireless telegraphy, but Carty convinced him of its importance in 1911. Yet none of these items gainsay his remarkable insight into how to build the business so that it worked.

Western Union and Elisha Grey, on the other hand, demonstrate the drawbacks of preservation on established perspectives. Grey could probably have invented the telephone at least a year before Bell had he realized its commercial value.[43] In 1875 in a letter to his patent lawyer Grey wrote: "Bell seems to be spending all his energies on (the) talking telegraph. While this is very interesting scientifically, it has no commercial value at present, for they can do more business over a line by methods already in use than by that system."[44] In another letter after the Philadelphia Centennial Exposition, he added: "Of course it may, if perfected, have a certain value as a speaking tube.... This is the verdict of a practical telegraph man."[45]

Hounshell points to a number of reasons for Grey's misjudgment: his extensive experience in telegraphy, his association with and his respect for the leaders of the telegraph industry, he committed the fallacy of historical analogy. He and Western Union thought of what the telephone could do to extend the existing telegraph system. Bell was a speech expert who approached the problems of telecommunications from the outside.

Hounshell illustrates the point by the story of one Western Union officer who anticipated the phone's use for transmitting speech between telegraphers. He could not visualize the elimination of the traditional telegrapher.[46]

Daniel Boorstin argues that Thomas Edison committed the same fallacy with the phonograph: he invented it as a repeater because he believed that few people would be able to afford their own telephone. His notion was that offices (such as telegraph offices) would use it to record spoken messages that would be transmitted via phone to a recorder at another office where the addressee could hear it.[47] Partly as a result of this misperception, it took Edison fifteen years to realize the entertainment potential of the phonograph.

Clearly capitalist investors or other market-oriented technical men can forecast badly, too. The combination of technical understanding and appreciation of the market may be a necessary condition for good assessment of a new technology. But capitalist investors fail more often than they succeed. History focuses on successes; failure is treated as a kind of environmental wasteland too dreary to gaze upon. And so innovators who followed the wrong path lost their money and have been forgotten.

Yet the melding of technical and economic considerations has been a key to whatever understanding successes of forecasting have occurred. Where those requisites have been present but foresight has failed, a common and easily identified reason has been a lack of imagination about the range of possible change and perseverance in an established way of doing things.[48]

Forecasts of Social Consequence

The record of social forecasting is far less impressive. To evaluate the forecast record on the telephone's social effects, we have looked at writings by journalists, historians, and sociologists. The first conclusion is that they have had very little to say on the subject.

We reviewed the indexes of some histories of technology. The result presented in table 9.1 shows that attention to transportation has been much greater than attention to communication. Among the references to communications, attention to the telephone is salient only in histories of American technology.

Table 9.2 presents a similar analysis of the number of paragraphs devoted to different technologies, mostly from the 1930s. The distribution reflects the bias of social scientists toward the present in contrast to the historians' focus on the past. The technologies the sociologists attended to most were the ones that were relatively new at the period when they wrote: radio, television, automobile, and aviation; the telegraph had receded into the past. But note that the telephone gets less

Table 9.1. Relative Concentration on Various Technologies in History of Technology Literature.

	Number of References to Different Technologies:*					
Reference	**Telephone**	**Telegraph**	**Radio**	**Television**	**Railroad**	**Automobile**
I Early Technology (1600–1900):	(9)	(27)	(–)	(–)	(123)	(40)
Kranzburg *Technology in Western-Civilization Vol. 1* (1976) (1600–1900)	7	14	–	–	62	6
Singer, ed. *A History of Technology* (1968) (1850–1900)	2	13	–	–	61	34
II General Technology Histories (Ancient to 1950 +):	(8)	(13)	(17)	(6)	(71)	(56)
Ferguson *Bibliography of the History of Technology* (1968)**	3	6	3	–	33	16
Lilley *Men, Machines, and History* (1965)	4	3	13	5	18	18
Armytage *A Social History of Engineering* (1961)	1	4	1	1	20	22
III American Technology (1700 +):	(77)	(60)	(96)	(47)	(231)	(152)
Boorstin *The Americans: The Democratic Experience* (1973) (1860–1970)	19	10	41	36	64	50
Oliver *History of American Technology* (1956) (1730–1950)	20	24	26	7	85	28
Allen *The Big Change* (1952) (1900–1950)	1	1	3	1	10	15
Burlingame *Engines of Democracy* (1940) (1865–1935)	37	25	26	3	72	59
Grand Totals	94	100	113	53	425	258
Totals II & III only	85	73	113	53	302	218

* Numbers indicate number of pages on which technology is mentioned plus number of different subtopics mentioned in index.
** Numbers for this book refer only to the number of documents on each technology cited in this bibliography.

Table 9.2. Relative Concentration on Various Technologies in Social Impact and Trend Literature of 1930s and 1940s.*

Reference	Telegraph	Telephone	Radio	Television	Railroad	Automobile	Aviation
Mumford *Technics and Civilization* (1934)	2	4	2	1	7	6	2
Leonard *Tools for Tomorrow*** (1935)	5	5	6	3	3	6	10
Gilfillan "Social Effects of Invention"*** (1937)	1	3	17	19	2	6	15
Ogburn *Machines and Tomorrow's World* (1938)	1	6	7	4	7	19	2
Roger *Technology and Society* ** (1941)	1	1	31	4	10	4	6
Ogburn *Technology and the Changing Family* (1955)	–	2	6	10	–	1	1
Totals	10	21	69	41	29	42	36

* Number of paragraphs related to technology except where noted.
** Number of references to technology in index, for these books only.
*** From Subcommittee on Technology of the National Resources Committee report, *Technological Trends and National Policy*, Ogburn Chairman, 1939.

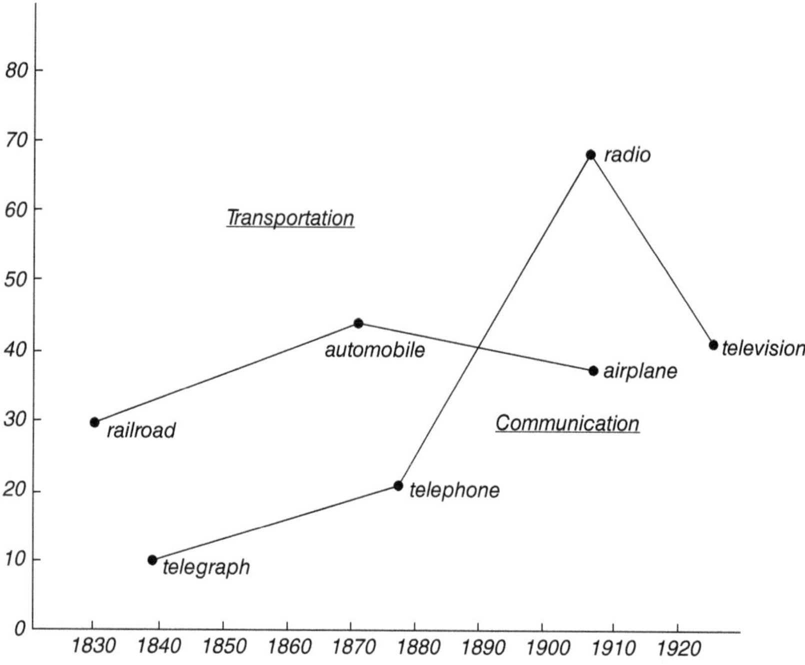

Figure 9.1. Relationship between Date Invented and Attention in the Social Impact Literature of the Thirties for Transportation and Communication Technology.

attention than railroads, even though it is younger. Figure 9.1 illustrates the greater focus on transportation than communication, age being held constant.

Quantity, however, is not the key thing; more disturbing is that historians, social scientists, journalists, and current commentators have given us very few significant forecasts or analyses on the telephone's social effects. What few there are tend to add the telephone to a list of forces that are all asserted to work in the same way. Sociological writing of the 1920s and 1930s was heavily shaped by a grand conception (which came to America from Germany about 1908) of the decline of *gemeinschaft* and the rise of *gesellschaft*: the decline of the traditional primary group and the growth of a complex society dominated by impersonal relations. In writing about any technology, the impulse was to make it fit that model. Writers discussed the growth of the city, the breakdown of the family, or some other aspect of this grand historical process, noted how the automobile or some other technical change led to it, and added (as an aside) "along with such other innovations as the telephone, the telegraph, or you-name-it."

Such metatheories without detailed cold-blooded study of the historical facts have obscured the telephone's real history. Its effect has not necessarily been in any single direction, nor in the same direction as other devices such as the mass media, the telegraph, or the automobile.[49] The telephone is a device with subtle and manifold effects which cannot be well guessed *a priori*. There are, in our society, significant problems of privacy, alienation, crime, and urban environment. In no instance is it clear what the telephone's net effect has been on any of these.

We should not be too harsh about forecasters, however; we have the benefit of hindsight now, yet it is not much easier to answer the questions about the past than about the present or future. Postdiction is almost as hard as prediction; aftcasts almost as hard as forecasts. What would have happened to American cities if the telephone had never been invented? Would there, perhaps, have been an enormous proliferation of teletypewriters to serve some of the same purposes? If so, would our cities be bigger or smaller than they are today, more densely settled or more dispersed? It is not much easier to answer the "what if" questions of history than the "what if" questions about the future.

Appendix

Kensington, March 25, 1878

To the capitalists of the Electric Telephone Company:

Gentlemen—It has been suggested that at this, our first meeting, I should lay before you a few ideas, concerning the future of the electric telephone, together with any suggestions that occur to me in regard to the best mode of introducing the instrument to the public.

The telephone may be briefly described as an electrical contrivance for reproducing, in distant places, the tones and articulations of a speaker's voice, so that conversation can be carried on by word of mouth between persons in different rooms, in different streets, or in different towns.

The great advantage it possesses over every other form of electrical apparatus consists in the fact that it requires no skill to operate the instrument. All other telegraphic machines produce signals which require to be translated by experts, and such instruments are therefore extremely limited in their application, but the telephone actually speaks, and for this reason it can be utilized for nearly every purpose for which speech is employed.

At the present time we have a perfect network of gas pipes and water pipes throughout our large cities. We have main pipes laid under the streets communicating by side pipes with the various dwellings, enabling the members to draw their supplies of gas and water from a common source.

In a similar manner it is conceivable that cables of telephone wires could be laid under ground, or suspended overhead, communicating by branch wires with private dwellings, counting houses, shops, manufactories, etc., uniting them through the main cable with a central office where the wire could be connected as desired, establishing direct communication between any two places in the city. Such a plan as this, though impracticable at the present moment, will, I firmly believe, be the outcome of the introduction of the telephone to the public. Not only so, but I believe in the future wires will unite the head offices or telephone companies in different cities, and a man in one part of the country may communicate by word of mouth with another in a distant place.

In regard to other present uses for the telephone, the instrument can be supplied so cheaply as to compete on favorable terms with speaking tubes, bells and annunciators, as a means of communication between different parts of the house. This seems to be a very favorable application of the telephone, not only on account of the large number of telephones that would be wanted, but because it would lead eventually to the plan of intercommunication referred to above. I would therefore recommend that special arrangements be made for the introduction of the telephone into hotels and private buildings in place of the speaking tubes and annunciators, at present employed. Telephones sold for this purpose could be stamped or numbered in such a way as to distinguish them from those employed for business purposes, and an agreement could be signed by the purchaser that the telephones should become forfeited to the company if used for other purposes than those specified in the agreement.

It is probable that such a use of the telephone would speedily become popular, and that as the public became accustomed to the telephone in their houses they would recognize the advantage of a system of intercommunication.

In conclusion, I would say that it seems to me that the telephone should immediately be brought prominently before the public, as a means of communication between bankers, merchants, manufacturers, wholesale and retail dealers, dock companies, water companies, police offices, fire stations, newspaper offices, hospitals and public buildings and for use in railway offices, in mines and other operations;

Although there is a great field for the telephone in the immediate present, I believe there is still greater in the future.

By bearing in mind the great object to be ultimately achieved, I believe that the telephone company cannot only secure for itself a business of the most remunerative kind, but also benefit the public in a way that has never been previously attempted.

I am, gentlemen, your obedient servant,

Alexander Graham Bell

Notes

1. Dilts, Marion May. *The telephone in a changing world.* New York: Longman's Green, 1941, p. 11.
2. Ibid., p. 16.
3. Ibid., p. 188ff.
4. Thomas P. Hughes (according to *Science* [November 21. 1975]: 763) notes that Edison was not only a "consummate inventor" but a "complete capitalist." His notebooks "while devising the nation's first public power system . . .

show on every other page calculations of the system's market potential, the price charged for competing gas illumination, the cost of copper wiring, and other entrepreneurial concerns."

5. That would have been particularly so, as Cherry has noted, without the switch board. As Arthur Vaughan Abbott calculated in 1894 (Engineering Series, *Bulletin of the University of Wisconsin* 1:4, p. 70), a system for 10,000 subscribers (the approximate number than in New York of Chicago) with a separate line between each pair of subscribers would have taken an underground conduit a yard square, or a pole above ground 1,000 feet high.
6. Dilts, *The telephone in a changing world*, p. 28.
7. In 1904, the AT&T *Annual report* asserted: "As a general principle, it seems perfectly certain that it will always be the case that the larger and more densely populated the community, the higher must be the standard rates for the comprehensive service required for that community. Not only the investment and the cost of operation, but the general difficulty of doing business which can only be overcome by enlarged expenditure, increase in passing from smaller towns and cities to the larger."
8. A further incentive for this change was the growing percentage of AT&T ownership of local phone companies in large cities such as New York. As long as AT&T's revenue was largely from franchise fees for the use of Bell equipment, the company stood to gain from the growth of local companies but not directly from their profitability. As their equity position grew, their direct concern for profitability did. too. Faced with competition from price-cutting independents (some using message rates), it became important to meet the competition at the low end while keeping revenues up. A pricing system that segmented the market maintained earnings. A message charge also served to discourage neighbors' using a telephone and thus increased the likelihood of their getting their own.
9. This figure, which was suggested to local companies for use in the Fundamental Plan, is a rather crude average. More detailed planning in AT&T, of course, used a variety of figures for different types of equipment.
10. Smith, Arthur B.; Campbell, William C. *Automatic telephony.* New York: McGraw Hill, 1915, p. 379.
11. In 1912, Arnold Bennett, in a series of *Harper's Monthly,* gave his impressions of the United States. He begins the fourth (vol. 125 [July 1912], pp. 191–92) commenting: "What strikes and frightens the backward European almost as much as anything in the United States is the efficiency and fearful universality of the telephone. [Just as buildings are pierced everywhere by elevator shafts full of movement so I think of cities as] threaded under pavements and over roofs and between floors and ceilings and between walls, by millions upon millions of live filaments that unite all the privacies of the organism—and destroy them in order to make one immense publicity. I do not mean that Europe had failed to adopt the telephone, nor that in Europe there are no hotels with the dreadful curse of an active telephone in every room. But I do mean that the European telephone is a toy, and a somewhat clumsy one, compared to the seriousness of the American telephone. Many otherwise highly civilized Europeans are as timid in addressing a telephone as they would be in addressing a royal sovereign. The average European middle-class householder still speaks of his telephone, if

he has one, in the same falsely casual tone as the corresponding American is liable to speak of his motor car . . . . Is it possible that you have been in the United States a month without understanding that the United States is primarily nothing but a vast congeries of telephone cabins?"

12. Dilts, *The telephone in a changing world,* p. 4.
13. Casson, Herbert N. "The telephone as it is today." *World's Work* 19 (1910): 12775. Vail understood the strategic advantage of controlling the long lines. From 1881 until 1897 the company issued a national telephone directory, like the national index directory today. Eventually it had to be abandoned for it became too big.
14. Burlingame. Roger. *Engines of democracy.* New York: Charles Scribner, 1940, p. 118ff.
15. Casson, "The telephone as it is today," p. 12776. Casson's tale simplifies slightly in that the Boston to New York was not an instant success. It was initially noisy and had the severe problems of all long-distance lines until adequate repeaters were developed. However, its very existence was a triumph, and quality of service gradually improved.
16. An article in *Current Literature* 50 (May 1911): 504, on "The Immediate Future of the Long-Distance Telephone," reports the laying of an experimental submarine telephone cable between France and England. Conversations between London and the whole European continent are, it says, now possible, and conversations are now possible over up to 1,700 miles of cable. The article looks forward to the time, far in the future, when the whole globe will be linked together.
17. Chapter 15 [from *The social impact of the telephone*] gives the data on the decreasing sensitivity of phone charges to distance.
18. It is worth noting that the same points can be made about Marconi and the history of wireless telegraphy. After Herzian waves were discovered in 1888, a number of scientists recognized that they could be used, as electrical transmissions over wires were already being used, for communications devices. Marconi's important insight, aside from his entrepreneurial ones, was his successfully demonstrated conviction that those waves could go long distances. His great triumph was his transatlantic transmission.
19. Alexander Bain outlines the principles of telegraphic transmission of pictures in a British patent in 1843.
20. Bruce, Robert V. *Bell.* Boston: Little Brown, p. 242.
21. Dilts, *The telephone in a changing world,* p. 22.
22. *World's Work* 20 (May 1910): 12916–17.
23. *The Independent* 73 (October 17, 1912): 886–91.
24. Proposed Report, Telephone Investigation. FCC, USGPO, 1938, pp. 238–39.
25. *Cosmopolitan Magazine* 43 (May 1907): 50–57.
26. Casson, Herbert. "The social value of the telephone." *The Independent* 71 (October 26, 1911): 903. See also Burlingame, *Engine of democracy,* p. 125, and Dilts, *The telephone in a changing world,* pp. 82, 95–96.
27. Dilts. *The telephone in a changing world,* p. 177. She quotes the *Worcester Telegram* on the capture of a gunman: "A bullet killed him, but radio and teletype and telephone had already doomed him" (p 178).
28. Leonard, V. A. *Police communication systems.* Berkeley: University of California Press, 1938.

29. Ibid., pp 6–7.
30. Ibid., p. 10.
31. Casson, Herbert. "The future of the telephone." *World's Work* (May 1910): 1908–13.
32. In Mumford, John Kimberly. "This land of opportunity, the nerve center of business." *Harper's Weekly* 52 (August, 1908): 23. The same point was made in the trade journal *Telephony* 4, no. 2 (1902).
33. Glaab, Charles N.; Brown, A. Theodore. *A history of urban America.* New York: Macmillan, 1967. pp. 144–45.
34. Ibid., p. 280.
35. Burlingame. *Engines of democracy,* p. 96.
36. We have noted several times how much worse European phone service was than American. Conversely, the local mail service was often very much better. In many big European cities express letters could be sent rapidly and reliably. There may have been some tradeoff between alternative communication devices for achieving the same goals.
37. Telephone, electric light, gas and trolley companies report that zoning is making it possible for them to eliminate much of their guesswork as to what services they must provide, said John Noland's book *City Planning* shortly after zoning was enacted in New York. Hubbard and Hubbard wrote: "The utility companies as a rule may be counted favorable to zoning. The general attitude of the telephone companies has been expressed in favor of the stability brought about by zoning."
38. Smith and Campbell. *Automatic telephony,* p. 379.
39. In the early years there was considerable concern about telephone wires and safety. The *American Architect and Building News* had a section in each issue on new inventions. It did not note the telephone in 1876, but by 1881 there had been ten references to the telephone in the magazine; four of these concerned safety. There was particular concern about the proliferation of overhead wires.
40. Hubbard, H. V.; Hubbard, T. K. *Your cities today and tomorrow.* Cambridge, MA: Harvard University Press, 1929, p. 93.
41. Smith and Campbell. *Automatic telephony,* p. 379.
42. However, occasionally phone companies took refuge in such restrictions. In *Young vs. Southwestern Telegraph and Telephone Co.* 192 F. 200, 1912, the Arkansas Circuit Court ruled that the phone company was not discriminating when it refused to construct a line beyond city limits.
43. Hounshell, David A. "Elisha Grey and the telephone: On the disadvantages of being an expert." *Technology and Culture* 16, no. 2, p. 159.
44. Ibid., p. 152.
45. Ibid., p. 157.
46. Ibid., p. 145.
47. Boorstin, Daniel. *The Americans: The democratic experience.* New York: Random House, 1973, p. 379.
48. When Vail left the company in 1887, the organization of engineering research fell to Hammond Hayes. Between 1887 and the management reorganization of 1907, the Bell company conducted little fundamental research. Rather, research activities focused upon improvements in apparatus. Sources outside the company contributed the significant breakthroughs in telephone: the

automatic exchange system by Strowger in 1889, the loaded coil by Pupin in 1900, and the vacuum tube by De Forest in 1907.

49. Vail's return in 1907 signaled a change in that research philosophy. The obvious frontier was "wireless" communication, made possible by the De Forest patents. Research in that area "would not only react most favorably upon our service where wires are used, but might put us in a position of control with respect to the art of wireless telephony should it turn out to be a factor of importance." (Quoted in Danielson. N. R. *AT&T: The story of industrial conquest.* New York: Vanguard, 1939. pp., 104–5.) The Bell interests rapidly acquired and developed wireless technology and moved on, in Vail's phrase, "to occupy the field" of telephonic research. That is, by 1910 the company was committed to the internal development of both fundamental research and of incremental engineering improvements. Today, the Bell Labs still follow the basic mandate and organization that followed from Vail's management. See chapters 5 and 8 [*The social impact of the telephone*] for a strong case for the difference between the social effects of the telephone and the mass media.

Part IV

Network Theory

Editor's Introduction

Contacts and Influence

This article, written with the mathematician Manfred Kochen, is one of Ithiel pool's most farsighted and original contributions. It begins to develop a set of analytical tools to study the rise of contact networks, which establish new avenues for political influence and social change.

Earlier in the twentieth century, it was more accurate to analyze politics as the study of groups. Social classes were more easily distinguished and there were moderate or strong correlations between social class and a wide range of attitudes and behavior. American politics typically involved the interaction of different organized groups: labor, business, political parties.

But today (the emphasis of humanists on social entrapment not withstanding) the correlation of social class with other variables has diminished steadily in advanced industrial nations, and traditional political loyalties also have loosened. At least in these countries, more people have wider choices about their lives, are more widely traveled, relate more as individuals, have a wider circle of acquaintances, and the verb "to network" has become commonplace.

Pool began to study contact networks by asking the probability that any two individuals, selected at random, would know each other; or, if not, would be able to contact one another through one step (a mutual friend); or through two steps; etc. Another way to pose the question is how many steps it would take, by personal acquaintance networks, to send a message to the President of the United States, or to any other selected target person in the world? Pool's line of inquiry often gave unexpected results, and it has become known as the "small world" phenomenon. A book and play, *Six Degrees of Separation,* were inspired by the ideas.[1]

Also (at the time of the publication of this volume in the late 1990s) the development of contact networks (supported and strengthened by the Internet) is becoming recognized as a powerful force in global humanitarian politics. It would be impossible to conceive of the global environmental movement, or the new world landmine treaty in the late 1990s, without recognizing the causal force of individuals and their network of relationships in producing results that earlier might have required support from the American government. The explicit measurement of these changes, an assessment of the depth of penetration, and of the new potential for political influence by well-connected individuals using new telecommunications technology are among the lines of research that can build upon this foundation.

Note

1. See Manfred Kochen (ed.), *The small world: A volume of recent research advance commemorating Ithiel de Sola Pool, Stanley Milgram, Theodore Newcomb.* (Norwood, NJ: Ablex publishing corp., 1989).

10

Contacts and Influence

with Manfred Kochen

Introduction

Let us start with familiar observations: the "small world" phenomenon, and the use of friends in high places to gain favors. It is almost too banal to cite one's favorite unlikely discovery of a shared acquaintance, which usually ends with the exclamation "My, it's a small world!" The senior author's favorite tale happened in a hospital in a small town in Illinois where he heard one patient, a telephone lineman, say to a Chinese patient in the next bed: "You know, I've only known one Chinese before in my life. He was from Shanghai." "Why that's my uncle," said his neighbor. The statistical chances of an Illinois lineman knowing a close relative of one of (then) 600,000,000 Chinese are minuscule; yet that sort of event happens.

The patient was, of course, not one out of 600,000,000 random Chinese, but one out of the few hundred thousand wealthy Chinese of Westernized families who lived in the port cities and moved abroad. Add the fact that the Chinese patient was an engineering student, and so his uncle may well have been an engineer too—perhaps a telecommunications engineer. Also there were perhaps some geographic lines of contact which drew the members of one family to a common area for travel and study. Far from surprising, the encounter seems almost natural. The chance meetings that we have are a clue to social structure, and their frequency an index of stratification.

Less accidental than such inadvertent meetings are the planned contacts sought with those in high places. To get a job one finds a friend to put in a good word with his friend. To persuade a congressman one seeks a mutual friend to state the case. This influence is peddled for

First published in *Social Networks* (1978).

5 percent. Cocktail parties and conventions institutionalize the search for contacts. This is indeed the very stuff of politics. Influence is in large part the ability to reach the crucial man through the right channels, and the more channels one has in reserve, the better. Prominent politicians count their acquaintances by the thousands. They run into people they know everywhere they go. The experience of casual contact and the practice of influence are not unrelated. A common theory of human contact nets might help clarify them both.

No such theory exists at present. Sociologists talk of social stratification; political scientists of influence. These quantitative concepts ought to lend themselves to a rigorous metric based upon the elementary social events of man-to-man contact. "Stratification" expresses the probability of two people in the same stratum meeting and the improbability of two people from different strata meeting. Political access may be expressed as the probability that there exists an easy chain of contacts leading to the power holder. Yet such measures of stratification and influence as functions of contacts do not exist.

What is it that we should like to know about human contact nets?

- For any *individual* we should like to know how many other people he knows, *i.e.* his acquaintance volume.
- For a *population* we want to know the distribution of acquaintance volumes, the mean and the range between the extremes.
- We want to know what kinds of people they are who have many contacts and whether those people are also the influentials.
- We want to know how the lines of contact are stratified; what is the structure of the network?

If we know the answers to these questions about individuals and about the whole population, we can pose questions about the implications for *paths* between pairs of individuals.

- How great is the probability that two persons chosen at random from the population will know each other?
- How great is the chance that they will have a friend in common?
- How great is the chance that the shortest chain between them requires two intermediaries; that is, a friend of a friend?

The mere existence of such a minimum chain does not mean, however, that people will become aware of it. The surprised exclamation "It's a small world" reflects the shock of discovery of a chain that existed all along.[1] So another question is:

- How far are people aware of the available lines of contact? A friend of a friend is useful only if one is aware of the connection. Also a channel is useful only if one knows how to use it. So the final question is, what sorts of people, and how many, try to exert influence on the persons with whom they are in contact: what sorts of persons and how many are opinion leaders, manipulators, politicists (de Grazia 1952; Boissevain 1974; Erickson and Kringas 1975)?

These questions may be answered at a highly general level for human behavior as a whole, and in more detail for particular societies. At the more general level there are probably some things we can say about acquaintanceship volume based on the nature of the human organism and psyche. The day has twenty-four hours and memory has its limits. There is a finite number of persons that any one brain can keep straight and with whom any one body can visit. More important, perhaps, there is a very finite number of persons with whom any one psyche can have much cathexis.

There are probably some fundamental psychological facts to be learned about the possible range of identifications and concerns of which a person is capable (Miller 1956).

These psychic and biological limits are broad, however. The distribution of acquaintanceship volumes can be quite variable between societies or social roles. The telephone makes a difference, for example. The contact pattern for an Indian villager *sans* radio, telephone, or road to his village is of a very different order from that of a Rotarian automobile dealer.

There is but little social science literature on the questions that we have just posed.[2] Even on the simplest question of the size of typical acquaintanceship volumes there are few data (Hammer, n.d.; Boissevain 1967). Some are found in anecdotal descriptions of political machines. In the old days there was many a precinct captain who claimed to know personally every inhabitant of his area. While sometimes a boastful exaggeration, there is no doubt that the precinct worker's success derived, among other things, from knowing 300+500 inhabitants of his neighborhood by their first names and family connections (Kurtzman 1935). At a more exalted level too, the art of knowing the right people is one of the great secrets of political success; James Farley claimed

10,000 contacts. Yet no past social science study has tested how many persons or what persons any politician knows. The estimates remain guesswork.

There exists a set of studies concerning acquaintanceship volume of delinquent girls in an institutional environment: J. L. Moreno and Helen Jennings asked girls in a reform school (with 467 girls in cottages of twenty-three or twenty-four apiece) to enumerate all other girls with whom they were acquainted (Jennings 1937). It was assumed they knew all the girls in their own cottage. Computed that way, the median number of acquaintances was approximately sixty-five. However, the range was tremendous. One girl apparently knew 175 of her fellow students, while a dozen (presumably with low I.Q.s) could list only four or fewer girls outside of their own cottage.

These figures have little relevance to normal political situations; but the study is valuable since it also tested the hypothesis that the extent of contact is related to influence, the girls were given sociometric tests to measure their influence. In each of two separate samples, a positive correlation (0.4 and 0.3) was found between contact range and influence.

One reason why better statistics do not exist on acquaintanceship volume is that they are hard to collect. People make fantastically poor estimates of the number of their own acquaintances (Killworth and Russell 1976). Before reading further, the reader should try to make an estimate for himself. Define an acquaintance as someone whom you would recognize and could address by name if you met him. Restrict the definition further to require that the acquaintance would also recognize you and know your name. (That excludes entertainment stars, public figures, etc.) With this criterion of acquaintance, how many people do you know?

The senior author tried this question on some thirty colleagues, assistants, secretaries and others around his office. The largest answer was 10,000 the smallest was fifty. The median answer was 522. What is more, there seemed to be no relationship between the guesses and reality. Older or gregarious persons claimed no higher figures than young or relatively reclusive ones. Most of the answers were much too low. Except for the one guess of 10,000 and two of 2,000 each, they were all probably low. We don't know that, of course, but whenever we have tried sitting down with a person and enumerating circles of acquaintances it has not taken long before he has raised his original estimate as more and more circles have come to mind: relatives, old school friends, merchants, job colleagues, colleagues on former jobs, vacation friends, club members, neighbors, and so on. Most of us grossly underestimate the number of people we know for they are tucked in the recesses of our minds ready to be recalled when occasion demands.

Perhaps a notion of the order of magnitude of acquaintanceship volume can be approached by a *gedankenexperiment* with Jennings's data on the reform school. The inmates were young girls who had not seen much of the world; they had but modest I.Q.s and memories; they had come from limited backgrounds; and in the recent past they had been thoroughly closed off from the world. We know that the average one knew sixty-five inmates. Is it fair to assume that we may add at least twenty teachers, guards, and other staff members known on the average? Somewhere the girls had been in school before their internment. Perhaps each knew forty students and ten teachers from there. These girls were all delinquents. They were usually part of a delinquent gang or subculture. Perhaps an average of thirty young people were part of it. They had been arrested, so they knew some people from the world of lawyers, judges, policemen, and social workers. Perhaps there were twenty of them. We have not yet mentioned families and relatives; shall we say another thirty? Then there were neighbors in the place they had lived before, perhaps adding up to thirty-five. We have already reached 250 acquaintances which an average girl might have, based solely on the typical life history of an inmate. We have not yet included friends made in club or church, nor merchants, nor accidental contacts. These might add another fifty. Nor have we allowed for the girls who had moved around—who had been in more than one school or neighborhood or prison. Perhaps 400 acquaintances is not a bad guess of the average for these highly constricted, relatively inexperienced young girls. Should we not suspect that the average for a mature, white-collar worker is at least double that?

Perhaps it is, but of course we don't know. All we have been doing so far is trying to guess orders of magnitude with somewhat more deliberation than was possible by the respondents to whom we popped the question "How many people do you know?" There has been no real research done to test such estimates.

It could be done by a technique analogous to that used for estimating a person's vocabulary. In any given time period during which we observe, a person uses only some of the words he knows and similarly has contact with only some of the people he knows. How can we estimate from this limited sample how many others are known to him? In each case (words and friends) we can do it by keeping track of the proportion of new ones which enter the record in each given time period. Suppose we count 100 running words. These may contain perhaps sixty different words, with some words repeated as many as six or seven times, but most words appearing once. Adding a second 100 running words may add thirty new ones to the vocabulary. A third hundred may add twenty-five new ones, and so on down. If we extrapolate the curve we reach a point where new words appear only every few thousand running words, and if we extrapolate to infinity we have an estimate of the person's total vocabulary. In the same way, on the first day one may meet thirty people. On the second day one may meet another thirty but perhaps only fifteen of them are new, the other fifteen being repeaters. On the third day perhaps the non-repeaters may be down to ten, and so on. Again by extrapolating to infinity an estimate of the universe of acquaintances may be made.

Extrapolation to infinity requires strong assumptions about the number of very rarely seen acquaintances. If there are very many who are seen but once in a decade, then a much longer period of observation is required. If the number of people seen once in two decades is not significantly smaller than the number seen in a shorter period, then there are methodological difficulties in estimation.

Two further cautions are necessary. It turns out that the lumpiness in the schedules of our lives makes this technique unusable except over long periods. Perhaps we start on Thursday and go to work. Friday we go to work and see almost the same people. Saturday we go to the beach and have an entirely new set of contacts. Then Monday, perhaps, we are sent on a trip to another office. In short, the curves are highly irregular. Long and patient observation is called for.

Also note that at the end of a lengthy experiment (say after one year), it is necessary to check back over the early lists to determine who are forgotten and no longer acquaintances. Just as new persons enter the acquaintanceship sphere, old ones drop out of it. In one record, for example, a subject recorded 156 contacts in five successive days, with 117 different persons whom he then knew. Two years and ten months later, though still working in the same place, he could no longer recall or recognize thirty-one of these; that is, 86 (or 74 percent) were still acquaintances.

It is important to collect more such empirical information. Section 2 of this paper describes some empirical findings that we have obtained. But before we can decide what to collect we need to think through the logical model of how a human contact net works. We shall do that roughly and nonmathematically in this introduction. Section 3 of the paper deals with it more formally.

One question that quite properly is raised by readers is what do we mean by acquaintanceship, or friendship, or contact. For the mathematical model, the precise definition of "knowing" is quite irrelevant. What the mathematical model gives us is a set of points each of which is connected with some of the other points. As we look away from our model to the world for which it stands, we understand that each point somehow represents a person, and each connection an act of knowing. The model is indifferent to this, however. The points could stand for atoms, or neurons, or telephones, or nations, or corporations. The connections could consist of collisions, or electric charges, or letters written, or hearing about, or acquaintanceship, or friendship, or marriage. To use the model (and satisfy ourselves that it is appropriate) we shall have to pick definitions of person (i.e., point) and knowing (i.e., connectedness) related to the problem at hand. But we start with a model that is quite general. We do indeed impose some constraints on the points and on their connections. These constraints are the substance of our theory about the nature of human contacts.

One simplification we make in our model is to assume that the act of knowing is an all-or-none relationship. That is clearly not true and it is not assumed by Hammer (n.d.), Gurevich (1961) and Schulman (1976). There are in reality degrees of connectedness between persons. There are degrees of awareness which persons have of each other, and there are varied strengths of cathexis. But we cannot yet deal with these degrees. For the moment we want to say of any person, A, that he either does or does not know any given other person, B.

The criterion of human acquaintanceship might be that when A sees B he recognizes him, knows a name by which to address him, and would ordinarily feel it appropriate that he should greet him. That definition excludes, as we have noted, recognition of famous persons, since as strangers we do not feel free to greet them. It excludes also persons whom we see often but whose names we have never learned; for example, the policeman on the corner. It is, however, a useful operational definition for purposes of contact net studies, because without knowing a name it is hard to keep a record.

Alternatively, the criterion might be a relationship which creates a claim on assistance. In politics, that is often the important kind of knowing. One might well find that a better predictor of who got a job was a man's position in the network of connections defined by obligation than his position in the network of mere acquaintance connections.

For some anthropological studies the connection with which we are concerned might be kinship. As many societies operate, the most important fact in the dealings of two persons is whether they are kin or not. Kinship creates obligations and thus provides a protection of each by the other. Blood kinship is a matter of degree fading off imperceptibly; we are all ultimately related to everyone else. But society defines the limit of who are recognized as kin and who are unrelated. This varies from society to society, and sometimes is hard to establish. In many societies, Brazil and India for example, the first gambit of new acquaintances is to talk about relatives to see if a connection can be established. For such societies kinship is clearly an important criterion of connectedness.

Another criterion of connectedness, of considerable relevance in the United States, is the first-name index. This makes a sharp distinction between levels of knowing, just as does *Sie* and *du* in German or *vous* and *tu* in French.

Whatever definition of knowing we choose to use, our model proceeds by treating connectedness as an all-or-none matter. In short, we are trying to develop not a psychological model of *the* knowing relationship, but a model for treating data about knowing relationships (however defined) which can be applied using whatever knowing relationship happens to be of interest.

The political scientist, using an appropriate definition, may use a contact net model to study influence (Gurevich and Weingrod 1976; n.d.). He asks the number of "connections" of a political kind a person has. The sociologist or anthropologist, using an appropriate definition, may use such a model to study social structure. He asks what kinds of persons are likely to be in contact with each other. The communications researcher may use such a model to study the channels for the flow of messages. Psychologists may use it to examine interrelationships within groups.

So far we have imposed only one restriction on the knowing relationship in our model, namely, that it be all-or-none. There are a few further things we can say about it. When a mathematician describes a relationship he is apt to ask three questions about it: Is it reflexive? Is it symmetric? Is it transitive? The "equals" (=) relationship is reflexive, symmetric, and transitive.

The knowing relationship about which we are talking is clearly not an equality relationship. Anything equals itself; that is, the equals relation is reflexive. Acquaintanceship is reflexive or not as one chooses to define it. The issue is a trivial one. One could say that by definition everyone knows himself, or one could say that by definition the circle of acquaintances does not include oneself. (We have chosen in our examples below to do that latter and so to define the knowing relation as nonreflexive.)

There is no reason why the knowing relation has to be symmetric. Many more people knew the film star Marilyn Monroe than she knew. If we use the definition of putting a face together with a name then, clearly, persons with good memories know persons with bad memories who do not know them. Similarly, it has been found in some studies that persons are more apt to know the names of persons with higher than lower social status. Thus, privates know each others' names *and* the names of their officers. Officers know each others' names and the names of those they serve, but not necessarily those of privates. Those served may only know servants categorically as, for example, "the tall blond waitress." All in all, to define any knowing relationship as a symmetric one is a great constraint on reality, but it is one which simplifies analysis enormously. It helps so much that for the most part we are going to make that assumption in the discussion below. And, for many purposes, it is largely correct. A kinship relationship is clearly symmetric; if A is a kin to B, B is a kin to A. Also the recognition relationship is mostly symmetric. Most of the time if A can recognize and greet B, B can recognize and greet A. It is generally convenient in our model to define away the minority of cases where this does not hold.

On the other hand, the assumption of transitivity is one that we cannot usefully make. If A knows B, and B knows C, it does not follow that A knows C. If it did follow, then all of society would decompose into a set of one or more cliques completely unconnected with each other. It would mean that everyone you knew would know everyone else you knew, and it follows that you could not know anyone who was outside the clique (i.e., not known to all your friends).[3] Clustering into cliques does occur to some extent and is one of the things we want to study. We want to measure the extent to which these clusters are self-contained, but they are not that by definition.

Thus one useful model of a contact network consists of a set of individuals each of whom has some knowing relationships with others in the set of a kind which we have now defined: all-or-none, irreflexive, symmetric, not necessarily transitive.

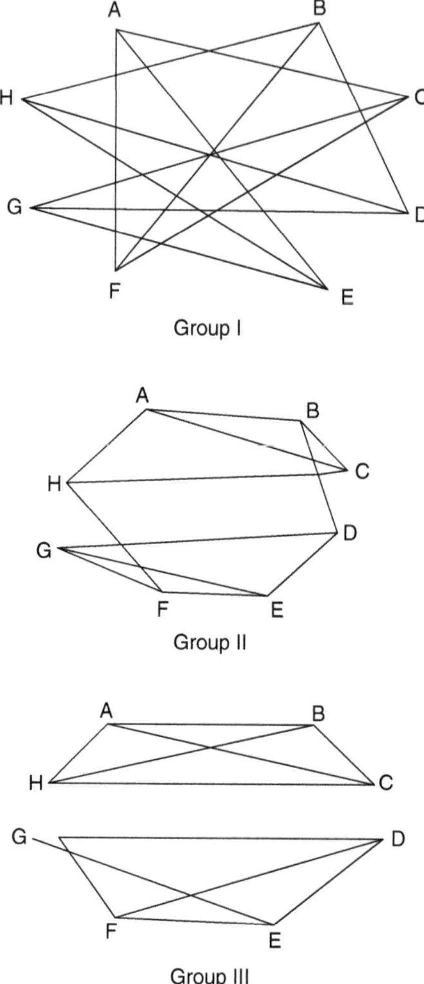

Figure 10.1. Networks of Different Structuredness.

We would like to be able to describe such a network as relatively unstructured or as highly structured. Intuitively that is a meaningful distinction, but it covers a considerable variety of strictly defined concepts. Figure 10.1 describes three hypothetical groups of eight people each, in which each individual has three friends. In the first there are no cliques, in the third there are two completely disjoint cliques, and the second group is intermediate. In the first any two people can be connected by at most one intermediary; in the second some pairs (e.g., A and E) require two intermediaries to be connected; in the third some individuals cannot be connected at all. We are inclined to describe the third group as the most stratified or structured and the first as least so, and in some senses that is true. But, of course, the first graph is also a rigid structure in the sense that all individuals are alike. In general, however, when we talk of a network as showing more social stratification or clustering in this paper, we mean that it departs further from a random process in which each individual is alike except for the randomness of the variables. The clustering in a society is one of the things which affects who will meet whom and who can reach whom.[4] Any congressman knows more congressmen than average for the general populace; any musician knows more musicians.

The simplest assumption, and one perhaps to start with in modelling a large contact net, is that the number of acquaintances of each person in the population is a constant. We start then with a set of N persons each of whom knows n persons from among the N in the universe; n is the same for all N persons.

If in such a population we pick two persons at random and ask what is the probability that they know each other, the answer can quickly be given from knowing N and n (or, if n is a random variable, the mean n). We know nothing about A and B except that they are persons from a population of size N each of whom on the average knows n other persons in that population. The probability that B is one of the n persons in the circle of acquaintances of A is clearly n/N. If we were talking of a population of 160,000,000 adults and each of them knew, on the average, 800 persons, the chances of two picked at random knowing each other would be one in 200,000.

Suppose we pick A and B who do not know each other, what is the probability of their having an acquaintance in common? The answer to that question, even with random choice of A and B, no longer depends just on n and N. The results now depend also on the characteristic *structure* of interpersonal contacts in the society, as well as on the size of the population and the number of acquaintances each person has. To see the reason why, we turn to an example which we outline diagrammatically in figure 10.2. This figure represents parts of two networks in which $n = 5$; that is, each person knows five others in the population. We start with A; he knows B, C, D, E, and F; this is his circle of acquaintances. Next we turn to B; he also knows five people. One of these, by the assumption of symmetry, is A. So, as the acquaintanceship tree fans out, four persons are added at each node.

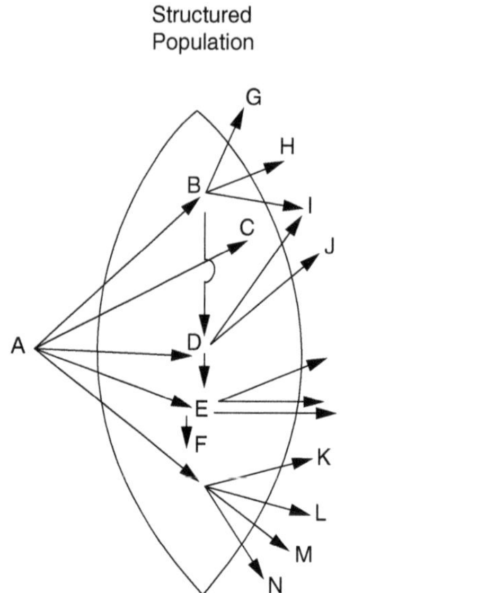

Figure 10.2. Structure in a Population.

However, here we note a difference between the structured and the unstructured population. In a large population without structure the chance of any of A's acquaintances knowing each other is very small (one in 200,000 for the U.S.A. figures used above). So, for a while at least, if there is no structure the tree fans out adding four entirely new persons at each node: A knows five people; he has twenty friends of friends, and eighty friends of friends of friends, or a total of 125 people reachable with at most two intermediaries. That unstructured situation is, however, quite unrealistic. In reality, people who have a friend in common are likely to know each other (Hammer, n.d.). That is the situation shown in the slightly structured network on the left side of figure 10.2. In that example one of D's acquaintances is B and another is E. The effect of these intersecting acquaintanceships is to reduce the total of different people reached at any given number of steps away from A. In the left-hand network A has five friends, but even with the same *n* only eleven friends of friends.

So we see, the more cliquishness there is, the more structure there is to the society, the longer (we conjecture) the chains needed on the average to link any pair of persons chosen at random. The less the acquaintanceship structure of a society departs from a purely random process of interactions, in which any two persons have an equal chance of meeting, the shorter will be the average minimum path between pairs of persons.[5] Consider the implications, in a random network, of assuming that *n*, the mean number of acquaintances of each person, is 1,000. Disregarding duplications, one would have 1,000 friends, a million ($1{,}000^2$) friends-of-friends, a billion ($1{,}000^3$) persons at the end of chains with two intermediaries, and a trillion (1.000^4) with three. In such a random network two strangers finding an acquaintance in common (i.e., experiencing the small-world phenomenon) would still be enjoying a relatively rare event; the chance is one million out of 100 or 200 million. But two intermediaries would be all it would normally take to link two people; only a small minority of pairs would not be linked by one of those billion chains.

Thus, in a country the size of the United States, if acquaintanceship were random and the mean acquaintance volume were 1,000, the mean length of minimum chain between pairs of persons would be well under two intermediaries. How much longer it is in reality because of the presence of considerable social structure in the society we do not know (nor is it necessarily longer for all social structures). Those are among the critical problems that remain unresolved.

Indeed, if we knew how to answer such questions we would have a good quantitative measure of social structure. Such an index would operationalize the common sociological statement that one society is more structured than another. The extent to which the mean minimum chain of contacts departs from that which would be found in a random network could be a convenient index of structuredness.

There are all sorts of rules for the topology of a network that can make its graph depart from random linkages. Perhaps the simplest and most important structure is that of triangular links among a given person's friends. If two persons both know person A, the odds are much better than otherwise that they will know each other; if they do know each other the acquaintanceship links form a triangle. For an example see figure 10.3. Disregarding the symmetric path (i.e., A knows B so B knows A), let us ask ourselves how many links it takes to go from A out to each of his acquaintances and back to A via the shortest path. If we start out on the path from A to B, we can clearly return to A via a triangle, A,B,D,A. We can also return by a triangle if we go from A to D or A to E. On the other hand, there is no triangle which will take one back if one starts on the path from A to F. Sooner or later there will be a path back, in this instance a path of eight links. (The only instance in which there would be no path back would be if the society

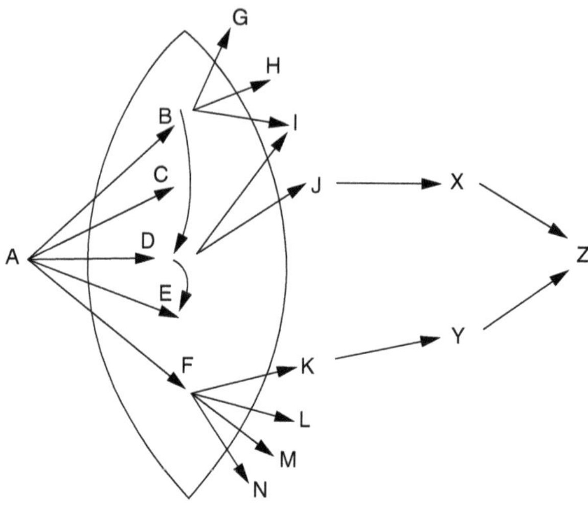

Figure 10.3. Effect of Structure.

were broken into two cliques linked at no point (see figure 10.1), or at only one point.) Clearly, the number of triangles among all the minimum circular chains is a good index of the tightness of the structure, and one that is empirically usable. It is perfectly possible to sample and poll the acquaintances of A to estimate how many of them know each other. That figure (which measures the number of triangles) then provides a parameter of the kind for which we are looking (Hammer, n.d., Wasserman 1977).

The fact that two persons have an acquaintance in common means that to some extent they probably move in the same circles. They may live in the same part of the country, work in the same company or profession, go to the same church or school, or be related. These institutions provide a nucleus of contacts so that one acquaintance in common is likely to lead to more. One way to describe that situation can be explained if we turn back to figure 10.3. Suppose we inquire of a person whether he knows A. If the answer is yes, then the chances of his knowing B are better than they would otherwise have been. Conversely if the answer is no, that reduces the chances of his knowing B. If he has told us that he does not know either A or B the chances of his knowing C are still further reduced. And so on down the list. This fact suggests that a second measure of structuredness would be the degree to which the chance of knowing a subsequent person on the list of acquaintances of A is reduced by the information that a person does not know the previous person on the list. In a society that is highly segmented, if two persons have any acquaintances in common they will have many, and so each report of nonacquaintanceship reduces more markedly than it otherwise would the chances of finding one common acquaintance on the list.

We require a measure, such as one of those two we have just been discussing, of the degree of clusteredness in a society, to deal with the question with which we started a few pages back, namely, the distribution of length of minimum contact chains: how many pairs of persons in the population can be joined by a single common acquaintance, how many by a chain of two persons, how many by a chain of three, and so on?

The answer depends on three values: N, n, and a parameter measuring structuredness. Increased social stratification reduces the length of chains between persons in the same stratum and at the same time lengthens the chains across strata lines. Thus, for example, two physicians or two persons from the same town are more likely to have an acquaintance in common than persons who do not share such a common characteristic. While some chains are thus shortened and others are lengthened by the existence of clusters within a society, it seems plausible to conjecture that the mean chain averaged over pairs of persons in the population as a whole is lengthened. Two persons chosen at random would find each other more quickly in an unstructured society than in a structured one, for most of the time (given realistic values of N, n, and clustering) persons chosen at random will not turn out to be in the same strata.

We might conjecture, for example, that if we had time series data of this kind running over the past couple of decades, we would find a decline in structuredness based on geography. The increased use of the long-distance telephone (and in the future of computer networks), and also of travel, probably has made acquaintanceship less dependent on geographic location than ever in the past.

In the final section of this paper we turn to an exploration of some of the alternative ways of modelling a network of the kind just described. The central problem that prevents an entirely satisfactory model is that we do not know how to deal with the structuredness of the population. Because of its lovely mathematical simplicity, there is an almost irresistible tendency to want to assume that whenever we do not know how the probability of acquaintanceship within two pairs of persons differs, we should treat it as equal; but it is almost never equal (Hunter and Shotland 1974; White 1970a). The real-world population lives in an n-dimensional space distributed at varying social distances from each other. But it is not a Euclidean space. Person A may be very close to both B and C and therefore very likely to know them both, but B and C may be very far from each other.

In the hope of getting some clues as to the shape of the distribution of closeness among pairs in real-world populations, we undertook some research on the actual contact networks of some twenty-seven individuals. These data we shall describe in the second part of this paper. While we learned a lot from that exercise, it failed to answer the most crucial questions because the most important links in establishing the connectedness of a graph may often be not the densely travelled ones in the immediate environment from which the path starts, but sparse ones off in the distance. How to go between two points on opposite sides of a river may depend far more critically on where the bridge is than on the roads near one's origin or destination. The point will become clear as we examine the data.

Empirical Estimates of Acquaintanceship Parameters

One is awed by the way in which a network multiplies as links are added. Even making all allowances for social structure, it seems probable that those whose personal acquaintances range around 1,000, or only about 1/100,000 of the U.S. adult population, can presumably be linked to another person chosen at random by two or three intermediaries on the average, and almost with certainty by four.

We have tried various approaches to estimating such data. We start with *gedankenexperiments,* but also have developed a couple of techniques for measuring acquaintance volume and network structure.

Consider first a rather fanciful extreme case. Let us suppose that we had located those two individuals in the U.S. between whom the minimum chain of contacts was the longest one for any pair of persons in the country. Let us suppose that one of these turned out to be a hermit in the Okefenokee Swamps, and the other a hermit in the Northwest woods. How many intermediaries do we need to link these two?

Each hermit certainly knows a merchant. Even a hermit needs to buy coffee, bread, and salt. Deep in the backwood, the storekeeper might never have met his congressman, but among the many wholesalers, lawyers, inspectors, and customers with whom he must deal, there will be at least one who is acquainted with his representative. Thus each of the hermits, with two intermediaries reaches his congressman. These may not know each other, though more likely they do, but in any case they know a congressman in common. Thus the maximum plausible minimum chain between any two persons in the United States requires no more than seven intermediaries.

This amusing example is not without significance. Viewed this way, we see Congress in a novel but important aspect, that of a communication node. The Congress is usually viewed as a policy choosing, decision-making instrument, which selects among preexisting public opinions which are somehow already diffused across the country. Its more important function, however, is that of a forum to which private messages come from all corners, and within which a public opinion is created in this process of confrontation of attitudes and information. Congress is the place which is quickly reached by messages conveying the feelings and moods of citizens in all walks of life. These feelings themselves are not yet public opinion for they are not crystallized into policy stands; they are millions of detailed worries concerning jobs, family, education, old age, and so on. It is in the Congress that these messages are quickly heard and are revised and packaged into slogans, bills, and other policy formulations. It is these expressions of otherwise inchoate impulses that are reported in the press, and which become the issues of public opinion. Thus the really important function of the Congress, distinguishing it from an executive branch policymaking body, is as a national communication center where public reactions are transformed into public opinion. Its size and geographically representative character puts it normally at two easily found links from everyone in the country. Its members, meeting with each other, formulate policies which express the impulses reaching them from outside. Through this communication node men from as far apart as the Okefenokee Swamps and the north woods can be put in touch with the common threads of each other's feelings expressed in a plank of policy. A body of 500 can help to weld a body of 100,000,000 adults into a nation.

While thinking about such matters has its value, it is no substitute for trying to collect hard data.

Empirical collection of contact data is possible but not easy:

First of all, people are not willing to reveal some or all of their contacts.

Second, it is hard to keep track of such massive and sequential data.

Third, because contacts run in clusters and are not statistically independent events, the statistical treatment of contact data is apt to be hard.

Reticence is probably the least serious of the difficulties. It is certainly no more of a problem for studies of contacts than for Kinsey-type research or for research on incomes or voting behavior, all of which have been successfully conducted, though with inevitable margins of error. As in these other areas of research, skill in framing questions, patience, proper safeguards of confidence, and other similar requirements will determine success, but there is nothing new or different about the difficulties in this field. Reticence is less of an obstacle to obtaining valid information about contacts than are the tricks played by our minds upon attempts at recall.

Indeed it is usually quite impossible for persons to answer questions accurately about their contacts. We noted above the bewilderment which respondents felt when asked how many people they knew, and how most gave fantastic underestimates. Over one day, or even a few hours, recall of contacts is bad. Given more than a very few contacts, people find it hard to recall whom they have seen or conversed with recently. They remember the lengthy or emotionally significant contacts, but not the others. The person who has been to the doctor will recall the doctor, but may neglect to mention the receptionist. The person who has been to lunch with friends may forget about contact with the waiter. In general, contacts which are recalled are demonstrably a highly selected group.

Most importantly, they are selected for prestige. A number of studies have revealed a systematic suppression of reports of contacts down the social hierarchy in favor of contacts up it (Warner 1963; Festinger et al. 1950; Katz and Lazarsfeld 1955). If one throws together a group of high status and low status persons and later asks each for the names of the persons in the group to whom he talked, the bias in the outcome is predictably upward. Unaided recall is not an adequate instrument for collecting contact data except where the problem requires recording only of emotionally meaningful contacts. If we wish to record those, and only those, we can use the fact of recall as our operational test of meaningfulness. Otherwise, however, we need to supplement unaided recall.

Some records of contacts exist already and need only be systematically noted. Noninterview sources of contact information include appointment books, committee memberships, and telephone switchboard data. The presidential appointment book is a fascinating subject for study.

Telephone switchboard data could be systematically studied by automatic counting devices without raising any issues of confidence. The techniques are already available and are analogous to those used for making load estimates. They could have great social science value too. A study, for example, of the ecology of long-distance telephone contacts over the face of the country would tell us a great deal about regionalism and national unity. A similar study of the origin and destination of calls by exchange could tell us a great deal about neighborhoods, suburbanism, and urbanism in a metropolitan region. This would be particularly interesting if business and residential phones could be segregated. The pattern of interpersonal contact could be studied by counting calls originating on any sample of telephones. (What proportion of all calls from any one phone are to the most frequently called other phone? What proportion to the ten most frequently called others?) How many different numbers are called in a month or a year? Would the results on such matters differ for upper and lower income homes, urban and rural, and so on?

In similar ways mail flows can tell us a good deal (Deutsch 1956, 1966). The post office data are generally inadequate, even for international flows, and even more for domestic flows. Yet sample counts of geographic origins and destinations are sometimes made, and their potential use is clear.

Not all the information we want exists in available records. For some purposes interviews are needed for collection of data. Various devices suggest themselves for getting at the range of a person's contacts. One such device is to use the telephone book as an *aide-memoire.* We take a very large book, say the Chicago or Manhattan book. We open it to a page selected by a table of random numbers. We then ask our respondent to go through the names on that page to see if they know anyone with a name that appears there or a name that would appear there if it happened to be in that book. Repeat the operation for a sample of pages. One can either require the subject to think of all the persons he knows with such names, which is both tedious and, therefore, unreliable, or assume that the probability of a second, third, or fourth known person appearing on a single page is independent of the previous appearance of a known name on the page. Since that is a poor assumption we are in a dilemma. Depending on the national origins of our respondent, he is apt to know more persons of certain names; he may know more Ryans, or Cohens, or Swansons according to what he is. Nationality is a distorting factor in the book, too. The Chicago phone book will contain a disproportionate number of Polish names, the Manhattan phone book a disproportionate number of Jewish ones. Also if the subject knows a family well he will know several relatives of the same name. In short, neither the tedious method of trying to make him list all known persons of the name, nor the technique in which one simply counts the proportion of pages on which no known name occurs (and uses that for p, $1 - p = q$, and then expands the binomial), gives a very satisfactory result. Yet with all those qualifications, this technique of checking memory against the phone book gives us a better estimate of approximate numbers of acquaintances than we now have.

One of the authors tried this technique on himself using a sample of thirty pages of the Chicago phone book and thirty pages of the Manhattan phone book. The Chicago phone book brought back names of acquaintances on 60 percent of the pages, yielding an estimate that he knows 3,100 persons. The Manhattan phone book, with 70 percent of the pages having familiar names, yielded an estimate of 4,250 acquaintances. The considerations raised above suggested that the estimate from the Manhattan phone book should be higher, for the author is Jewish and grew up in Manhattan. Still the discrepancy in estimates is large. It perhaps brings us closer to a proper order of magnitude, but this technique is still far from a solution to our problem.

To meet some of these problems we developed a somewhat better method which involves keeping a personal log of all contacts of any sort for a number of sample days. Each day the subject keeps a list (on a pad he carries with him) of all persons whom he meets and knows. The successive lists increasingly repeat names which have already appeared. By projecting the curve one hopes to be able to make estimates of the total size of the acquaintanceship volume, and from the lists of names to learn something of the character of the acquaintances.

The rules of inclusion and exclusion were as follows:

1. A person was not listed unless he was already known to the subject. That is to say, the first time he was introduced he was not listed; if he was met again on a later day in the 100 he was. The rationale for this is that we meet many people whom we fail to learn to recognize and know.

2. Knowing was defined as facial recognition and knowing the Person's name—any useful name, even a nickname. The latter requirement was convenient since it is hard to list on a written record persons for whom we have no name.

3. Persons were only listed on a given day if when the subject saw them he addressed them, if only for a greeting. This eliminated persons seen at a distance, and persons who the subject recognized but did not feel closely enough related to, to feel it proper to address.

Table 10.1. 100–Day Contacts of Respondents.

Sex	Job	Age	(*a*) No. of different persons seen in 100 days	(*b*) No. of contact events	Ratio *b/a*
Blue collar					
M	Porter	50–60	83	2946	35.5
M	Factory labor	40–50	96	2369	24.7
M	Dept. store receiving	20–30	137	1689	12.3
M	Factory labor	60–70	376	7645	20.3
M	Foreman	30–40	510	6371	12.5
F	Factory labor and unemployed	30–40	146	1222	8.4
White collar					
F	Technician	30–40	276	2207	8.0
F	Secretary	40–50	318	1963	6.2
M	Buyer	20–30	390	2756	7.1
M	Buyer	20–30	474	4090	8.6
M	Sales	30–40	505	3098	6.1
F	Secretary	50–60	596	5705	9.5
Professional					
M	Factory engineer	30–40	235	3142	13.5
F	T.V.	40–50	533	1681	3.2
M	Adult educator	30–40	541	2282	4.2
M	Professor	40–50	570	2175	3.8
M	Professor	40–50	685	2142	3.1
M	Lawyer-politician	30–40	1043	3159	3.0
M	Student	20–30	338	1471	4.4
M	Photographer	30–40	523	1967	4.8
M	President*	50–60	1404**	4340**	3.1**
Housewives					
F	–	30–40	72	377	5.2
F	–	20–30	255	1111	4.4

(Continued)

Table 10.1. (Continued)

Sex	Job	Age	(*a*) No. of different persons seen in 100 days	(*b*) No. of contact events	Ratio *b*/*a*
F	–	20–30	280	1135	4.0
F	–	30–40	363	1593	4.4
F	–	30–40	309	1034	3.3
F	–	50–60	361	1032	2.9
Adolescent					
M	Student	10–20	464	4416	9.5

* Data estimated from Hyde Park records.
** Record for 85 days.

4. Telephone contacts were included. So were letters written but not letters received. The rationale for the latter is that receiving a letter and replying to it is a single two-way communication such as occurs simultaneously in a face-to-face contact. To avoid double counting, we counted a reply as only half the act. Of course, we counted only letters written to people already known by the above criterion.

5. A person was only listed once on a given day no matter how often he was seen. This eliminated, for example, the problem of how many times to count one's secretary as she walked in and out of the office.

The task of recording these contacts is not an easy one. It soon becomes a tedious bore. Without either strong motivation or constant checking it is easy to become forgetful and sloppy. But it is far from impossible; properly controlled and motivated subjects will do it.

The data on twenty-seven persons were collected mostly by Dr. Michael Gurevich (1961) as part of a Ph.D. dissertation which explored, along with the acquaintanceship information itself, its relation to a number of dependent variables. As table 10.1 shows us, the respondents, though not a sample of any defined universe, covered a range of types including blue collar, white collar, professional, and housewives.

Among the most important figures in the table are those found in the right-hand column. It is the ratio between the number of different persons met and the number of meetings. It is what psychologists call the type-token ratio. It is socially very indicative, and is distinctive for different classes of persons.

Table 10.2. Number of Acquaintances by Occupation.

	Subject's occupation				
Acquaintances' occupation	**Blue collar (%)**	**Housewife (%)**	**White collar (%)**	**Professional (%)**	**Entire group (%)**
Professional	11	24	20	45	24
Managerial	9	7	19	14	14
Clerical	13	7	13	7	11
Sales worker	5	6	19	4	11
Craftsman, foreman	15	5	6	5	7
Operative	25	1	3	5	8
Service worker	9	2	2	1	3
Laborer	4	1	1	–	1
Housewife	4	35	10	12	13
Student	2	3	1	5	3
Farmer	–	–	–	–	–
Dont' know	4	10	8	3	6
	100*	100*	100*	100*	100*

* Figures may not add up to 100% because of rounding.

Blue collar workers and housewives had the smallest number of different contacts over the 100 days. They both lived in a restricted social universe. But in the total number of interpersonal interactions the blue collar workers and housewives differed enormously. Many of the blue collar workers worked in large groups. Their round of life was very repetitive; they saw the same people day in and day out, but at work they saw many of them. Housewives, on the other hand, not only saw few different people, but they saw few people in the course of a day; they had small type-token ratios. They lived in isolation.

In total gregariousness (i.e., number of contact events) there was not much difference among the three working groups. Blue collar workers, white collar workers, and professionals all fell within the same range, and if there is a real difference in the means, our small samples do not justify any conclusions about that. But in the pattern of activity there was a great difference. While blue collar workers were trapped in the round of a highly repetitive life, professionals at the other extreme were constantly seeing new people. They tended to see an average acquaintance only three or four times in the hundred days. One result of this was that the professionals were the persons whose contacts broke out

Table 10.3. Subject's Age Compared with His Acquaintance's Age.

	Subject's age			
Acquaintance's age	**20–30** (%)	**31–40** (%)	**41–50** (%)	**Over 50** (%)
Under 20	7	2	2	1
20–30	21	19	11	15
31–40	30	39	33	20
41–50	21	22	27	32
Over 50	21	19	27	33
	100*	100*	100*	100*

* Figures may not add up to 100% because of rounding.

of the confines of social class to some extent. They, like the others (see table 10.2) tended to mix to a degree with people like themselves but, to a slightly greater degree than the other classes, they had a chance to meet people in other strata of society.

The tendency of society to cluster itself as like seeks like can also be seen in Tables on contacts by age, sex, and religion (see tables 10.3, 10.4 and 10.5). These data reflect a society that is very structured indeed. How can we use the data to estimate the acquaintanceship volume of the different respondents? We found that over 100 days the number of different persons they saw ranged between seventy-two for one housewife and 1,043 for one lawyer-politician. Franklin Roosevelt's presidential appointment book, analyzed by Howard Rosenthal (1960), showed 1,404 different persons seeing him. But that leaves us with the question as to what portion of the total acquaintance volume of each of these persons was exhausted.

One of the purposes of the data collection was to enable us to make an estimate of acquaintance volume in a way that has already been described above. With each successive day one would expect fewer people to be added, giving an ogive of persons met to date such as that in figure 10.4. In principle one might hope to extrapolate that curve to a point beyond which net additions would be trivial.

Fitting the 100–day curve for each subject to the equation (acquaintanceship volume) = At^X gave acquaintanceship volumes over twenty years ranging from 122 individuals for a blue-collar porter in his fifties to 22,500 persons for Franklin Roosevelt.

However, that estimation procedure does not work with any degree of precision. The explanation is that the estimate of the asymptote is

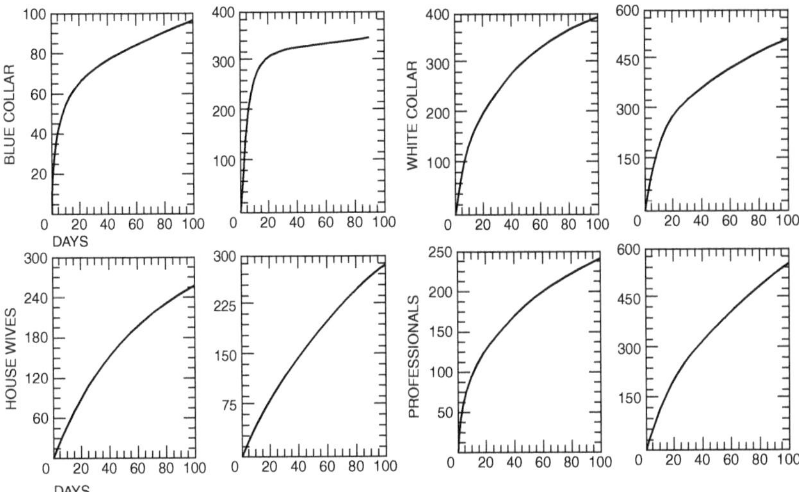

Figure 10.4. Acquaintanceship Ogives.

sensitive to the tail of the distribution (Granovetter 1976). Such a large proportion of the respondent's acquaintances are seen only once or twice in 100 days that any estimate which we make from such data is very crude. Table 10.6 shows the figures. Except for blue-collar workers, half or more of the acquaintances were seen only once or twice in the period.

One may think that the way around this problem would be to rely more heavily or the shape of the curve in its more rugged region where contact events are more frequent. The problem with that is that the nature of the contacts in the two parts of the curve are really quite dissimilar. To explain that perhaps we should look more closely at a single case; we shall use that of one of the author's own contact lists.

In 100 days he had contact with 685 persons he knew. On any one day the number of contacts ranged from a low of two other persons to a high of eighty-nine, the latter in the Christmas season. The mean number of acquaintances with whom he dealt on a day was 22.5. The median number was nineteen. There were several discreet typical patterns of days, resulting in a multimodal distribution. There was one type of day, including most weekend days, when he would typically meet seven to nine people, another type of day with typically around seventeen contacts, and a third type of day of highly gregarious activity which involved dealing with about thirty people.

Table 10.4. Sex of Subject and Sex of Acquaintance.

	Acquaintances		
Subject	**Male (%)**	**Female (%)**	**Total(%)**
Blue collar Male	83	17	100
White collar Male	65	35	100
Female	53	47	100
Professional Male	71	29	100
Housewife Female	45	55	100

Table 10.5. Religion of Subject and Religion of Acquaintance.

	Acquaintance's religion				
Subject's religion	**Protestant (%)**	**Catholic (%)**	**Christian (didn't know denomination) (%)**	**Jewish (%)**	**Religion known (%)**
Protestant	46	25	25	4	100*
Catholic	15	57	23	5	100*
Jewish	9	16	27	47	100*

* Figures may not add up because of rounding and omission of other religions.

Only about half of the 685 persons were seen more than once in the 100 days. The mean frequency was 3.1 times per person. The distribution, however, is highly skewed (table 10.7).

These figures, however, are somewhat misleading. It seems that we are actually dealing with two distributions: one which includes those persons living in the author's home and working in his office whom he saw during his regular daily routine, and the other including all his other acquaintances in the seeing of whom all kinds of chance factors operated. All individuals seen nineteen or more times are in the former group; so are all but two individuals seen thirteen or more times. Removing fifty-one such family members and co-workers gives us the data that are really relevant to estimating the large universe of occasional contacts, but in that sample more than half the persons listed were seen only once and 91 percent five times

Table 10.6. Frequency Distribution of Contacts with Acquaintances.

Frequency of contact over 100 days	Blue collar group				
	Case A (%)	Case B (%)	Case C (%)	Case D (%)	Case E (%)
1	4.8	23.9	29.0	9.3	23.5
2	2.4	11.4	11.6	5.0	10.7
3	–	4.1	6.5	3.9	8.4
4	–	4.1	4.3	3.4	4.7
5	1.2	3.1	3.6	3.4	4.9
6–10*	2.4	0.4	1.7	3.4	2.2
11–20*	0.8	0.5	1.2	2.1	1.3
21–30*	1.0	0.6	1.0	1.3	1.0
31–40*	1.8	0.6	0.6	0.9	0.7
41–50*	1.7	0.3	0.5	0.5	0.4
51–60*	1.7	1.4	0.1	0.4	0.2
61–70*	0.6	1.1	–	0.7	0.1
71–80*	0.1	0.1	0.07	–	0.02
81–90*	–	–	–	–	–
91–100*	0.2	0.2	0.07	0.05	0.02
	100%	100%	100%	100%	100%

Frequency of contact over 100 days	White collar group					
	Case G (%)	Case H (%)	Case I (%)	Case J (%)	Case K (%)	Case L (%)
1	43.4	44.3	27.2	30.8	47.7	37.7
2	11.5	16.9	20.0	12.4	13.1	12.9
3	7.9	7.5	10.7	9.0	6.5	7.5
4	4.3	3.7	6.1	6.9	7.1	4.5
5	3.2	3.4	6.1	4.0	3.2	3.0
6–10*	1.9	1.8	2.3	2.8	1.9	2.3
11–20*	0.7	0.8	0.7	1.1	0.6	0.9
21–30*	0.4	0.3	0.%	0.4	0.2	0.3
31–40*	0.3	–	0.2	0.2	0.2	0.3
41–50*	0.5	0.09	0.1	0.2	0.1	0.3
51–60*	0.1	0.1	0.2	0.2	0.1	0.4
61–70*	–	0.2	–	0.1	0.06	0.1
71–80*	–	–	–	–	–	–
81–90*	–	–	–	–	–	–
91–100*	0.04	0.03	0.03	0.02	0.02	0.02
	100%	100%	100%	100%	100%	100%

(Continued)

Table 10.6. (Continued)

Frequency of contact over 100 days	Professionals				Housewives		
	Case M (%)	Case O (%)	Case P (%)	Case Q (%)	Case V (%)	Case W (%)	Case X (%)
1	39.5	53.0	43.3	49.6	56.0	54.6	47.9
2	7.7	12.3	17.5	18.5	18.8	18.9	16.5
3	4.3	7.5	12.2	10.9	7.8	7.8	8.8
4	3.9	4.2	5.9	4.7	1.5	3.2	6.8
5	3.0	3.6	5.2	3.8	3.9	2.5	4.4
6–10*	1.2	2.3	1.8	1.3	1.1	1.3	1.6
11–20*	1.6	0.4	0.5	0.3	0.3	0.4	0.3
21–30*	0.4	0.09	0.07	0.09	0.04	0.04	0.2
31–40*	0.4	0.07	0.02	0.06	0.08	0.04	0.03
41–50*	0.3	0.05	0.05	0.01	0.04	–	0.1
51–60*	0.7	0.07	0.02	0.01	0.08	0.1	–
61–70*	0.1	–	–	–	–	–	–
71–80*	–	–	–	–	0.04	0.07	–
81–90*	–	–	–	–	–	–	0.03
91–100*	0.1	0.02	0.02	0.01	0.08	0.04	0.03
	100%	100%	100%	100%	100%	100%	100%

* The percentages in each entry are average percentages for a single day, not for the 5—or 10–day period.

or less. No easily interpretable distribution (such as Poisson which would imply that there is no structure among these contacts) fits that distribution, and with such small frequencies the shape of the distribution is unstable between respondents. It is possible that the projection of the 100–day data for this author to a year's time could come out at anywhere between 1,100 and 1,700 persons contacted. That is not a very satisfactory estimate, but it is far better than the estimates we had before.

This estimate is way below our telephone book estimates, which it will be recalled ranged from 3,100 to 4,250 acquaintances. The discrepancy is more revealing than disturbing. It suggests some hypotheses about the structure of the universe of acquaintances. It suggests that there is a pool of persons with whom one is currently in potential

Table 10.7. Contact Frequency Distribution for One Person.

Number of days on which contact was had during the 100 days	Number of persons with that frequency of contact	Days	Persons	Days	Persons
1	335	11	4	24	1
2	125	12	4	26	2
3	74	13	1	30	1
4	32	14	2	33	2
5	26	15	4	34	1
6	12	16	2	36	1
7	16	18	1	45	1
8	5	19	1	51	1
9	8	20	4	92	1
10	4	23	2		

contact, and a larger pool in one's memory, which for the senior author is about two to three times as large. The active pool consists of acquaintances living in the areas which one frequents, working at the activity related to one's occupation, belonging to the groups to which one belongs. Random factors determine in part which persons out of this pool one happens to meet, or even meet several times during any set period. But in one's memory there are in addition a considerable number of other persons whose names and faces are still effectively stored, but who are not currently moving in the same strata of contacts as oneself. These are recorded by the telephone book measure; they will not appear in the record of meetings except for the rarest kind of purely chance encounter. Needless to say, these two pools are not clearly segregated, but merge into each other. Yet, our data would suggest that they are more segregated than we would otherwise have suspected. The probabilities of encounter with the two types of persons are of quite different orders of magnitude.

We have now established plausible values for some of the parameters of the contact net of one of the authors. He typically deals with about twenty people in a day. These are drawn from a set of some 1,500 persons whom he actively knows at the present time. At the same time he remembers many other persons and could still recognize and name perhaps 3,500 persons whom he has met at some point in the past. (Incidentally, he has never regarded himself as good at this.)[6]

The remaining parameter which we would wish to estimate is the degree of structuredness in this acquaintanceship universe. The indicator that we proposed to use was the proportion of the acquaintances of the list-keeper who knew each other; that is, the proportion of triangles in the network graph. When the 100–day data collection was finished, we took the lists of some of the respondents and turned them into a questionnaire. To a sample of the people who appeared on the respondent's list of contacts, we sent a sample of the names on the list and asked, regarding each, "Do you know that person?" This provided a measure of the degree of ingrowth of the contact net. It can be expressed as the percentage of possible triangles that are completed (Wasserman 1977). The values for five subjects from whom we got the data ranged from 8 to 36 percent, and we would speculate that a typical value lies toward the low end of this range.

We have indicated above that the degree of structure affects how much longer than chance the minimum chain between a pair of randomly chosen persons is apt to be. We can go no further in specifying the effect of structure on the chains in this qualitative verbal discussion. Any more precise conclusion depends on the treatment of this subject in a much more formal mathematical way. We turn, therefore, to a restatement of our presentation in a mathematical model.

Mathematical Models of Social Contact

To describe with precision the structure of human acquaintance networks, and the mechanisms by which social and political contacts can be established within them, it is necessary to idealize the empirical situation with a model. Models have been used effectively in a number of related fields. Rapoport and others have modelled the flow of messages in a network (Rapoport and Horvath 1961; Foster et al. 1963; Foster and Horvath 1971; Rapoport 1963; Kleinrock 1964). Related models use Markov chains, queuing theory and random walks (White 1970b, 1973). Most such models, however, depend critically upon an assumption that the next step in the flow goes to other units in the model with a probability that is a function of the present position of the wanderer. The problem that we are addressing does not lend itself to that kind of model; the probability of contact between any two persons is a function of a long-established continuing relationship that inheres in them. The model required for our purposes must be one which retains a characterization of the relationship of each pair of individuals.

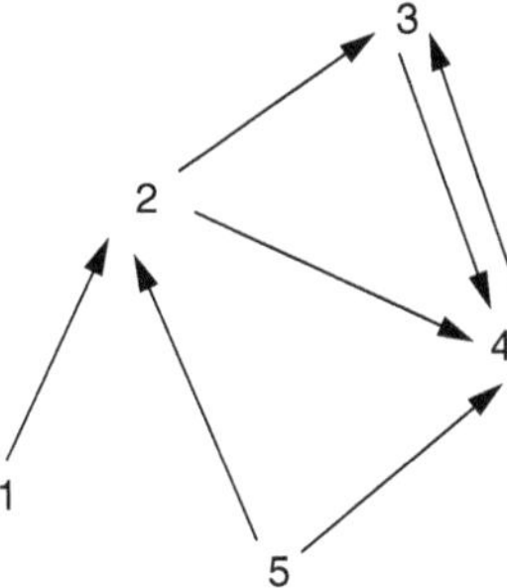

Figure 10.5. A Directed Graph.

	1	2	3	4	5
1	–	1	0	0	0
2	0	–	1	1	0
3	0	0	–	1	0
4	0	0	1	–	0
5	0	1	0	1	0

Figure 10.6. An Incidence Matrix.

Nonetheless, it is useful to begin our analysis with the simplest models in order to develop the needed framework within which to formulate the essential problems. Two extreme situations are relatively easy to analyze. The first is one in which the number of individuals is sufficiently small so that combinatorial methods are still feasible. The second is one in which there are so many individuals that we can treat it as an infinite ensemble, applying methods similar to those used in statistical mechanics. The hard problems deal with conditions between these two extremes.

Graph-Theoretic Models

Let P denote a group of N people. We shall represent the individuals by integers $1,\ldots,i,\ldots,N$. We draw a directed line or arrow from individual i to individual j to indicate that i knows j. This can be presented as a directed graph, shown in figure 10.5 for $N = 5$, and also represented by an incidence matrix in figure 10.6, where a one is entered in the cell of row i and row j if i knows j and a zero otherwise. If we assume the knowing relation to be symmetric, then every arrow from i to j is side by side with an arrow from j to i—and the incidence matrix is symmetric as well—and we may as well use undirected edges. Let M be the total number of edges or mutual knowing bonds.

The incidence matrix has N rows and N columns, but only $(N^2-N)/2$ of its elements can be chosen freely for a symmetric irreflexive (or reflexive) knowing relation. Thus, there can be at most $(N^2-N)/2$ pairs or edges. Generally, $0 \leq M \leq (N^2-N)/2$. If M takes the largest value possible, then every individual knows every other; if $M = 0$, then no individual knows any other. There is just one structure corresponding to each of these extreme cases. If $M = 1$, there are $(N^2-N)/2$ possible structures, depending on which pair of people is the one. If $M = 2$, there are $\binom{N^2-N/2}{2}$ possible structures, and there are altogether 2 possible structures corresponding to $M = 0,1,2,\ldots,(N^2-N)/2$. The number of possible structures is largest when $M = (N^2-N)/4$.

Let U denote the symmetric incidence matrix, and let u_{ij} be (0 or 1) its element in row i, column j. Let $u_{ij}^{(k)}$ denote the corresponding element in the symmetric matrix U^k. This represents the number of different paths of exactly k links between i and j (Luce 1950; Doreian 1974; Peay 1976; Alba 1973). A path is an adjacent series of links that does not cross itself. Two paths are called distinct if not all the links are identical. Thus, there are exactly two 2-step paths from 5 to 3 in figure 10.5, one via 4 and one via 2; multiplying U by itself (with 0 in the diagonals) gives

$$\begin{bmatrix} 0 & 0 & 1 & 1 & 0 \\ 0 & 0 & 1 & 1 & 0 \\ 0 & 0 & 1 & 0 & 0 \\ 0 & 0 & 0 & 1 & 0 \\ 0 & 0 & 2 & 1 & 0 \end{bmatrix}$$

and the element in row 5, column 3 is clearly 2, since matrix multiplication calls for the sum of the products of the elements in row 5, (0 1 0 1 0), and the elements in column 3, (0 1 0 1 0), which is $0 \cdot 0 + 1 \cdot 1 + 0 \cdot 0 + 1 \cdot 1 + 0 \cdot 0 = 2$.

It follows that $u_{ii}^{(3)}$ is the number of triangles that start and end with individual i. Each individual could be the start-end point of as many as $\binom{N-1}{2}$ different triangles, or as few as 0. If $u_{ii}^{(3)} = 0$ for all i, then there cannot be any tightly knit cliques; if $u_{ii}^{(3)} \geq 1$ for all i, then there is a considerable degree of connectedness and structure.

Let n denote the number of others each individual knows. This is the number of 1's in each row and each column of the incidence matrix or the number of edges incident on each node of the graph. Let a_k be the sum of all the elements in U^k. It follows that $a_1 = 2M$, and a_2 is twice the number of length-2 paths, which could serve as an index of clustering.

If each of a person's n acquaintances knew one another, U would consist of $N\,(n+1) \times (n+1)$ matrices consisting of all 1's (except for the diagonal) strung out along the diagonal, assuming that $n + 1$ divides N. Here no individual in one cluster knows anyone in a different cluster.

Such combinatorial, graph-theoretic approaches are intuitively appealing and have considerable descriptive power. There is also a number of theorems for counting the number of different configurations, such as Polya's theorem, as well as computer-based techniques for eliminating structures, such as Lederberg's creation of a language, DENDRAL, for representing the topology of molecules. Graph-theoretic theorems, however, have to ignore reality to introduce assumptions leading to mathematically interesting applications or else follow the scientifically unnatural approach of starting with strong but farfetched assumptions and relaxing them as little as possible to accommodate reality. The limitations of combinatorial methods become clearest when their computational complexity is studied. Multiplying matrices is of polynomial complexity, requiring of the order of N^3 multiplications; for sparse incidence matrices this can be reduced. But tracing out various configurations or finding a specified path can be much more complex, so that it cannot even be done by computer. Moreover, there is no realistic way that data can be obtained to fill in the elements of U for a nation,[7] and different ways of representing acquaintanceship among millions of people must be found. Even storing who knows whom among millions is a non-trivial problem, and more efficient ways of processing such data than are provided by conventional ways of representing sets such as P by ordering its elements $1,\ldots,N$ must be used. The problems of processing data about social networks and drawing inferences from them have received considerable attention, but still face serious obstacles (Wasserman 1977; Holland and Leinhardt 1970; Breiger et al. 1975; Granovetter 1974; Newcomb 1961).

Statistical Models with Independence and No Structure

We now take advantage of the large size of N, typically 10^8 or greater, corresponding to the population of a country such as the U.S. We select any two individuals A and B at random from such a large population P.

We would like to estimate the distribution of the shortest contact chain necessary for A and B to get in touch.

Let $k = 0$ mean that A and B know one another, that a direct link exists. We have a chain of one link with $k = 0$ intermediaries. But $k = 1$ means that A and B do not know one another, yet have a common acquaintance. It is a chain with two links and one intermediary, $k = 2$ means that A and B do not even have a mutual acquaintance but A knows someone who knows B. It is a chain with three links and two intermediaries.

Let p_k be the probability of a chain with exactly k intermediaries, $k = 1,2,\ldots$. We approximate p_0 by n/N, the ratio of each person's total number of acquaintances to the total population size. Thus, if A knows 1,000 people out of 100,000,000 Americans (other than A) then the probability of his knowing a randomly chosen person B among the 100,000,000 is $10^3/10^8 = 10^{-5}$.

Let q_0 be the probability that B does not know A. This is $q_0 = 1 - p_0$. It is the probability that one of A's acquaintances is not B. If we now make the strong assumption that the corresponding probability of a second of A's acquaintances is also not B, nor is it affected by knowledge of the probability of the first of A's friends not being B, then the probability that none of the n of A's acquaintances is B is q_0^n. This corresponds to a random or unstructured acquaintance net.

The probability p_1 that A and B are not in direct contact but have at least one common acquaintance is $q_0(1 - q_0^n)$. This assumes that B not being in direct contact with A is also independent of B not being in direct contact with each of the n people whom A knows.

Similarly, we estimate:

$$p_2 = q_0 q_0^n (1 - q_0^{n^2})$$

This uses another simplifying assumption: each of A's n acquaintances has n *new* acquaintances that will not include any of A's n acquaintances nor any acquaintance of his acquaintances. Thus, there are altogether n^2 different people who are the friends of A's friends. Thus if A knows 1,000 people, their friends number a million people not assumed to be counted so far.

If we extend these assumptions for the general case, we have

$$\begin{aligned} p_k &= q_0 q_0^n q_0^{n^2} \cdots q_0^{n^{k-1}} (1 - q_0^{n^k}) \\ &= (1 - p_0)^{(n^k - 1)/(n-1)} [1 - (1 - p_0)^{n^k}] \quad k = 1,2,3,\ldots \end{aligned} \tag{1}$$

Table 10.8. Distribution of Contact in an Unstructured Net.

	$n = 500$	$n = 1000$	$n = 2000$
p_0	0.00000500	0.00001000	0.00002000
p_1	0.00249687	0.00995012	0.03921016
p_2	0.71171102	0.98999494	0.96076984
$\sum_{k=3}^{n-1} p_k$	0.28578711	0.00004495	0.00000000
Mean	2.28328023	1.99007483	1.96074984
Variance	0.20805629	0.00993655	0.03774959

Table 10.8 shows some typical numbers for $N = 10^8$ The numbers were computed using equation I on the University of Michigan 470/V6. Note that the average number of intermediaries is 2 (when $n = 1{,}000$), and the average chain is three lengths, with very little variation around that mean. Nor is that average sensitive to n, a person's acquaintance volume. This is not implausible for, according to the above assumptions, if a person knows 1,000 people (in one remove), then in two removes he reaches $1{,}000 \times 1{,}000$, and in three removes 10^9, which exceeds a population of 10^8, according to a simple and intuitive analysis. This result is, however, very sensitive to our independence assumption. The probability of a randomly chosen person C knowing A, given that he knows a friend of A, is almost certainly greater than the unconditional probability that C knows A. (The latter should also exceed the conditional probability of C knowing A, given that C does not know any friend of A.) We turn next to models that do not depend on this independence assumption.

The Number of Common Acquaintances

The independence assumptions of the last section imply that the probability of A having exactly k acquaintances in common with randomly chosen B is $\binom{n}{k} p_0^k q_0^{n-k}$. Here, p_0^k the probability that k out of the n acquaintances of A each knows B and that each of his remaining $n - k$ acquaintances do not know B; there are $\binom{n}{k}$ ways of selecting these k from the n people whom A knows. The mean of this binomial distribution is np_0 and the variance np_0q_0.

If $n = 10^3$ and $N = 10^8$ then $p_0 = 10^{-5}$, $q_0 = 1 - 10^{-5}$ and the average number of common acquaintances is approximately 0.01 with a variance of 0.01. This is far too small to be realistic, and it points out the weakness of the independence assumption.

One way to replace it is to define p_0', the conditional probability that a randomly chosen friend of A knows randomly chosen person B′ given that B′ also knows A. This should exceed p_0 or n/N. A plausible estimate for the probability that two of A's friends know each other is $1/(n-1)$, because there are $n-1$ people from whom a friend of A could be chosen with whom to form an acquaintance bond. The probability that k of A's friends each knows another friend could now be estimated to be $(p_0')^k$ or $(n-1)^{-k}$, if we assume independence of acquaintance among A's friends. Similarly, $(1-p_0')^{n-k}$ is an estimate of the probability that $n-k$ of A's friends do not know another of A's friends. As before, the mean number of common acquaintances is $n\ p_0'$, which is, $n/(n-1)$, or close to 1, with a variance of $n\, p_0'\, q_0'$, which is close to 0. This, too, is too small for realism, however.

Consider next an approach that relates recursively the average number of acquaintances common to k individuals chosen at random. Call this m_k and assume that

$$m_{k+1} = am_k, \qquad m_1 = n, \qquad k = 2, 3, \ldots \tag{2a}$$

This means that the average number of acquaintances common to four people is smaller than the average number common to three by a fraction, a, which is the same proportion as the number of friends shared by three is to the number shared by two. This constant a is between 0 and 1 and would have to be statistically estimated. It is assumed to be the same for all $\binom{n}{k}$ groups of k people.

p_0, the probability of A knowing a randomly chosen person B, is n/N or m_1/N, as before. If $m_2 = am_1$, then $n/N = (m_2/a)/N$ and $a = m_2/n$. Thus, if we could estimate the number of acquaintances shared by two People, we could estimate a. Thus, we can set the number of common acquaintances, m_2, to any value we please, and use it to revise the calculation of p_k from what it was in the last section.

p_1, the probability that A does not know randomly chosen B but knows someone who knows B, is $(1-p_0) \times$ Prob {A and B have at least one common acquaintance}. The latter is the number of ways of choosing a person out of the n people A knows so that he is one of the m_2 common acquaintances, or m_2/n. Thus,

$$p_1 = (1-p_0)m_2/n$$

and

$$p_2 = (1-p_0)(1-p_0)\,p_2'$$

To calculate p_2', the probability that B knows someone who is a friend of one of A's n acquaintances, we need n', the number of different persons known to the n acquaintances of A. Then we could estimate by p_2' by

$$p_2' = \binom{n'}{1}\frac{m_1}{N} - \binom{n'}{2}\frac{m_2}{N} + \binom{n'}{3}\frac{m_3}{N} - \binom{n'}{4}\frac{m_4}{N} + \cdots \pm \binom{n'}{n'}\frac{m_{n'}}{N} \qquad \text{(2b)}$$

Here $\binom{n'}{k}m_k$ is the number of ways that B could be one of the m_k acquaintances common to some k of the n' friends of A's friends. It follows from eqn. (2a) that

$$m_2 = am_1,$$

$$m_3 = am_2 = a(am_1) = a^2 m_1,$$

and generally that

$$m_k = a^{k-1} n \qquad \text{(2c)}$$

Substituting into eqn. (2b), we can show that

$$p_2' = \frac{n}{aN}[1-(1-a)^{n'}]$$

To estimate n', we note that of all A's n friends, m_2 are also known to one other person, m_3 to two others, *etc.* Thus,

$$\begin{aligned} n' &= \binom{n}{1}m_1 - \binom{n}{2}m_2 + \binom{n}{3}m_3 - \binom{n}{4}m_4 + \ldots \pm \binom{n}{n}m_n \\ &= n\left[\binom{n}{1} - \binom{n}{2}a + \binom{n}{3}a^2 - \binom{n}{4}a^3 + \ldots \pm \binom{n}{n}a^{n-1}\right] \\ &= \frac{n}{a}\left[\binom{n}{1}a - \binom{n}{2}a^2 + \binom{n}{3}a^3 - \ldots \pm \binom{n}{n}a^n\right] \qquad \text{(2d)} \\ &= \frac{n}{a}[1-(1-a)^n] \text{ by the Binomial theorem} \end{aligned}$$

Hence,

$$p_2 = (1 - p_0)(1 - p_1)(n/aN)[1 - (1 - a)^{n'}]$$

and

$$p_3 = (1 - p_0)(1 - p_1)(1 - p_2)(n/aN[1 - (1 - a)^{n''}]$$

where

$$n'' = (n/a)[1 - (1 - a)^{n'}]$$

We can set up a recursive equation for p_k in general; We can also require it to hold for $k = 1$, in which case we should expect that

$$m_2/n = (n/aN)[1 - (1 - a)n'] = a \tag{2e}$$

If $n = 10^3$ and $N = 10^8$, then a should be such that $(10^{-5}/a)[1 - (1 - a)^{1000}] = a$. This is a transcendental equation to be solved for a, and the value of $a = 0.003$ is an approximate solution because $10^{-5}[1 - (1 - 0.003)^{1000}]$ is approximately $(0.003)^2$ or 9×10^{-6}, which is reasonably close. A value for $a = 0.003$ or $m_2 = 3$ is no longer so unreasonable for the number of acquaintances common to two people chosen at random. The assumption expressed in eqn. (2a) now implies that m_3, the number of acquaintances common to three people, is $(0.003) \times 3$ or 0.009, which is effectively zero. This is too small to be realistic. Using these values, we obtain,

$p_0 = 0.00001$,	as before
$p_1 = 0.003$	compared with 0.009949
$p_2 = 0.00332$	compared with 0.99001
$p_3 = 0.00330$	
$n' = 381{,}033$,	$n'' = 333{,}333$

The distribution of k is now considerably flattened, with chains of short length no less improbable than chains of greater length. This is due to a value of a greater than 10^{-5}, as specified by a chosen value of m_2 and eqn. (2e).

The above analysis, though more realistic, is still limited by an independence assumption and the low value of $m_3, m_4, \ldots$. Yet it may be fruitful to explore it further by exploiting the sensitivity of these results to m_2, or replacing eqn. (2a) by one in which a is not constant. We now proceed, however, to replace this approach by defining the following conditional probabilities.

Let K_A be A's circle of acquaintances, with $\overline{K}_A$ its complement. Let $A_1, ..., A_n$ denote the individuals in it. Consider:

$\text{Prob}(B \in \overline{K}_{A_1}), \text{Prob}(B \in \overline{K}_{A_2} | (B \in \overline{K}_{A_1}), \text{Prob}(B \in \overline{K}_{A_3} | (B \in \overline{K}_{A_2}, B \in \overline{K}_{A_1})$ etc. The product of these probabilities is $\text{Prob}(B \in \overline{K}_{A_1} \cap \overline{K}_{A_2} \cap \overline{K}_{A_3} \cap ...)$, the probability that a randomly chosen B is not known to each of A's acquaintances.

A simple and perhaps plausible assumption other than independence is that of a Markov chain:

$$\text{Prob}(B \in \overline{K}_{A_k} | B \in \overline{K}_{A_{k-1}}, \ldots B \in \overline{K}_{A_1}) = \text{Prob}(\overline{K}_{A_k} | \overline{K}_{A_{k-1}}) = b$$

where b is a constant to be statistically estimated.

Thus,

$$\text{Prob}(\overline{K}_{A_n}, \overline{K}_{A_{n-1}}, \ldots, \overline{K}_{A_1}) = \text{Prob}(\overline{K}_{A_1}) b^{n-1} = (1 - n/N) b^{n-1}$$

For $k = 2$,

$$\text{Prob}(\overline{K}_{A_2}, \overline{K}_{A_1}) = (1 - n/N) b = 1 - 2n/N + m_2/N$$

Hence

$$b = \frac{1 - 2n/N + m_2/N}{1 - n/N}$$

This gives more freedom to choose m_2. If $m_2 = 10$, $n = 10^3$, $N = 10^8$, then $b = 0.9999900999$. Now

$$p_0 = n/N = 0.00001 \quad \text{as before}$$

and

$$p_1 = (1 - p_0)[1 - (1 - n/N) b^{n-1}] = 0.001$$
$$p_2 = (1 - p_0)(1 - p_1) p'_2$$

Where

$$p_2' = \text{Prob(B Knows at least one of the } n' \text{ friends of A's friends)}$$
$$= 1-(1-n/N)b^{n'-1}$$

$$n' = \binom{n}{1}m_1 - \binom{n}{2}m_2 + \binom{n}{3}m_3 - \binom{n}{4}m_4 + \ldots \pm \binom{n}{n}m_n \text{ as before}$$

To estimate m_k we need Prob(K_1,..., K_k), the probability of B being known to k randomly chosen people, and we shall assume this to be Prob(K_1) · c^{k-1}, where c = Prob($K_k|K_{k-1}$). If $k = 2$, then

$$\text{Prob}(K_1, K_2) = m_2/N = \text{Prob}(K_1) \cdot c = (n/N)c$$

so that $c = m_2/n$. Hence,

$$m_k = N \cdot (n/N)\,(m_2/n)^{k-1} = n(m_2/n)^{k-1} \qquad k = 1, 2, \ldots$$

Therefore,

$$n' = \sum_{k=1}^{n}(-1)^{k-1}\binom{n}{k} \cdot n(m_2/n)^{k-1}$$
$$= \frac{n}{m_2/n}\sum_{k=1}^{n}(-1)^{k-1}\binom{n}{k}(m_2/n)^k$$
$$= (n^2/m_2)[1-(1-m_2/n)^n]$$

If $m_2 = 10$, then $c - 10/100 = 0.01$ and $n' = 10^5(1 - e^{-10}) = 99996$. Thus

$$p_2' = 1-(1-0.00001)(0.9999900999)^{99996}$$
$$\approx 1-(0.99999)(0.3716)$$
$$\approx 0.6278$$

and

$$p_2 = (0.99999)(0.999)(0.6278) \simeq 0.627$$

To compute p_3 we shall need p'', the number of different people who are the friends of the acquaintances of the n people whom A knows.

$$
\begin{aligned}
n'' &= \sum_{k=1}^{n'} (-1)^{k-1} \binom{n'}{k} n(m_2/n)^{k-1} = (n^2/m_2)\left[1-(1-m_2/n)^{n^{n'}}\right] \\
&\simeq (10^6/10)[1-(1-10^{-2})^{10^5}] \simeq 10^5(1-e^{-10000}) \simeq 10^5 \simeq n' \\
p_3' &= 1-(1-n/N)b^{n''-1} = 1-(1-10^{-5})(0.9999900999)^{10^5} \simeq 0.6278 \\
p_3 &= (1-p_0)(1-p_1)(1-p_2)p_3' \sim (0.999)(0.373)(0.6278) = 0.234
\end{aligned}
$$

This calculation leads to more plausible results, but it still does not have an underlying rationale to warrant attempts to fit data.

Contact Probabilities in the Presence of Social Strata

In a model of acquaintanceship structure it is desirable to be able to characterize persons as belonging to subsets in the population which can be interpreted as social strata. We show how the distribution for the length of minimal contact chains can be computed when strata are introduced. We begin by partitioning the entire population into r strata, with the ith stratum containing m_i members. Let h_{ij} denote the mean number of acquaintances which a person who is in stratum i has in stratum j. The mean number of acquaintances of a person in stratum i is then $n_i = \Sigma_{j=1}^{r} h_{ij}$.. The conditional probability p_{ij} that a person picked at random in stratum j is known to someone in stratum i, given j, is $h_{ij}/m_j = p_{ij}$. The $r \times r$ matrix (p_{ij}) is symmetric, and doubly stochastic because we have assumed that the "knowing" relation is symmetric.

We now select two people, A and C, with A in stratum i and C in stratum j. To obtain the probability that there is no 2-link contact chain from A to C, with the intermediary being in a specified stratum k, let K_i be the set of A's h_{ik} friends in stratum k. Combinatorially, Prob$\{K_i \cap K_j = \phi\}$ is the number of ways of selecting h_{ik} and h_{jk} out of m_k elements such that $K_i \cap K_j = \phi$, divided by the total number of ways of selecting h_{ik}, h_{jk} out of m_k elements, assuming independent trials without replacement. Thus,

$$
\begin{aligned}
\text{Prob}\left\{K_i \cap K_j = \phi\right\} &= \frac{m_k!/[h_{ik}!h_{jk}!(m_k - h_{ik} - h_{jk})!]}{\binom{m_k}{h_{ik}}\binom{m_k}{h_{jk}}} \\
&= \frac{(m_k - h_{ik})!(m_k - h_{jk})!}{m_k!(m_k - h_{ik} - h_{jk})!}
\end{aligned}
\tag{3}
$$

The probability that there is no chain from A in stratum i to C in stratum j *via* some mutual acquaintance in any stratum is

$$\prod_{k=1}^{r} \frac{(m_k - h_{ik})!(m_k - h_{jk})!}{m_k!(m_k - h_{ik} - h_{jk})!} \equiv q_{ij}'$$

While data about all the elements of (h_{ij}) are not likely to be readily obtainable, the variables m_i, n_i and h_{ii} for $i = 1, \ldots, r$ may be estimable. We now make a methodological simplification and assume these variables equal for all i, with $m_i = m = N/r$, $n_i = n$, $h_{ii} = h$ and

$$h_{ij} = \frac{n-h}{r-1} = h' \text{ for all } i \neq j \qquad (4)$$

To compute q_1', the probability that there is no chain of length 1—or that there is *no* mutual acquaintance—between two individuals A and C, it is necessary to consider two cases:

(1) that in which A and C are in the same stratum;
(2) that in which A and C are in different strata.

In the first case, $q_1' = uv^{r-1} \equiv q_1'$ (1) (the number in parentheses refers to case 1), where u is the probability that B, the intermediary between A and C, fails to be in the same stratum as A and C, and v is the probability that he fails to be in a different stratum. Using eqn. (3), it is readily seen that

$$u = \frac{(m-h)!^2}{m!(m-2h)!} \qquad (5)$$

$$v = \frac{(m-h')!^2}{m!(m-2h')!} \qquad (6)$$

By similar reasoning,

$$q_1'(2) = w^2 v^{r-2}$$

where w is the probability that the stratum of B is the same as that of A but not of C; this is equal to the probability that the stratum of B is the same as that of C but not of A. This is, by eqn. (3),

$$w = \frac{(m-h)!(m-h')!}{m!(m-h-h')!} \tag{7}$$

With the help of Stirling's formula and series expansions we can derive a useful approximation for w. It is

$$w \simeq (1 + hh'/m^2)e^{-hh'/m} \simeq e^{-hh'/m} \tag{8}$$

As before, let p_1 denote the probability that A and C do not know each other, but that they have at least one common acquaintance. Then

$$p_1(i) \simeq (1 - p_0)[1 - q_1'(i)] \quad i = 1, 2$$

To estimate p_1, we could take a weighted average,

$$p_1 = (1/r)p_1(1) + (1 - 1/r)p_1(2)$$

The above relation is written as an approximation, because $q_1'(i)$ is not a conditional probability given that A and C do not know each other, but the error is negligible. The number in the parentheses, 1 or 2, refers to whether or not A and C are in the same stratum, respectively. Thus,

$$p_1(1) \simeq (1 - n/N)(1 - uv^{r-1})$$

Because u can also be approximated by $\exp(-h^2/m)$ and v by $\exp(-h'^2/m)$, we can approximate $p_1(1)$ by

$$1 - \exp[-(h^2/m) - (h'^2/m)(r-1)]$$

Substituting $m = N/r$, this becomes

$$p_1(1) \simeq 1 - \exp\{-(r/N)[h^2 + h'^2(r-1)]\} \tag{9}$$

If A has more friends in a given stratum not his own than he has in his own stratum then $h' > h$. If almost all of A's friends are in his own stratum then $h' \ll h$, and $h \simeq n$. If r is large enough, $p_1(1)$ can be very close to 1. For instance, if $N = 10^8$, $h = 100$, $n = 1000$ and $r = 10$, we have that $h' = 900/9 = 100$, and $p_1(1) \simeq 0.00995$, as in the case of independence.

Next,

$$p_1(2) \simeq (1 - n/N)(1 - w^2 v^{r-2})$$

$$\simeq 1 - \exp\{-(2/\mathrm{N})[2hh' + (\mathrm{r}-2)h'^2]\} \tag{10}$$

For the same numerical values as above,

$$p_1(2) \simeq 1 - \mathrm{e}^{-10^{-2}} \approx 0.00995 \text{ also}$$

We now wish to compute $p_2{}^*$, the joint probability that A and C do not know each other, *and* that they have no common friends, *and* that A has some friends, at least one of whom knows some friend of A. As before, we shall compute the conditional probability that A has some friends, at least one of whom knows some friend of C, given that A and C neither know each other, nor have a common acquaintance. We shall denote this conditional probability by $p_2{}'^*$, so that $p_2{}^* = (1 - p_0)(1 - p_1{}'^*)p_2{}'^*$. To say that A has some friends, at least one of whom knows some friend of C, is to say that there is at least one person, B, who knows A *and* who has at least one friend, D, in common with C. By the assumed symmetry of the knowing relation, this is the same as saying: there exists $\mathrm{B} \in \mathrm{K_C}$, where $\mathrm{K_C}$ is the set of all people who can be linked to C by a minimal chain of length 1 (one intermediary). Select B at random and consider the choice fixed. $\mathrm{Prob}(\mathrm{B} \in \overline{\mathrm{K}}_\mathrm{C}) = 1 - p_1{}^*$, averaged over all strata. Assuming independence, the probability that any n B's, and in particular the n friends of A, all fail to be connected to C by a minimal chain of length 1 is $(1 - p_1{}^*)^n$. Hence, neglecting a small correction due to the condition in the definition of $p_1{}'^*$, we can estimate:

$$p_2'^* = 1 - (1 - p_1{}^*)^{\mathrm{n}} \simeq 1 - \exp(-p_1{}^* n)$$

for $p_1{}^*$ very small.

To obtain a more precise estimate of $p_2'^*$ we proceed as follows. Let s(A) denote the stratum of A. Consider first the case $i = 1$, where s(A) = s(C). Now suppose that s(B) = s(A). Then the probability that no chain of length 1 links B and C is uv^{r-1} as before. If s(B) ≠ s(A), however, B can be in any one of $r - 1$ strata, and for each stratum the probability that no chain of length 1 links B and C is w^2v^{r-2}. Hence the probability that no chain of length 2 links A and C with s(A) = s(C) is

$$\begin{aligned} q_2'(1) &= u^h v^{h(r-1)} (w^2 v^{r-2})^{(r-1)h'} \\ &= u^h v^{(r-1)h+(n-1)(r-2)h'} w^{2(r-1)h'} \end{aligned} \tag{11}$$

Consider next the case $i = 2$, where s(A) ≠ s(C). If s(B) = s(A), the probability that no chain of length 1 links B and C is $(w^2v^{r-2})^h$. If s(B) ≠ s(A), this probability is the product of:

(a) the probability of no 1-chain linking B and C when s(B) = s(C)—this is $(uv^{r-1})^{h'}$; and

(b) the same probability when s(B) ≠ s(C), *i.e.* $(w^2v^{r-2})^{(r-2)h'}$. Hence, the probability that no chain of length 2 links A and C when s(A) ≠ s(C) is

$$\begin{aligned} q_2'(2) &= (w^2 v^{r-2})^h (uv^{r-1})^{h'} (w^2 v^{r-2})^{(r-2)h'} \\ &= u^{h'} v^{h(r-2)h+h'(r-1)+(r-2)^{2h'}} w^{2h+2(r-2)h'} \\ &= u^{h'} v^{h(r-2)+h'(r^2-3r+3)} w^{2[h+(r-2)h']} \end{aligned} \tag{12}$$

As before, we may estimate the conditional probability that A and C are linked by at least one 2–chain given that A does not know C or any friend of C by

$$\begin{aligned} 1 - p_2'^* = q_2'^* &= (1/r) u^h v^{(r-1)h+(r-1)(r-2)h'} w^{2(r-1)h'} + \\ &+ (1 - 1/r) u^{h'} v^{h(r-2)-h'(r^2-3r+3)} w^{2[h-(r-2)h']} \end{aligned}$$

Note that effects due to the two conditions have been neglected and that independence has been assumed throughout.

Observe also that we could have written

$$q_2'(1) = [q_1'(1)]^h [q_1'(2)]^{h'(r-1)}$$

$$q_2'(2) = [q_1'(1)^{h'} [q_1(2)]^h [q_2(2)]^{h'(r-2)}$$

$$q_2'^* = (1/r) q_2'(1) + (1 - 1/r) q_2'(2)$$

The above relation suggests a recursive scheme of generalizing the calculation. That is:

$$p_k = (1-p_0)(1-p_1'^*)(1-p_2'^*)\dots(1-p_{k-1}'^*)(1-q_k'^*)$$

$$q_k'^* = (1/r)q_k'(1) + (1-1/r)\,q_k'(2)$$

$$q_k'(1) = [q'_{k-1}(1)]^h[q'_{k-1}(2)]^{h'(r-1)}$$

$$q_k'(2) = [q'_{k-1}(1)]^{h'}[q'_{k-1}(2)]^{h+h'(r-2)} \qquad k = 2, 3, 4, \dots$$

Using the cruder method suggested in the first paragraph of the above section,

$$p_k'^* = 1-(1-p_{k-1}'^*)^n \qquad k = 2, 3, 4, \dots$$

There is another iterative method that could be used to compute p_k^*. If k is odd (*e.g.*, $k = 3$), compute $q'_k(1)$ and $q_k(2)$ using formulas (9) and (10) but substituting $p'_{k-1}(1)m$ for h and $p'_{k-1}(2)m$ for h'. Similarly, if k is even, use formulas (11) and (12) with the same substitutions for h and h'.

In the Appendix we develop further approximations to facilitate the calculation of p_0^*, p_1^*, and p_2^*, which we find to be 0.00001, 0.00759, and 0.9924, respectively, with the parameters used previously.

Note the departure from the model without strata is not very great. That is a significant inference. Structuring of the population may have a substantial effect on p_1. (It has no effect, of course, on p_0.) However, in a connected graph (which we believe any society must be) the nuclei get bridged by the longer chains quite effectively, and so the mean length of chains between randomly chosen pairs is only modestly affected by the structuring. We would therefore conjecture that, despite the effects of structure, the modal number of intermediaries in the minimum chain between pairs of Americans chosen at random is 2. We noted above that in an unstructured population with $n \simeq 1000$ it is practically certain that any two individuals can contact one another by means of at least two intermediaries. In a structured population it is less likely, but still seems probable. And perhaps for the whole world's population probably only one more bridging individual should be needed.

Monte-Carlo Simulation Models

To achieve greater understanding of the structural aspects of acquaintance nets, we approached an explanation of the dynamics of how acquaintance bonds are formed with the help of a stochastic model that was simulated by computer. We regarded each individual to be located as a point in a social space, which we regarded as a square region in the two-dimensional Euclidean plane, to start with. As before, we let N be the number of individuals. Each individual can change his position in time $t + 1$ to time by $(\Delta x, \Delta y)$ where

$$\Delta x = \begin{cases} s & \text{with probability } p \\ -s & \text{with probability } q \text{ where } p + q + r = 1 \\ 0 & \text{with probability } r \end{cases}$$

and with Δy defined similarly, and statistically independent of Δx. Each individual is confined to remain in a $D \times D$ square, so that if his location at t is $z(t)=[x(t), y(t)]$, then in the next simulation cycle it is

$$\left[x(t) + \Delta x \bmod D,\ y(t) + \Delta y \bmod D\right] = [x(t+1), y(t+1)]$$

We now define e_{AB} to be 1 if the line connecting $[x_A(t), y_A(t)]$ and $[x_A(t+1), y_A(t+1)]$ intersects the line from $[x_B(t), y_B(t)]$ to $[x_B(t+1), y_B(t+1)]$, and $e_{AB} = 0$ if these paths do not intersect. The event E_{AB} corresponding to $e_{AB}(t) = 1$ at time t is interpreted as a contact between A and B on day t. $(1/t)\sum_{\tau=1}^{t} e_{AB}(\tau)$ denotes the frequency with which A and B have met during the first t days.

Next, let $K_A(t)$ be the set of all people whom A has met by day t, or {all B:$e_{AB}(\tau) = 1$ for $\tau \leq t$}. We now extend $K_A(t)$ to include A and define the center of that group or cohort on day t as follows:

$$c_A(t) = [\bar{x}_A(t), \bar{y}_A(t)]$$

With

$$\bar{x}_A(t) = \frac{x_A(t) + \sum_{B \in K_A(t)} x_B(t) \sum_{\tau=1}^{t} e_{AB}(\tau)}{1 + \sum_B \sum_\tau e_{AB}(\tau)}$$

and $\bar{y}_A(t)$ is similarly defined. The x-coordinate of the center is the average of the x-coordinates of A and all the people he has met, weighted by how frequently they were contacted.

The probabilities p and q also vary with time and with each individual, as follows with $z_A(t) = (x_A(t), y_A(t))$.

If $c_A(t) > z_A(t)$, then
$$p_A(t+1) = p_A(t) + e$$
$$q_A(t+1) = q_A(t) - e/2$$
$$r_A(t+1) = r_A(t) - e/2$$

If $c_A(t) < z_A(t)$, then
$$p_A(t+1) = p_A(t) - e/2$$
$$q_A(t+1) = q_A(t) + e$$
$$r_A(t+1) = r_A(t) - e/2$$

If $c_A(t) = z_A(t)$, then the probabilities do not change. Initially $[p(0), q(0), r(0)] = (1/3, 1/3, 1/3,)$ and no probability must ever fall outside $[\delta, 1 - \delta]$ to ensure that the system remains stochastic; when these values are reached, the probabilities stay there until the z's and c's change.

After considerable experimentation with several values of the different parameters, we chose:

Number of individuals	$N = 225$
Size of one side of square grid	$D = 15$
Social responsiveness or elasticity	$e = 0.2$
Lower bound on probability of position change	$\delta = 0.01$
Unit increment in position change	$s = 1$

Well before the 10th iteration, clustering begins and by the 20th iteration it clusters into a single group. For realism, we would expect several clusters to emerge (corresponding to social strata) that exhibit both local and global structure, which are not too rigidly determined by the Euclidean structure of the social space. We have not explored the model sufficiently to determine if it has these properties, if small changes in the model could provide it with these properties, or if this approach should be abandoned. Computation cost increases as N^2 and the number of iterations, and took a few minutes per iteration on the MIT 370–186 system in 1973. This cost could be reduced by sampling, resulting in a fractional decrease that is the sample size divided by N. After enough iterations have produced what appears to be a realistic but scaled-down acquaintance net in such an idealized social space, a second program (also written by Diek Kruyt) to compute the distribution of chain lengths is then applied. Its cost varies as N^3.

Our present decision—held since 1975—is to explore the use of a computer program that constructs an acquaintance net according to a simulation that uses the data we obtained from the 100–day diaries kept by our 27 respondents (see § 2). The basic inputs to this program are:

The total number of individuals	$N = 1000$
The number of people seen by person A on any f days in 100	$Y(f)$ = data
The number of different people that A did not see in 100 days	$Y_A(0)$
The number of people, each of whom has exactly k acquaintances in common with A	$M_A(k)$ = data

Outputs include the distribution of chain length. The program starts by selecting A and linking to him all the $Y(100)$ people he sees daily (chosen at random from the $N - 1$ in the program). This might, for example, be the nucleus of his circle of acquaintances consisting of $Y(100) = 3$ people. Call them B, C, and D, and we have

A — B, C, D

so far.

Next proceed with the first of A's friends just chosen, say B. Link to him all $Y(100)$ others chosen randomly from $N - 1$, but including A. This might generate the following list of B's friends: A, C, F. Repeat this for all people labeled so far, *e.g.*, C, D, F, *etc.*, until there are no more new "target" people. Then repeat this procedure for $Y(99)$ in place of $Y(100)$, but eliminating certain randomly chosen links if they do not satisfy the following constraint.

Our data suggested that there are fewer people who have one acquaintance in common with A than there are who have two acquaintances in common with A, *etc.*, but that only a few people have very many acquaintances in common with A. Thus, there is a value, M, for which $M(k)$ is greatest, where $M = M(K)$ For example, if $M(1) = 2$, $M(2) = 3$, $M(4) = 5$, $M(5) = 4$, *etc.*, then $M = 5$, $K = 4$. We must ensure that M people among those chosen so far each have K acquaintances in common with A, also with the people he sees daily. We then repeat these steps with $Y(98)$ in place of $Y(99)$ and replace the constraint that M friends have K acquaintances in common with A, *etc.*, by one requiring that $M(K-1)$ people have $K-1$ acquaintances in common with A, B, *etc.* This is continued until $Y(0)$ and $M(1)$ replace $Y(1)$ and $M(2)$, respectively.

Effective and efficient algorithms for making these selections subject to the given constraints have yet to be developed. The computational complexity of this algorithm must also be determined, and hopefully is a polynomial in N. Hopefully also, such a program can be run for N large enough so that distribution of chain length does not change significantly as N is increased. Fruitful next steps seem to us to be the further development and analysis of the models sketched in this section. When these are found to have properties we consider realistic for large social contact nets and are the result of plausible explanatory inferences, then some difficult problems of statistical estimation must be solved. Hopefully, then we will have reached some understanding of contact nets that we have been seeking.

Appendix

Some approximations using Stirling's formula have already been derived and analyzed.

There is another very useful approximation based on a slightly different model in the general case.

Let q'_{ij} be defined as in eqn. (2), but rewrite it as

$$\frac{(m_k-h_{ik})!(m_k-h_{jk})!}{m_k!(m_k-h_{ik}-h_{jk})!}$$

$$=\frac{(m_k-h_{ik})!(m_k-h_{jk})(m_k-h_{jk}-1)\ldots(m_k-h_{jk}-h_{ik}+1)(m_k-h_{jk}-h_{ik})!}{m_k(m_k-1)\ldots(m_k-h_{ik}+1)(m_k-h_k)!(m_k-h_{jk}-h_{ik})!}$$

$$=\left(1-\frac{h_{jk}}{m_k}\right)\left(1-\frac{h_{jk}}{m_k-1}\right)\left(1-\frac{h_{jk}}{m_k-2}\right)\ldots\left(1-\frac{h_{jk}}{m_k-h_{ik}+1}\right)$$

(h_{ik} terms)

It is easily seen that this represents the probability of failing to draw a sample of h_{ik} red balls from an urn having m_k balls of which h_{ik} are red, but sampling without replacement. If we sample with replacement, the above formula becomes $q_{jk}^{h_{ik}}$, where $q_{jk}=(1-h_{ik}/m_k)$. This represents the probability that none of A's h_{ik} friends in stratum k is known to C (s(A) = i, s(C)= j), where it is possible to count the same friend more than once. The fractional error committed by this assumption is

$$\varepsilon = \left[\prod_{k=1}^{r} q_{jk}^{\ h_{ik}} - \prod_{k=1}^{r} \prod_{l=0}^{h_{jk}-1} \left(1 - \frac{h_{jk}}{m_k - l} \right) \right] \Big/ \prod_{k=1}^{r} q_{jk}^{\ h_{ik}}$$

This will be estimated later. Now,

$$\log q'_{ij} \simeq \sum_{k=1}^{r} h_{ik} \log\left(1 - \frac{h_{jk}}{m_k} \right)$$

If $h_{ik} << m_k$ for all k, we can further approximate this by

$$-\sum_{k=1}^{r} h_{ik} \frac{h_{jk}}{m_k} = -\sum_{k=1}^{r} h_{ik} \frac{h_{kj}}{m_j} = -\frac{1}{m_j} \sum_{k=1}^{r} h_{ik} h_{kj}$$

with a fractional error of about $h_{jk}/2m_k$, which is less than $(h + h')^2/2m$, as in the previous approximation. Furthermore, this approximation permits matrix multiplication and greater generality than only two values of h_{ij}. If we denote the matrix (h_{ij}) by **H** and ($\log q_{ij}$) by **L**, then $\mathbf{L} = \mathbf{H}\overline{\mathbf{H}}$, $\overline{\mathbf{H}}$ being the transpose of **H**.

To estimate the error, we take

$$\varepsilon = 1 = \prod_{k=1}^{r'} \prod_{l=0}^{h_{ik}-1} \left[\frac{1 - h_{jk} / (m_k - l)}{1 - h_{jk} / m_k} \right]$$

The term in brackets is approximated by the series

$$\left(1 + \frac{h_{jk}}{m_k} + \frac{h_{jk}^2}{m_k^2} + \ldots \right) - \frac{h_{jk}}{m_k - l} \left(1 + \frac{h_{jk}}{m_k} + \ldots \right)$$

$$= 1 + h_{jk} \left(\frac{1}{m_k} - \frac{1}{m_{k-l}} \right) + \frac{h_{jk}^2}{m_k} \left(\frac{1}{m_k} - \frac{1}{m_k - l} \right) + \ldots$$

$$= 1 - \frac{1}{m_k (m_k - l)} \left(h_{jk} + \frac{h_{jk}^2}{m_k} + \ldots \right)$$

$$= 1 \quad \frac{h_{jk}}{m_k^2} l$$

$$\varepsilon \simeq 1 \prod_{k=1}^{r} \exp\left(\frac{-h_{jk}}{m_k^2} \sum_{l=0}^{h_{ik}-1} l \right)$$
$$= 1 - \prod_{k=1}^{r} \exp\left(\frac{-h_{jk}}{m_k^2} \frac{(h_{ik}-1)h_{ik}}{2} \right)$$
$$= 1 - \prod_{k=1}^{r} \exp\left(\frac{-h_{jk}h_{ik}^2}{2m_k^2} \right)$$
$$= 1 - \exp\left(-\frac{1}{2m_j^2} \sum_{k=1}^{r} h_{ik}^2 h_{kj} \right)$$

According to this estimate, the approximation is good only when

$$\sum_{k=1}^{r} h_{ik}^2 h_{kj} < m_j^2$$

To compare this with the exponential approximation, let $h_{ik} = h$ if $i = k$, h' if $i \neq k$, so that

$$\sum_k h_{ik}^2 h_{kj} = h^2 h' + hh'^2 (r-2)h'^3 \qquad i \neq j$$
$$= h^3 + (r-1)h'^3 \qquad i = j$$

Hence, it would be required that $(h + h')^3 r < m^2$, $(h + h')^{3/2} \sqrt{\ } r < m$, compared with $(h + h')^2 < m$.

For the above simplified situation, the replacement model gives

$$q'_{ii} \simeq \exp\left[\frac{-h^2 + (r-1)h'^2}{m} \right]$$
$$q'_{ij} \simeq \exp\left[\frac{-2hh' + (r-2)h'^2}{m} \right] \qquad i \neq j$$

As an example where the departure from the results obtained when stratification was disregarded becomes more pronounced than in the illustrations chosen so far, let $N = 10^8$, $n_i = n = 10^3$ for all i, $m_j = m = 10^4$ for all j, $r = 10^4$, $h_{ii} = h = 500$, $h_{ij} = h' = 500/(10^4 - 1) = 5 \times 10^{-2}$ for all $i \neq j$.

(1) $p_0{}^* = n/N = 10^{-5}$

(2) $p_1{}^* = (1-p_0)p_1'^* = (1-p_0)(1-q_1'^*)$

$$q_1'^* = \frac{1}{r}q_1'(1) + \left(1-\frac{1}{r}\right)q_1'(2)$$

$$q_1'(1) = \exp\left(-\frac{25\times 10^4}{10^4} + \frac{25\times 10^{-4}}{10^4}\times 10^4\right) \simeq e^{-25} \simeq 0$$

$$q_1'(2) = \exp\left(-\frac{2\times 500\times 5\times 10^{-2}}{10^4} + \frac{10^4\times 25\times 10^{-4}}{10^4}\times 10^4\right) \approx 0.9925$$

$$q_1'^* \simeq 0.99241$$

$$p_1{}^* \simeq 0.00759$$

(3) Recall that $u \simeq \exp(-h^2/m)$, $v \simeq \exp(-h'^2/m)$, $w \simeq \exp(-hh'/m)$ so that

$$q_2'(1) = \exp\left(-\left[\frac{h^3}{m} + \frac{h'^2}{m}(r-1)h + (r-1)(r-2)h' + 2\frac{hh'^2}{m}(r-1)\right]\right)$$

$$= \exp\left(-\left[\frac{h^3}{m} + 3\frac{hh'^2}{m}(r-1) + \frac{h'^3}{m}(r-1)(r-2)\right]\right)$$

$$\approx \exp\left(-\frac{1}{m}(h^3 + 3rhh'^2 + r^2h'^3)\right)$$

$$q_2'(2) = \exp(-\frac{1}{m}\{h^2h' + [h(r-2) + h'(r^2-3r+3)]h'^2 + \\ +2[h+(r-2)h']hh'\})$$

$$\approx \exp\left(-\frac{1}{m}[h^2h' + hrh'^2 + h'^3r^2 + 2h^2h' + 2(r-2)hh'^2]\right)$$

$$\approx \exp\left(-\frac{1}{m}(3h^2h' + 3rhh'^2 + r^2h'^3)\right)$$

Then,

$$q_2'(1) = \exp[-10^{-4}(125\times10^{6}+3\times125\times10^{-2}\times10^{4}+10^{8}\times$$
$$\times125\times10^{-6})]$$
$$=\exp[-(12500+5)]\simeq 0$$
$$q_2'(2) = \exp[-10^{-4}(3\times125\times10^{2}+3\times10^{4}\times125\times10^{-2}+$$
$$+10^{8}\times125\times10^{-6})]$$
$$=\exp(-8.75)\simeq 0.00016$$

Hence,

$$p_2{}^* \simeq (1-10^{-5})(1-0.00759)(1-0.00016)$$
$$\simeq 0.9924$$

Notes

* MIT, Center for International Studies, 30 Wadsworth Street, Cambridge, Mass. 02139, U.S.A.

** Mental Health Research Institute, The University of Michigan, Ann Arbor, Mich. 48104, U.S.A.

1. In the years since this essay was first written, Stanley Milgram and his collaborators (Milgram 1967; Travers and Milgram 1969; Korte and Milgram 1970) have done significant experiments on the difficulty or ease of finding contact chains. It often proves very difficult indeed.
2. In the last few years, however, the literature on human networks has started proliferating. There are articles dealing with information and help-seeking networks in such fields as mental health (Saunders and Reppucci 1977; Horowitz 1977; McKinlay 1973). There is also some anthropological literature on networks h different societies (Nutini and White 1977; Mitchell 1969; Jacobson 1970).
3. Most sociometric literature deals with "liking" rather than "knowing". Preference relationships do tend to be transitive (Hallinan and Felmlee 1975).
4. A growing literature exists on structures in large networks (Boorman and White 1976; Lorrain 1976; Lorrain and White 1971; Rapoport and Horvath 1961; Foster *et al.* 1963; Foster and Horvath 1971; Wolfe 1970; McLaughlin 1975; Lundberg 1975; Alba and Kadushin 1976).
5. Let us state this more carefully for a network of n nodes and m links, in which $n! > m$, but all nodes are reachable from all nodes. In that case, m pairs know each other. The question is what structure will minimize the average number of steps between the $n! - m$ remaining pairs. Whenever the m pairs who know each other are also linked at two steps, then the two-step connection is wasted. The same is true for pairs linked by more than one two-step route. Such wastage occurs often when there are dense clusters of closely related nodes in a highly structured network. It happens rarely (because n! > m) in a random network structure—but it does happen. The

minimum average chain would occur not in a random structure, but in one designed to minimize wasted links. However, when n! > m, the random structure will depart from that situation only to a small extent.

6. The $n = At^x$ fitted curve for this author's ogive reached that level in just 5 years, but without taking account of forgetting.
7. The use of bibliometric data—for example, who co-authored with whom, who cited whom, which can be obtained in computerized form from the Institute for Scientific Information in Philadelphia for much of the world's scientific literature—may be a practical source. Mathematicians have for some time used the term "Erdös number", which is the distance between any author and Paul Erdös in terms of the number of intermediary co-authors; *e.g.,* A may have co-authored with B who co-authored with C who co-authored with Erdös, making the Erdös distance 2 from A. The use of co-citation and similar data also appears promising (Griffith *et al.* 1973).

References

Alba, R. 1973. "A graph-theoretic definition of a sociometric clique." *Journal of Mathematical Sociology 3*:113–126.Alba, R. and C. Kadushin. 1976. "The intersection of social circles: a new measure of social proximity in networks." *Sociological Methods and Research* 5:77–102.Boissevain, J. 1974. *Friends of Friends: Networks, Manipulators, and Coalitions.* New York: St. Martin's Press.

Boorman, S. and H. White. 1976. "Social structures from multiple networks." *American Journal of Sociology 81*:1384–1446. Breiger, R., S.

Boorman and P. Arabie. 1975. "An algorithm for clustering relational data with applications to social network analysis and comparison with multidimensional scaling." *Journal of Mathematical Psychology 12*: 328–383.

de Grazia, A. 1952. *Elements of Political Science.* New York: Free Press.

Deutsch, K. 1956. "Shifts in the balance of communication flows." *Public Opinion Quarterly 20*:143–60.

———. 1966. *Nationalism and Social Communication.* Cambridge, MA: MIT Press

Doreian P. 1974. "On the connectivity of social networks." *Journal of Mathematical Sociology* 3:245–258.

Erickson, B. and P. Kringas. 1975. "The small world of politics, or, seeking élites from the bottom up." *Canadian Review of Sociology and Anthropology 12*:585–593.

Festinger, L., S. Shachter and K. Back. 1950. *Social Pressures in Informal Groups.* New York: Harper.

Foster, C. and W. Horvath. 1971. "A study of a large sociogram III: reciprocal choice probabilities as a measure of social distance." *Behavioral Science 16*:429–435.

Foster, C., A. Rapoport and C. Orwant. 1963. "A study of large sociogram II: elimination of free parameters." *Behavioral Science 8*:56–65.

Granovetter, M. 1974. *Getting a Job: A Study of Contacts and Careers.* Cambridge, MA: Harvard University Press.

———. 1976. "Network sampling: some first steps." *American Journal of Sociology 81*:1287–1303.

Griffith, B., V. Maier and A. Miller. 1973. *Describing Communications Networks Through the Use of Matrix-Based Measures.* Unpublished. Drexel University, Graduate School of Library Science, Philadelphia, PA.

Gurevich, M. 1961. *The Social Structure of Acquaintanceship Networks.* Cambridge, MA: MIT Press.
Gurevich, M. and A. Weingrod. 1976. "Who knows whom—contact networks in Israeli national élite." *Megamot 22*:357–378.
———. n.d. *Human Organization.* To be published.
Hallinan, M. and D. Felmlee. 1975. "An analysis of intransitivity in sociometric data." *Sociometry 38*:195–212.
Hammer, M. n.d. *Social Access and Clustering of Personal Connections.* Unpublished.
Holland, P. and S. Leinhardt. 1970. "A method for detecting structure in sociometric data." *American Journal of Sociology 70*:492–513.
Horowitz, A. 1977. "Social networks and pathways to psychiatric treatment." *Social Forces 56*:81–105.
Hunter, I. and R. L. Shotland. 1974. "Treating data collected by the small world method as a Markov process." *Social Forces 52*:321–332.
Jacobson, D. 1970. "Network analysis in East Africa: the social organization of urban transients." *Canadian Review of Sociology and Anthropology 7*:281–286.
Jennings, H. 1937. "Structure of leadership—development and sphere of influence." *Sociometry 1*:131.
Katz, E. and P. Lazarsfeld. 1955. *Personal Influence.* Glencoe, IL: Free Press.
Killworth, P. and B. Russell. 1976. "Information accuracy in social network data." *Human Organization 35*:269–286.
Kleinrock, L. 1964. *Communication Nets: Stochastic Message Flow and Delay.* New York: McGraw-Hill.
Korte, C. and S. Milgram. 1970. "Acquaintanceship networks between racial groups: application of the small world method." *Journal of Personality and Social Psychology 15*:101–108.
Kurtzman, D. H. 1935. *Methods of Controlling Votes in Philadelphia.* Philadelphia: University of Pennsylvania.
Lorrain, F. 1976. *Social Networks and Classification.* Manuscript.
Lorrain, F. and H. White. 1971. "Structural equivalence of individuals in social networks." *Journal of Mathematical Sociology 1*:49–80.
Luce, R. 1950. "Connectivity and generalized cliques in sociometric group structure." *Psychometrika 15*:169–190.
Lundberg, C. 1975. "Patterns of acquaintanceship in society and complex organization: a comparative study of the small world problem." *Pacific Sociological Review 18*:206–222.
McKinlay, J. 1973. "Social networks, lay consultation and help-seeking behavior." *Social Forces 51*:275–292.
McLaughlin, E. 1975. "The power network in Phoenix. An application of the smallest space analysis." *The Insurgent Sociologist 5*:185–195.
Milgram, S. 1967. "The small world problem." *Psychology Today 22*:61–67.
Miller, G. 1956. "The magical number seven plus or minus two." *Psychological Review 63*:81–97.
Mitchell, J. C. (Ed.) 1969. *Social Networks in Urban Situations—Analysis of Personal Relationships in Central African Towns.* Manchester: University Press.
Newcomb, T. 1961. *The Acquaintance Process.* New York: Holt, Rinehart, and Winston.

Nutini, H. and D. White. 1977. "Community variations and network structure in social functions of Compradrazgo in rural Tlaxcala, Mexico." *Ethnology 16*:353–384.

Peay, E. 1976. "A note concerning the connectivity of social networks." *Journal of Mathematical Sociology 4*:319–321.

Rapoport, A. 1963. "Mathematical models of social interaction." *Handbook of Mathematical Psychology.* New York: Wiley, pp. 493–579.

Rapoport, A. and W. Horvath. 1961. "A study of a large sociogram." *Behavioral Science 6*:279–291.

Rosenthal, H. 1960. *Acquaintances and Contacts of Franklin Roosevelt.* Unpublished B.S. thesis: MIT.

Saunders, J. and N. Reppucci. 1977. "Learning networks among administrators of human service institutions." *American Journal of Community Psychology 5*:269–276.

Schulman, N. 1976. "Role differentiation in urban networks." *Sociological Focus 9*:149–158.

Travers, J. and S. Milgram. 1969. "An experimental study of the small world problem." *Sociometry 32*:425–443.

Warner, W. L. 1963. *Yankee City.* New Haven, CT: Yale University Press.

Wasserman, S. 1977. "Random directed graph distributions and the triad census in social networks." *Journal of Mathematical Sociology 5*:61–86.

White, H. 1970a. "Search parameters for the small world problem." *Social Forces 49*:259–264.

———. 1970b. *Chains of Opportunity.* Cambridge, MA: Harvard University Press.

———. 1973. "Everyday life in stochastic networks." *Sociological Inquiry 43*:43–49.

Wolfe, A. 1970. "On structural comparisons of networks." *Canadian Review of Sociology and Anthropology 7*:226–244.

Part V

Social Science in Political Contexts

Editor's Introduction

"But the scores of methodological and ideological essays about new approaches to the study of communications can hardly be honored by the term "ferment." There is a simple recipe for these essays: avoid measurement, add moral commitment, and throw in some of the following words: social system, capitalism, dependency, positivism, idealism, ideology, autonomy, paradigm, commercialism, consciousness, emancipation, cooptation, critical, instrumental, technocratic, legitimation, praxiology, repressive, dialogue, hegemony, contradiction, problematic."

—Ithiel Pool, pp. 271–72 below

"How could it be that in free universities in a free society we came so close to a major debacle, with little awareness of what was going on. and with relative quiescence by students and faculties alike?"

—Ithiel Pool, p. 289 below

"Most movements that are self-described as radical are highly urbanistic, or nationalistic, or oriented to obsolete class structures, or to central bureaucratic planning. The changes that we can see on the horizon are much more drastic than that . . . People who think about social change in traditional political terms cannot begin to imagine the changes that lie ahead. Conventional reformers cast their programs in terms of national policies, or in terms of laws and central planning. But in the end, what will shape the future is a creative potential that inheres in the new technologies."

—Ithiel Pool[1]

Plato's *Republic* argued that improved education of future leaders was a key to better government: he recommended an ideal of philosopher-kings. Beginning in the 1930s, American universities supported the growth of social science that began at the University of Chicago and have added another (scientific) ideal and option for undergraduate and graduate training in public affairs.

The development of social science continues to face political challenges in America: when it is used to recommend greater effectiveness for contentious policies; from the unexpected tenacity and competition of simple and familiar ideological ideas; from (in Ithiel's view) deconstructionism and other misdirected wastes of time; and from government. These issues are addressed in the first four selections:

"Some Facts About Values"

During the Cold War Ithiel Pool shared the anti-Communist commitment of the American foreign policy Establishment. When America became militarily involved in Vietnam, he contracted to direct a series of major research projects in Vietnam to improve the war effort. He also was a public supporter of the war. Leading academic opponents of the Vietnam War brought the integrity of his scientific work under attack, alleging (in part) that it should have been value free.

In the first essay, "Some Facts About Values," Ithiel Pool responds to this criticism and the deeper issue of whether the disciplined detachment of science is inconsistent with strong moral and political commitments.[2]

"What Ferment?"

Ithiel Pool was deeply educated in the humanities. Thus, there was a degree of surprise and frustration when a movement of deconstructionists and other humanists began to criticize the scientific study of communication processes. As the quotation at the beginning of this section illustrates, Pool had scant sympathy for their elusive and impassioned conversations of words with other words, especially if these were presented as progress. It may help to explain his views by making three points:

1.) As I noted in the introduction to this volume: To Ithiel Pool's generation of social scientists, it was already obvious that social reality was invented and that people often were entrapped and manipulated by the cultures, societies, and political systems in which they lived. As an undergraduate during the 1930s, at the University of Chicago, he was a passionate Trotskyite and student leader. Later, he studied Nazi propaganda during World War II as armies marched at the behest of demagogic leaders. Afterward, he studied political development in decades when millions more died in the Chinese revolution and other nationalist/decolonial revolutions; and Soviet-American confrontations, intensified by ideology, threatened nuclear wars.[3]

The commitment to freedom was implicit: Pool believed that social science, itself, is liberating and provides an independent, steadier, truer, and more realistic alternative to the frameworks and choices that the political world provides.

2.) Deconstruction has been done for decades—perhaps more usefully—with help from scientific methods. Any scientist who researches America's pluralist political system quickly recognizes that feminists, Republican businessmen, Black nationalists, religious fundamentalists, authoritarians, etc. "write" different stories and interpretations of national political reality, their own identities, and their relationship to government. The alleged single "objective" reality of a good social scientist typically is a picture of many individual's realities, only partially shared—just as (in section two of this volume) Pool described the Kaiser and the Tsar as living in distinct realities, although with common elements. Another example (also from section two): when Abelson, Pool, and Popkin used a computer to simulate the American political system they began with 80,000 respondents (from statistically representative samples), immediately "deconstructed" any crude effort to tell one story about political reality by systematically identifying 480 voter types, and reconstructing the stories of each type's different relation to the political election with respect to 52 political issues! Just as "deconstructing" the physical world into 100+ physical elements by *scientific* methods allows you to see how it is put together, and is empowering, so Ithiel believed that the social scientific way of pursuing the aims of deconstructionist liberation also would be more productive.

3.) The contention between some humanist writers and social scientists is not whether social reality is made-up. Indeed, a key task of social scientists is to create and line-up independent and dependent variables, invent stories (i.e., alternative causal theories) and chose among them. An American physician could be challenged by a witch doctor, on the grounds that both "make up" versions of reality, but the rejoinder of an American physician would be "What is your cure rate?" Until their debate moved to this second question, Ithiel believed critics were missing the point, and power, of uniting the humanities with science to create social science as an aid to democratic problem solving.

"Who Rules America?"

The third selection is Ithiel Pool's critical review of a book by a distinguished contemporary and political scientist at Yale, Charles Lindblom. Lindblom's book, *Politics and markets,* was a public affairs book that made strong ideological arguments blended with the language of social science.

Ordinarily, Pool did not review public affairs books, which typically require simple and bold themes and proscribe words like "hypothesis"—it would be unfair to hold them to scientific standards. In Lindblom's case he made an exception, perhaps because the book received an award from the American Political Science Association as a scientific contribution. Too, the unexpected tenacity of simple ideological ideas to diagnose and solve national problems has continued to restrict the growth of social science and the review was an opportunity to alert readers, with a degree of frustration, that social science is capable of a better analysis of the issues that Lindblom addressed.[4]

"Human Subjects Regulations on the Social Sciences"

Ithiel Pool's scientific views about the conditions of well-functioning democracy are included in a companion volume, also published by Transaction Books.[5] He believed that many other institutions in society must be strong and well-run, with a degree of respected independence and self government, for a democracy to be strong. The value of healthy, independent institutions was evident in his own life in the strength provided by his family and Jewish traditions: he was descended from a long line of distinguished scholars and rabbis (on both sides) and his father, David deSola Pool, had been the head of the Sephardic congregation in New York City. And he cared about scientific integrity and building strong institutions: he built the MIT Political Science Department to be one of the best in the world and cared deeply about the quality of teaching and the humanity and rigor of the Department's daily operation.

The essay concerns an attempt by the federal government to impose requirements for prior ethical review of all university research involving human subjects, *even* when no government funds are used for the research. The attempts to assure ethical rules may seem well-intentioned to the reader (and, perhaps, they were). Thus, Ithiel Pool's reasons for leading the national fight against them might be especially instructive: he felt that basic truths, supported by social science research, were being forgotten—or had never sunk-in—among many faculty and administrators at American universities.[6] At the time, it was alarmingly easy for university administrations to be unconcerned or to acquiesce in the face of such well-intentioned motives for bureaucratic review—and the reader should be forewarned that, except for

Ithiel's personal initiative, commitment, and credibility with scientists throughout the country, the erosion probably would have occurred.

"What's Next? The Intellectual Legacy of Ithiel de Sola Pool" by Lloyd Etheredge

This final paper discusses the potential contribution of several of the methods from this volume to improve our understanding and foresight about the new forces that are shaping the world. Especially as these methods are made more practical by the exponential improvements in computer technology. The reader may especially want to consider Ithiel Pool's view (expressed in the quotation at the beginning of this section) that emerging social science research will show that the traditional categories of thinking about political reform are becoming outmoded and that better guidance in securing a freer world, and more humane politics, can be provided by the development of social science.

The paper also seeks to express the spirit of Ithiel Pool's scientific work. It discusses elements of his life, his civic engagement with the issues of his time, his instinct for scientific leadership, and his passionate commitment to a world with freedom and human dignity. The paper was presented at an MIT symposium honoring a communication research program that Ithiel Pool had begun three decades earlier, a symposium that—in Ithiel's spirit—looked forward to the new research issues raised by the transitions to new media on the threshold of the twenty-first century.

Notes

1. Ithiel de Sola Pool, "Four unnatural institutions and the road ahead," in Lloyd S. Etheredge (ed.). *Politics in wired nations: Selected writings of Ithiel de Sola Pool* (New Brunswick, NJ: Transaction Publishers, 1998), pp. 227–237, p. 237.
2. Readers who are familiar with the Vietnam period and Ithiel Pool's views may wish to have a further discussion of the issues raised by his involvement. The questions deserve to be addressed separately, after copies of the research are declassified, but several comments may be useful to future scholars:

   There were seven main Simulmatics projects in Viet Nam between June, 1966 and the Tet offensive: 1.) a study of the Chieu Hoi or Open Arms Program to understand the original recruitment of Viet Cong members and increase the effectiveness of the program in securing and maintaining defections. (The study included observations of reception centers and several hundred interviews, including 84 depth interviews.) 2.) A study, under Dr. Philip Worchel, to improve the effectiveness of the Regional and Popular Forces of South Vietnam. Over 700 troops from effective and ineffective RF/PF squads were interviewed, along with their wives and fellow-villagers (a total of about 1300 subjects); reliability was checked by a second series of interviews three months later and the results were cross-validated with untested units and villagers. 3.) New methods to measure combat effectiveness, a project directed by Dr. Frederick Rockett. 4.) An independent assessment of the reliability of the data provided by American advisers concerning the progress in pacification of rural areas. 5.) Assessment of elements of Vietnamese culture and tradition which aided US authorities in communicating effectively with the Vietnamese population. 6.) A three wave panel survey, designed by Ithiel Pool and Dr. Ralph K. White (George Washington University), to assess the impacts of introducing television to rural areas of Vietnam, which was never completed. 7.) Studies of special groups within the Vietnamese population to assess how to help mobilize these groups for the war effort and national reconstruction. The study included students, the labor movement, the Chinese community, the Hoa Hao (a religious sect that have successfully checked Communism in provinces under its control), and the entrepreneurial class in both metropolitan areas and small towns. Participants included Dr. Arthur Smithies (Harvard). Dr. John Donnell (Temple), Dr. Milton Sacks (Brandeis), and Dr. Frederick Yu (Columbia). Source: Ithiel de Sola Pool. "Simulmatics efforts in Viet Nam." February, 1968. Xerox. Attachment 7 to a post Tet-offensive memorandum by Ithiel de Sola Pool, "Achieving pacification in Viet Nam." Xerox, no date.

B.) In judging Pool's relationship to the war effort, it is relevant that he was highly respected in Cambridge and enjoyed a unique and direct access to the National Security Advisers of Presidents involved in the war, especially McGeorge Bundy (Presidents Kennedy and Johnson) from Harvard and Walt Rostow (President Johnson) who was a former MIT colleague. It seems likely that the contracts to Ithiel Pool's Simulmatics corporation were designed to give an independent and direct channel of scientific assessment and well-informed advice at a high level, in the same spirit as related contracts to the RAND Corporation. Thus Pool's belief that he could influence the war effort as an in-house critic and adviser had a realistic basis. If there is criticism due on this score, it is probably that Ithiel Pool over-estimated the capacity and commitment of the American government to act on the assessments and recommendations he provided, even if they were favored by the National Security Adviser.

C.) The question of impact needs to be judged carefully. Ithiel Pool's advice for winning the war was not accepted, but his research concerning the problems that needed to be solved may have confirmed a pessimistic and skeptical analysis in the Washington intelligence community, especially concerning problems of motivation of the military forces of South Vietnam compared with the Viet Cong and the acute disconnection between local villages and the political elites in Saigon. (For example, in his post-Tet memorandum (cited above) Ithiel Pool recommended a vigorous improvement of the war effort, but also summarized current progress candidly: "Most of these 150,000 to 175,000 [PF—Popular Force soldiers in the villages of Viet Nam] are poorly led." "PF unlike (sic) ARVN [the army of South Viet Nam] seldom abuse the villagers." "The interface of the village and the district governments is the interface between a grass roots meaningful organization and Mandarin authoritarianism . . . responsible [national] government in

Viet Nam that will command the people's loyalty" has not been achieved. See Leslie Gelb and Richard Betts, *The irony of Vietnam: The system worked* (Washington, DC: Brookings Institution, 1979.)

3. In America, there also was a steady progression of liberation and reform movements during his lifetime: union organizing, the civil rights and environmental movements of the 1960s, women's liberation, and many others.
4. A reader who is familiar with Pool's work will recognize that his earlier book about the influence of American business on Congress (R. Bauer, I. Pool, and L. Dexter, *American business and public policy: The politics of foreign trade.* (NY: Atherton Press of Prentice-Hall, 1963)) is the type of grounded analysis that he believed Lindblom should have done before making statements about the influence of business in American politics.
5. Etheredge (ed.), *op. cit.*
6. The scientific base for these views concerning civil society is discussed more fully in his "The Public and the polity," reprinted in Lloyd S. Etheredge (ed.), *op. cit.*, pp. 263–290.

11

Some Facts About Values

Leading articles in both the current issue of *APSR* (Winter 1969–70) and of *PS* (Fall 1969) attack an identical quotation from my chapter in "The Public and the Polity" in *Contemporary Political Science.* In reply to Professor Sheldon Wolin's article in APSR, I wrote a short reply for he clearly misinterpreted the quotation in an otherwise serious article. Professor Surkin's piece, "Sense and Nonsense in Politics" in *PS* frustrates all my attempts at a short reply, for the issue is not the text of a particular quotation that has become a minor *cause célebre,* but rather the central thesis of his article that is in error. His is an error that has become sufficiently widely diffused these days that it needs a serious reply.

The issue is the role of value judgments in political science. The common error is the assertion that modern political science has been non-normative and value-free, or at least has aimed at being so. The statement is usually made in criticism of so-called behavioral political science and in favor of a supposed post-behavioral revolution, which is alleged to be seeking a new concern for relevance. Professor Surkin's article is a particular variant on that theme. He states that his purpose is to show that a particular social science methodology, namely, "claimed objectivity and value neutrality" leads to a "non-objective role for social science knowledge in the service of the dominant institutions in American society." Here is an important set of allegations. To phrase them in less pejorative terms: (1) behavioral social scientists claim to be objective and value-neutral; (2) in fact they are not so; (3) by claiming to be so they actually support evil institutions.

There are at least three lines of thought (mutually inconsistent with each other) that exist in the American social science community in answer to these allegations: (1) There are a few people, but I would argue that they are very few, who would accept the goal of value-neutrality,

First published in *PS* (1970).

but deny the assertion that their methodology serves the dominant institutions. (2) There are an even smaller number (indeed I can't think of any) who might accept both the goal of value-neutrality and the allegation that it serves the dominant institutions in society, but who would argue that the validity of the scientific methodology has to be judged on its own merits, and that its social effects are whatever they are. (3) The bulk of political scientists, and myself among them, would argue that the so-called value-free approach is not now and never was a goal or characteristic of political science. The attack in short, is against a figment of imagination, and what the consequences of this figment of imagination might have been or might be, had it ever existed, is speculative and "iffy" at best.

The record of the moral concerns of the behavioral school is fairly clear. Certainly no topic in the past thirty years has received more attention from behavioral political scientists than political participation. There are studies of voting and nonvoting, of community power structure, and of citizen politics. The underlying concern in all of these is with democratic values and the implicit preference is equalitarian and participatory. Even those studies that have explored the limits of effective democracy have reflected the moral anguish of those committed to a goal which they were forced to concede was not entirely within their grasp. A second major focus of the so-called behaviorists has been on political development. Again clearly there has been a deep moral commitment toward the achievement of modernization and development in the third world. Another major area of interest to the behaviorists was the operation of pressure group politics, again clearly because of a concern to achieve genuine representation. A fourth recent area of active interest has been peace research, which by its very name is clearly not non-normative. Finally, but perhaps most significant, civil rights, race, and prejudice has been a persistent subject of study, and almost without exception by people whose concern was on the equalitarian side of those issues. The historical closet is almost bare of merely non-normative research.

Furthermore, the values of behavioral scientists have not been hidden. Many leading behavioral scientists have been quite explicit in their value concerns. If any one man is a symbol of behavioral political science it is Harold Lasswell, and if any social scientist's work has been value-laden it is his. In 1951 he published a book called *The Policy Sciences*, which was a kind of manifesto for those of us who were concerned with making social science useful. From the beginning Harold

Lasswell saw the study of man not as a matter of idle curiosity but a tool for promoting the dignity of man. As he put it in talking about content analysis, it was important for its "contribution . . . to the special objectives of humane politics."[1] Much of Lasswell's other writings were concerned with what he calls "the developing science of democracy." He stated that "the developing science of democracy is an arsenal of implements for the achievement of democratic ideals." In another essay he wrote that "modern procedures do make it possible for the first time in history of large-scale social organization to realize some of the aims of democracy." He saw in social science an instrument for humane politics: "the aim of humane politics is a commonwealth in which the dignity of man is accepted in theory and fact."[3]

These are not unusual quotations pulled out of context. They are quite characteristic aphorisms that could be matched a thousand times over from most political scientists who wrote in the 1940s, 1950s, or 1960s. Whether they talked of policy sciences, like Lasswell, or of applied social science, or more recently, systems analysis, whether they worked for the government in the war, for organizations combating prejudice, for agencies working on international propaganda, for economic development or for peace-keeping, most social scientists have been involved in applied purpose activity of one sort or another.

Differences of opinion will, of course, exist about these activities. Mr. Surkin and those who feel as he does, will of course regard many, if not most of them as on the wrong side. That, however, is a very different statement than the one that they were passing under the guise of non-normative objectivity.

What accounts for the widespread acceptance of Surkin's obviously ahistorical stereotype of the claims of behavioral science? It is easy enough to brush the stereotype aside as nonsense, but it is more fruitful to ask how such a stereotype gained its hold. As with most popular myths, if one looks closely one can find a kernel of badly distorted truth. The discovery of that kernel is more worthwhile than the nailing of any distortions.

There are two truths, logically unrelated though historically related, that underlie the current misperception of so-called value-free social science. The first is an empirical observation about the personality traits that make for effectiveness as a scientist or other user of knowledge; the second is a logical proposition about the evidential basis for empirical vs. non-empirical statements.

1. Highly charged emotional states of various kinds restrict cognitive skill. Thus excessive involvement in one's own value preferences may inhibit accurate observation. It certainly does not follow that the scientist or other knowledge-using professional must avoid having preferences. Consider the surgeon. He has a highly valued goal, the saving of the life of his patient. He is a more skillful surgeon, however, if his personality or training make him cool and detached enough to permit him calmly to cut or not cut, and to sleep despite grim facts of failure and death. So it is for everyone in a knowledge-using activity (that is to say a profession) whether he is a social worker, a general, a political campaign manager, a lawyer, or a scientist, he will do his job better if he is personally capable of a measure of temporary suspension of passion in the process of achieving his highly valued goals. It is that psychological capability which is referred to by the terms "objectivity" and "detachment," and they are certainly essential for a good social scientist.

2. The other truth often confused with the psychological one is the proposition that irreducible value judgments have a different evidentiary status in logic than do empirical statements of fact. In modern logic two classes of statements are distinguished: those in which the evidence is sensory observations and those which rest upon postulation and analysis. In the latter class belong mathematics, logic itself, definitions, and also irreducible value judgments. The statement "I consider X . . . Y to be the basis for evaluating something good," stands logically in the same situation as the statement "I define word N as meaning X . . . Y." Clearly neither is a statement to be subjected to experimentation for verification. Clearly both are in that sense arbitrary or postulational decisions by the analyst.[4] To say that, however, is not to denigrate them any more than to say that mathematics and logic are analytical rather than empirical disciplines is to denigrate them. Nor do these distinctions make it illegitimate for the researcher to use a value statement any more than he is excluded from using a definition, a principle in logic, or a mathematical method. He may feel that he is less skilled as a moralist than as an empirical researcher, in the same way as he may feel his inadequacy as a logician or a mathematician. That, however, is a psychological and factual statement about an individual. It does not lead to the conclusion that he should not apply normative statements about his goals (as every medical researcher does when he discusses a cure) any more than it precludes him from introducing logic, mathematics, and definitions where he needs them.

The two quite distinct and valid conclusions about the psychology of knowledge on the one hand and about the structure of evidence on the other have been intertwined in the intellectual history of what Surkin mislabels non-normative social science. A brief sketch of the history might be helpful in putting some of the ideas in perspective.

In the modern world it was Karl Marx who initiated that detachment from values among social scientists which has made it possible for them to stand off from values and look at them as social facts to be explained, rather than as part of the explanatory theory itself. In turning Hegel on his head and formulating the concept of historical materialism, Marx denied to ideas and values any inherent truth of their own, treating them as mere ideologies expressing the state of development of the productive forces and the interests of the resulting classes. Marxist social scientists therefore claimed to have a way to look at values objectively from the point of view of scientific knowledge of the historical facts. They for the first time carried out what claimed to be value-free analysis of historical developments based upon an objective material reality that the Marxist historian knew. (It is ironical that the nearest thing to fitting the new left stereotype of value-free social science was the social science of the old left, of whose history the new left, it must be recognized, is profoundly ignorant).

Of course it would be highly misleading to fail to recognize Marx's hidden values. He was a revolutionist and crusader committed to changing society. Nevertheless, he railed incessantly against those of his utopian socialist colleagues who claimed that their reason for wishing to change society was that the socialist society would be better in some moral sense. Marx was willing to describe the communist future as representing a higher stage of development, meaning by that further down some sequence of necessary historical law. He was willing to make such factual statements as that it represented expanded levels of productivity. But the irreducible value statement that it was better was to Marx pure ideology, even if, in this case the ideology of the new proletarian class, rather than that of the bourgeoisie. Marx as a social scientist would never permit himself such indulgence in normativeness.

Out of such Marxist and semi-Marxist objective analysis of society came much of the significant sociology of the nineteenth and early twentieth centuries. This kind of detached analysis of values is represented for example in Mannheim's *Ideology and Utopia*. It is also represented in a significant way in Max Weber, who more than any other social scientist formulated the prevailing orthodoxy regarding facts and values in the social sciences. Just as Marx had stood Hegel on his head, so Weber stood Marx on his head, and sought by partial incorporation to retain what he saw as the merits of Marxist analysis on behalf of liberal values. Weber, in his discussion of the ethic of the scientist and of the role of values in social science, said in effect to the Marxist school: Yes one can look at values in a value-free way as a sociologist, but one does not therefore have to deny that values shape history just as much as do the material forces of production. Thus he preserved for social science the intellectual power gained by a detached willingness to look at values as ideology without at the same time accepting the incubus of a clearly inadequate historical law that denied to values the casual significance that they often have.

The Marxist-Weberian trend of sociological detachment in looking at the evolution of thought was in turn reinforced by developments in the history of philosophy and logic, specifically, logical positivism in its various manifestations including logical empiricism. Historically, there was substantial interaction between Marxist materialism and logical positivism as evidenced, for example, in Lenin's *Materialism and Empirio-Criticism.* The Marxists found reinforcement in their rejection of so-called idealism and their embrace of materialism (meaning by that in this context assignment of truth value to physical observables) in the positivists' attack upon metaphysics and their analysis of validation as arising from empirical confirmation. The logical empiricists made the sharp distinction whose validity we accepted above between that class of statements which were subject to empirical confirmation and that class such as those in mathematics, logic, evaluation, and definition, which were not empirically testable. In their more extreme phase in the 1930s some of the successors of the Vienna School tended to call these other kinds of statements nonsense, and it must be conceded for a period treated them with substantial scorn as mere metaphysics incapable of proof. It is some time since such scorn was in fashion in philosophic circles. What remains is a fairly indisputable logical distinction.

It must be recognized that not only critics stemming from the so-called New Political Science, but also many self-designated behaviorists have tended to confuse the scientific norm of maintaining a mood of detachment and objectivity with a logical distinction between analytic and empirical statements. Researchers in any science are seldom very clear about the logical status of what they are doing. That is an exercise left to philosophers of science. Thus the kernel of truth that one can concede to Professor Surkin and to others who rant against supposedly value-free social science is that these various psychological and logical notions that we have just been reviewing did get wound up in the day-to-day frame of thought (or ideology if you wish) of practicing social scientists into a highly useful set of liberal professional norms.

The social scientist has a hard job to do. He conducts research on topics that are extremely sensitive and emotionally charged. He looks at situations full of human passions, of love and hate, conflict and ambition. He is a human being as he looks at them. In that respect he as a scientist is not unique, but belongs in a large class of professions that must be able to suspend judgment enough to understand, while at the same time being able to judge. The psychotherapist must have the same qualities; he must learn enough discipline not to fall in love with his patient. The journalist, to do a good reporting job, must also have such qualities; so must the social worker or politician. They are, in short, the qualities required by anyone with a role where he must be involved in human problems, but open to questioning and change. It is a legitimate question for social scientists to ask "What were Stalin's personal relations like?" or "What does it feel like to be a peasant in a contested Vietnamese hamlet?" To answer such questions one needs traits of personality and learned habits of discipline that both permit empathy and prevent oneself from becoming so emotionally involved that one can no longer perceive reality. One must learn to conduct oneself at three levels simultaneously: One at which one empathizes with the perceptions of the person observed, one in which one can be detachedly critical of those perceptions and place them into some theoretical context, and a third in which one can apply one's own value standards to them. These are not easy skills to learn, and they are not learned by militants who think that the test of truth is the passionateness with which one describes evils.[5] It is because of such difficult and somewhat unnatural professional norms of scientific behavior that behavioral social science shocks the "true believer," first because it coolly looks at his beliefs as a datum to be explained, and second because it recognizes logical constraints on its ability to "prove" or "disprove" those beliefs by its ordinary scientific tools, and thirdly, and most importantly, because it takes temporarily a calm and reasoned approach to even the most repulsive aspects of the human experience. None of that, however, is the same as saying that the behavioral sciences have been value-free and non-normative.

One is bothered by the glib assertions to the contrary that are appearing with increasing frequency among political scientists, not so much because the statement is wrong, (it shares that with a lot of other widely believed statements) but because of the extraordinarily low standard of evidence and scholarship revealed by those making the allegation. Surkin's article is a case in point. The quotation from me which led to this reply appeared in *Contemporary Political Science,* a book containing the plenary session papers of the 1966 convention of the APSA. That book is a codification of what a number of leaders of the profession, all of them in what roughly might be called the behavioral persuasion, saw as the relationship between political theory and contemporary empirical political science. It is a mystery that any scholar claiming to write about behavioral political science would not have examined that volume, yet the quotation Surkin uses is picked up second-hand from Noam Chomsky, whose remarkable work in linguistics is matched by his generally recognized chronic incapacity to quote accurately anyone who disagrees with him. As a result, Surkin ends up with some extraordinary interpretations; for example, he quotes indirectly from an article I wrote in *Asian Survey,* dealing with possible postwar settlements in Vietnam, and advocating certain policies that generally go under the name of accommodation (clearly that was policy-advocacy and not value-free). There, in stating the alternatives that I was going to discuss I said, "I rule out of consideration here a large range of viable political settlements," specifically, those that involve "the inclusion of the Viet Cong in a coalition government, or even the persistence of the Viet Cong as a legal organization in South Viet Nam." What I was discussing was how a successful non-communist government of Vietnam might proceed "despite the persisting great political power of the Viet Cong." These passages quoted by Surkin from me via Chomsky led Surkin to say "Social scientists deny that this sort of analysis is ideological, claiming instead that these studies conform to the scholarly objective rigor of his discipline. This is sheer nonsense. Take for example, the following proposition by Professor Pool on restructuring government as an empirical formulation." He then proceeds to the above quotations. Clearly no one who reads the original could have interpreted those introductory sentences restricting the range of alternatives that I was going to analyze as an "empirical formulation" or for that matter as a finding of any kind. Indeed I characterized other alternatives as also "viable"—the only empirical statement in that quote. Mr. Surkin may not be much interested in those alternatives whereby the government of Vietnam could establish a peaceful society under its rule. That is his privilege. It is also my privilege to be interested in that range of questions, but it is nobody's privilege, not even a Chomsky's or a Surkin's, or some combination of distortions arising out of a two-step process of quotation to take a simple statement limiting the subject of an article, and to treat it as it the author thought that these were empirical statements about the external world.

It is only by such processes of lack of attention to what in fact the original sources say that Surkin is enabled to establish a supposed distinction between the three methodological approaches to science which he calls (1) the New Mandarin (of which I am supposed to be an example), (2) the public advocate, and (3) the persuasive neutralist. While he attacks all three, he insists on some imaginary distinctions between them based upon whether the "professed mission" of the social scientist is "to serve the public good" or to serve "the government or the corporation." Clearly, the purpose of all of us is to serve the public good.[6] Equally clearly, that goal is sometimes served by helping governments and corporations and sometimes by criticizing them. To talk as though there was a choice between seeking to improve the institutions of which society consists, and seeking to help the people who are that society is not radicalism but inanity.

It must be conceded that in appealing to the facts, I am not answering Mr. Surkin's argument fully for he explicitly renounces liberal standards of scientific evidence. He says that "to plead for reason, detachment, objectivity or patience in the face of abject poverty, political repression or napalmed women and children is absurd." After making his analysis of the nature of modern society he says that "to argue to the contrary is of no avail, since this generation has experienced . . . its own poverty, powerlessness, alienation." In this view, in his words "the Wallacites and the new left, right extremists and left extremists, and other so-called social deviants have correctly perceived the insane world of reason from which they rebel." Against such arguments there is no reply for there is no common ground of rational premises from which to proceed.

Why then pay any attention to such an untenable position or to some of the historical myths that are used to bolster it? The answer is not clear. The anti-intellectual theses of which the attack on supposedly non-normative social science is a part raise the age-old fundamental question of how seriously a liberal scientific discipline needs to address itself to the claims of a mysticism which challenges its fundamental premises. How seriously should chemistry take alchemy? How seriously should psychology take parapsychology? The challenge to contemporary political science from the anti-scientists raises exactly the same questions. As a liberal intellectual I must concede that I do not know the answer. The scientific philosophy of knowledge recognizes that there is never any absolute or final disproof of any theory, no matter how low it ranks on the junk heap of discredited miasmas. We will continue to listen and to discuss but we are hardly likely to be persuaded by people who do not look at the facts carefully enough to describe even the last two decades of history accurately.

Notes

1. I have analyzed Harold Lasswell's concerns with the social and moral significance of content analysis in "Content analysis and the intelligence function," in Arnold Rogow, ed., *Politics and personality in social science in the 20th century: Essays in honor of Harold D. Lasswell* (Chicago: University of Chicago Press, 1969). [See also pp. 19–41 in this volume—Ed.]
2. L. D. White, ed. *The future of government in the United States: Essays in honor of Charles E. Merriam* (Chicago: University of Chicago Press, 1942); reprinted in R. D. Lasswell, *The analysis of political behavior* (New York: Oxford University Press, 1947), p. 1, and "The relation of ideological intelligence to public policy," *Ethics*, 53 (1942): 27; reprinted in Lasswell, *Analysis of political behavior*, p. 122.
3. Harold D. Lasswell, ed., *Language of politics* (Cambridge. MA: MIT Press, 1965), p. 51.
4. Of course a logical distinction of this sort is not to be confused with a differentiation in natural language. The meaning of any statement in natural language is a confused mixture of statements of various sorts arising from the multiple denotative meanings of words, their connotations, accent, emphasis, context, and sheer ambiguity. Thus the statement "Americans love apple pie" may be a pure report of facts drawn from a dietetic survey or if said by an American in an affective context it may be a normative expression of identification, or in many cases it may be a little of each in some indeterminate ratio.
5. Many scientists, of course, make sharp distinctions between their thoughtful and critical behavior in the laboratory and their behavior in such other realms as religion and politics. There is no *a priori* reason why a man's values should be maintained consistently across these different realms of life. One cannot exclude either the empirical existence of or the normative validity of such disjointed ways of life. Nonetheless, there is some psychological congruity between liberal values in general and the kind of scientific liberalism involved in being willing to listen to evidence and accept the conclusions on the basis of the evidence. It is therefore, understandable that most scientists

in most societies tend (with many obvious exceptions) to a generally liberal persuasion.

6. The Persuasive Neutralists are supposed to be at the opposite end of some scale from the New Mandarins, yet I as the ostensible representative of the latter, can find nothing in the extensive quotations from Heinz Eulau, the ostensible representative of the former, with which I'm not in 100 Percent agreement.

12

What Ferment?: A Challenge for Empirical Research

What used to be called the conservative critique of empiricism is now often called the radical critique, but it is neither of these—it is simply beside the point.

I wish there were some ferment, but I fail to find it. Fermentation is a productive process; the enzymes produce a feisty brew. Is current communications research in ferment, or is it at a dead end? Is anything new and productive being done, or are we treading water?

My answer is an optimistic one, but more because of what the world is doing to the discipline than because of what is happening within the discipline. That is not abnormal; it is the way the social sciences usually move. Most social research is motivated by social problems or social changes; researchers respond to real-world crisis by coming up with ideas for research. If these turn out to be fruitful, they are mined over and over till the vein begins to run out. Then social changes stimulate a new surge of different research.

The period from the 1930s through the 1960s was a great era in communications research. The exogenous stimulus was the new dominance of the mass media, which had begun with the rotary press and power press about a century earlier. In the first two decades of the twentieth century, some interesting sociological writing had appeared on the phenomenon of journalism, with Simmel, Weber, Lippmann, and others making real contributions.

Then came the dramatic development of nonprint mass media: movies, radio, and television. These led to an unprecedented era in which, to take one example, two-thirds of the population of the United States

First published in *Journal of Communication* (1983).

was exposed for two to four hours a day to the same messages—or at least one out of three or four limited alternatives. There never was such a mass society before and there probably will never be one again.

This social change posed enormous challenges for social research, with the obvious question to explore that of media effects. What impact did this torrent of mass media stimuli have? Paul Lazarsfeld asked what effects radio news had on newspaper reading and what effects media campaigns had on voters and buyers. Psychologists asked what effects the introduction of mass media had on children; political scientists asked what effects they had on traditional societies.

With the marvelous new observational techniques of psychological experimentation and survey research at hand to shed light on these questions, a great deal was learned.

We came to understand notions that are now banalities only because we have been over the ground so often—learning curves and forgetting curves, inconsistency theories of attitude change, persuasibility as a personality factor, the patterns of diffusion of innovation, the interaction between mass media information and personal influence in politics or marketing.

Sometimes the discussion of effects was trivialized in a silly debate about the so-called minimal effects hypothesis. It is true, of course, that social research dramatically debunked lay generalizations about the enormous controlling effects of the new mass media. Hundreds of studies showed that human beings and societies somehow absorbed these stimuli without being overwhelmed by them. But whether the effects of mass media are "big" or "small" is hardly a serious question for social science. The significant research questions concern the kinds of effects that occur under different circumstances and the processes by which these effects take place. Thus, long-term and short-term influences were compared, as was reinforcement and conversion, attitude change and action.

Nonetheless, one of the major problems in that type of research has been that the empirical instruments used were often too crude to note small changes that could be of great significance as they were compounded over time. For example, it might be hard to detect short-term attitude changes in an audience that result from the content of the network evening news; yet, compounded over years, those effects might be profound.

Probably the most important recent progress in communications research has been in the improvement of measurement instruments that make these small changes, in the past lost in the "noise," observable. Some of the rhetoric about the present state of the field portrays this development as a disproof of the minimal effects hypothesis or as a swing toward belief in large effects. It is nothing of the kind. It is, however, genuine progress to be able to analyze and evaluate short-term effects, which can in turn permit much more sophisticated analysis of the cumulative long-term effects. Patterson's reanalysis of what Lazarsfeld, Berelson, and McPhee did in the 1950s on the effects of election campaigns is a case in point.

This work, however, involves no strikingly new ideas or paths of research; we are in a period of marginal improvement and perfection of work that was pioneered a quarter century ago.

So where is the ferment? There is, of course, a large and dull literature that claims to have overthrown empirical behavioral research. It condemns quantification and controlled observation as arid, naive, banal, and even reactionary and immoral. I choose not to digress into a debate about the morality of acquiring knowledge. The important point here is that, if knowledge of the world is a good thing to have, there is no other way of acquiring it except by observing carefully and with well designed controls. Indeed, some of the same people who write tirades about "the old paradigms" or about "positivism" do nothing different in their own work, and they have produced some rather interesting studies, especially on communications industries and on communications in developing countries.

But the scores of methodological and ideological essays about new approaches to the study of communications can hardly be honored by the term "ferment." There is a simple recipe for these essays: avoid measurement, add moral commitment, and throw in some of the following words: social system, capitalism, dependency, positivism, idealism, ideology, autonomy, paradigm, commercialism, consciousness, emancipation, cooptation, critical, instrumental, technocratic, legitimation, praxiology, repressive, dialogue, hegemony, contradiction, problematic. Nothing is particularly new in these critiques of empirical research, though the dictionary of in-words changes with each generation. From the thirties onward, each decade has had essays attacking the aridity of empirical studies and accusing such scientific efforts of failure to take account of the full human and historical context and of not assuming the moral stances that are so vital to the communications professions. What used to be called a conservative critique of empiricism is now often called a radical critique of empiricism. The critique is neither conservative nor radical; it is simply beside the point. Yet I agree with such critics that empirical research at the present moment is not very exciting, though I disagree in that I feel that it was quite exciting in the past. What of the future? If there is to be a new wave of exciting research on communications, it is likely to be on new questions made salient by drastic changes in the communications situation. While we can expect to make some marginal progress in understanding the effects of the mass media, I see no reason to anticipate a major breakthrough in this area. But new technologies raise different questions than do the mass media. For example, because mass media are one-way, controlled by a small population of producers and consumed in the same form by millions of people, we are naturally curious about the "effects" of such heavy stimuli.

But this is not the salient question to ask about an information retrieval system. If people have access to an enormous range of information and are able to choose what they want out of it, they may have all sorts of problems in skill and motivation in finding just what they want, but no one is telling them what ought to be heard or seen. This situation makes the user more interesting than the effects of the messages on that user. We are likely to see interesting research being done on people's motivation to seek knowledge, on their styles of search, on their gains of knowledge, and on their creativity in learning, as well as on how they interact with one other when each retrieves different information.

An information retrieval system is not the sole format of communications for the coming age, any more than the mass media are the sole formats of communications today, but it is the prototype of what is becoming increasingly important. The chief characteristic of the new electronic media is that they provide diverse material on demand to individuals. Whether it is a Xerox copier, one channel on a hundred-channel cable system, a videodisc or cassette player, or a microcomputer, each of the new media allows a more active control by a consumer who chooses to exercise it. The new media also allow for fragmentation of the mass audience and even for quite individualized communications.

I am not asserting that these things will happen in any radical way. Exactly what *will* happen is, in fact, the research question. When blue-sky futurists foresaw people being manipulated by the mass media's power, social scientists urged caution. Now, with highly individualized and user-controlled media, blue-sky futurists are forecasting that what has become technically possible will actually happen. The social scientist again must note that the questions are more complicated than that. How will people actually behave when the available media permit highly individualistic interactive use? Who will use them that way, and who will passively demand to be guided? Who will work alone, and who will create group processes for reinforcement? Will people use the new media to their full potential, reject them, use them less than optimally, ask for social regulation? And how will the media themselves be institutionalized and modified to meet what is socially demanded rather than what they are technically capable of?

These questions may lead us to other, fascinating questions about cognitive processes and group formation. But they will be different questions than those that had priority in the now-waning era of the mass media.

13

How Powerful Is Business?

Charles Lindblom's thesis of the power of business in democratic societies is a familiar one: business exercises excessive power. I shall not argue for or against the point; I am not sure that I know whether business influence is too great, too small, or just about right. What I wish to evaluate is the logic of the argument.

First of all, Lindblom confuses business—namely, the for-profit sector that encompasses the large majority of the American workers—with a small group of top executives in large corporations. Sometimes he talks about one and sometimes the other, traveling between the two conceptions with marvelous ease.

Business, he asserts, exercises an influence quite different from that of other interest groups. It has far more influence than labor, or the intelligentsia, or the press, he says. But since we do not know which of his two conceptions of "business" he is using here, it is hard to judge whether the claim is true.

Lindblom argues that business exercises its power not only through economic blackmail and political shenanigans but also by somehow capturing the minds of the rest of us. Some sort of "false consciousness" (though he distinguishes his view in some details from Marx's use of that term) leads us to refrain from challenging the basic business viewpoint.

There is nothing remarkable in the argument as I have sketched it. It has appeared in thousands of tracts and articles over the past century and a half. It is the ABC of the radical critique of capitalist society. What distinguishes Lindblom's statement from 99 percent of the rest is not the case or its accuracy but the sophistication with which he makes it.

Lindblom starts by flagging a fact that might be embarrassing to his case, namely, that "liberal democracy has arisen only in nations

---

From *Does Big Business Rule America?* (1981).

that are market-oriented" (*Politics and Markets,* p. 5). He sets up four categories of societies:

1. market-oriented and "polyarchic" (his word for democratic);
2. market-oriented and authoritarian;
3. centrally planned and polyarchic;
4. centrally planned and authoritarian.

Category 3 is empty of examples; there are no polyarchies in countries without a market economy.

Having proceeded in proper rhetorical fashion to present the strongest argument against his case, Lindblom now tells us we should not fear that if we move away from a market orientation, democracy (or polyarchy) will be undermined. There is, he says, "no compelling reason for the two to be tied together." How does he support that? One might expect that, having shown a strong historical correlation, he would have to go on to show that the correlation was a historical accident. If there is a strong indication that centrally planned economies erode the very basis of democratic decision making, then we should demand strong evidence that the causal relation was an illusion before we consider experimenting with central planning.

But instead of evidence Lindblom offers a brief semantic comment. He explains that the facts to which the term "polyarchy" refers are different from the facts to which "market-oriented" refers; one refers to the economy, the other to the polity. Since the two definitions pertain to different spheres, we need not fear that we can't have one without the other.

A less compelling argument is hard to imagine. We can certainly agree that a term referring to the economy and a term referring to the polity cannot be synonymous. But Lindblom has conceded that there is an empirical relationship between these two things—that is, a relationship not in the realm of logic but in history. He does nothing to help us understand why we should not assume this relationship to be one of cause and effect.

If it were true that political controls over market allocations brought no unintended consequences, this would be a happy world. The market, as Lindblom among others has helped us to understand, is just one way of making economic decisions, and it has both advantages and disadvantages. Indeed, the whole political process in market-oriented democracies is devoted to correcting unacceptable results of the working of the market. Majority rule is a legitimate means for imposing public control on undesirable market outcomes. But to impose controls on the market has bad as well as good consequences, loss of some freedom being among the bad ones.

Public control, Lindblom notes, has rarely been considered a supreme end in its own right. The most desirable arrangement is that each person be able to do as he wishes. Only in situations where that creates difficulties for others is there reason for the majority to impose its preferences on the minority.

Are Collective Problems Growing?

Lindblom understands that historically democracy has been viewed not as an end in itself but as a means to liberty, and he offers us little reason to retreat from that view. At one point he mentions a series of great public issues that obviously call for collective decision, such as environmental degradation and the avoidance of atomic holocaust. But, although he asserts that we are in a new era in which collective problems are of growing weight relative to the ones that can best be handled by individual decisions, he offers no evidence on this point.

A number of factors operating in the contemporary world favor a withering away of central decision making. One is the increasing affluence in industrial societies. More and more people have some accumulated resources. To have money in the bank is a prime condition for individual independence. Slavery, feudalism, sharecropping, and various other forms of personal dependence reflected the historical fact that in most societies most people could not live even a few weeks on their own accumulated resources.

Another factor favoring pluralistic decision making is international geographic mobility. Single nations may have socialistic tendencies within them, leading to growing government controls, but increasingly business operates on a global basis, locating activities wherever conditions are most favorable.

A more important factor favoring individual decision making is the technology of electronics. The use of computers and other modern electronic systems permits the individualization of what were formerly mass activities.

Whether Marx was right in expecting postindustrial developments to lead to the withering away of the state, or whether Lindblom is right in expecting more collectivism, is an open question. Lindblom does not attempt to prove his claim. On this as on so many other points he proceeds by dicta, not data.

For Lindblom (as also for socialists over the past 150 years) the most decisive reason for turning over more economic decisions to the political authorities is dissatisfaction with the way businessmen are making those decisions. Whether the language chosen is Marx's phrase "capitalist exploitation" or such terms as "200 families" and "robber barons" or Lindblom's more scholarly words about the "extraordinarily disproportionate influence" of a "dominating minority," the argument is the same. Businessmen are portrayed as the dominant elite of our society.

In some respects, of course, the portrayal is true. The great majority of our labor force is in the for-profit sector, and the greatest part of our GNP is produced by that sector. Since for-profit business enterprise is the most prevalent activity, persons who rise to the top decision-making positions in that sector do play a very important role in our society. Collectively, they provide the leadership in society's major activity.

It is also true that these business leaders are not democratically chosen. For better or for worse, our society has chosen to rely more on corrective processes of competition and on a pluralism of self-constituted groups than on representative election, except in the government. A good case can be made for the introduction of democratic processes at various places in business. Experiments with worker participation in some areas of decision making are an example. But the basic principle of letting private entrepreneurs make their own decisions, corrected and chastened by the marketplace, is certainly a sound one for much activity. The case for representative government in that one organization to which willy-nilly we all belong, the state, does not hold for Mom and Pop's grocery store, or for Edwin Land's Polaroid Corporation, or even for General Motors. If we do not like what General Motors does we can deal with Ford, or even with Saab.

The "Grand Issues"

Lindblom recognizes that businessmen do not agree about everything. However, there are, he says, certain "grand issues" on which "business tends to speak with one voice." Business influence over the media and over government keeps these "grand issues" from coming under public discussion; the issues are kept out of political debate.

One can readily agree with Lindblom that the market-oriented democracy has some largely unchallenged consensual views. As he says, "a set of unifying beliefs that assert the virtues of the fundamentals of social organization will be found in any stable society" (p. 230). But when Lindblom starts to list these fundamental and unchallenged assumptions, one is aghast. Issues that he says are kept out of the political debate in the market-oriented democracies of North America and Western Europe include: the privileged position of business, the association of private enterprise with political democracy, preservation of the status quo in income distribution, close consultation between business and government, and the restriction of union demands to those consistent with business profitability.

Now really! I wish Lindblom would name the country he is talking about, the one in which the privileged position of business is excluded from political debate; where no politician wins votes by proposing to soak the rich; where there are no labor or socialist parties; where books like Lindblom's *Politics and Markets* are never published; where hardly any young intellectuals read and discuss the works of Marx; where there is no consumer movement; where there are no magazines that can be described as belonging to the left; where the left is not critical of business. What is the country in which income distribution is not a political issue; in which there is no debate in the parliament about such matters as income taxes and capital-gains taxes; in which social security payments are not a significant expenditure or a widely discussed political matter? If it is the United States that Lindblom has in mind when he says that close consultation between business and government is kept from becoming a political issue, one wonders how he would explain the press attention given to such news items as Bert Lance's bank loans or the campaign contributions to CREEP (the Nixon reelection committee). And would he say that Senate committees dealing with confirmation show little interest in the investment portfolios of rich appointees to public office?

It is perfectly plain that the central issues of politics in Western democracies are precisely those of the distribution of property and wealth. The dividing line in most countries is between a socialist party that defines its fundamental goal as the socialization of the means of production and a capitalist party. Although there is no significant socialist party in the United States, the fundamental political issues have nonetheless been the power of business and the distribution of wealth. Far from being excluded from politics, these issues are at its heart.

True, the socialists have not succeeded in displacing the market-based system in any democracy, even those in which they have held office. Perhaps their programs are so impracticable that people see through them, or perhaps when their programs are tried they turn out to be catastrophic failures. But Lindblom's case is not that somehow business has won its battle to stay alive as the major sector in the economy; his argument is that it has not even had a battle to fight because it has captured men's minds. That is clearly absurd. Orthodox Marxists who talk about class struggle (while also indulging in myths of sorts) are far closer to the truth than is Lindblom's fantasy of a society in which business is so strong that it is not even politically embattled.

There are, of course, in market-oriented democracies, some values that are truly consensual and are removed from political debate. Among the values upon which consensus smiles are the family, the nationstate, peace as a fundamental goal, individual integrity, individual property, work, and comfortable living standards. On each of these there is occasional dissent, but it is of no lasting political consequence. No one would argue that these items of political consensus constitute mere "business ideology." Indeed, the very reason that they are items of consensus is that they cut across the beliefs of all major sectors of the population.

Why Government Protects Business

What remains, then, of Lindblom's thesis that business is not just one interest group among others, like labor, the intelligentsia, or the press? Something does. Business, if by that we mean the for-profit sector, is by far the largest sphere of activity in the society, employing most people, generating most of the GNP. It is certainly true, as Lindblom tells us, that government officials are usually protective of business activity—as they are of the activity of smaller sectors such as nonprofit institutions and the press. Any responsible government wants the major institutions of its society to work well. Government leaders are happy when businessmen invest, when new jobs are created, and when trade expands, and they regard it as a legitimate aim of policy to promote such developments. They are receptive to suggestions from business about means to achieve such goals, though they may be highly suspicious of possible personal motives as they listen to individual businessmen.

To the extent that government desires to see the major sector of the economy progress, it is, as Lindblom emphasizes, protective of and beholden to business. It is not free to act with irresponsible disregard for the interests of business.

But from that obvious point Lindblom jumps to some extraordinary statements about government and "businessmen." Businessmen, he maintains, are, apart from government officeholders, the most powerful persons in our society. They have a special relationship with public officials; they control vast amounts of money; they dominate the media and other institutions. Presumably by "businessmen" Lindblom means the top officials of the Fortune 500 corporations—vice presidents and above—plus a certain number of very wealthy investors. Clearly the picture he is drawing does not include the rental agent of an apartment house, or the owner of the local laundry, or a traveling salesman, though all these persons would call themselves businessmen.

In fact, of course, there is a distribution of power in every sector. It makes no sense to compare the power of the president of the Chase Manhattan Bank with that of a college professor or an unpublished poet; yet that is the way the argument is often made. If we look at comparable levels in various professional areas, the differences are not very great. James Reston, at the power peak of journalism, is probably a more powerful man than the head of the Chase Bank. The president of Harvard is certainly in the league. Charles Lindblom, an eminently successful professor, is not in the same league of power, but he is certainly more influential in American life than any but a couple of thousand top businessmen; few businessmen can blow as frightening a trumpet as he can. And the same is true for the top few hundred Washington or foreign correspondents, columnists, and editors.

The Special Interests of Businessmen

In Lindblom's vocabulary, then, "businessmen" means the top executives of corporations and major money managers. These persons, like any other distinguishable set, have certain special interests that include, but are not identical with, the general health of the institutions that they head. They are in that respect no different from any other employees. Like union members they want "more" for themselves, while at the same time they have an interest in seeing their firms succeed. The personal concerns of top corporation executives are focused on such matters as taxes, SEC rules, bonuses, and pensions. Bankers and investors have slightly different special interests, though all of them share a general concern for business growth, or what is generally called prosperity.

The special situation of corporate executives in the United States and how it differs from that of capitalists in the classic sense deserves a lot more attention than it gets from Lindblom's broad brush. Corporate executives in the United States today are highly paid but insecure employees. They can get rich by the standards of a college professor or government official, but not by the standards of those with great fortunes. People with AT&T, by most measures the largest corporation in the country, are fond of pointing out that no one in the company ever made a fortune. The corporation is essentially a bureaucracy, with high salaries at the top but no opportunity to make what a successful—smart and lucky—buccaneer on the stock or commodities market can make.

The reader may be tempted to object that AT&T is a special case because it is a regulated industry; but the fact that the government does regulate that and other businesses serves as further evidence that the government is not a servant of business.

The people who have influence are the ones who can come in and say, "I speak for 50,000 jobs." They may be corporate executives, or bankers, or hired managers of investment funds, such as pension funds. They may be union leaders. When they speak for their own self-interest, their credibility and influence is small. Often they speak for themselves under the guise of speaking for the sector of the economy that they represent, as when they ask for less discouraging tax rates at the higher levels on the grounds of stimulating investment. But their greatest influence comes when they really speak for workers in their sector, with no self-interest except the general interest that any leader has in the success of his institution.

In this respect businessmen do not differ from union leaders, educators, and people from the mass media. But Lindblom fails to see that. He talks about the power and influence of business and translates that into the power and influence of businessmen in serving their self-interest. Then he talks about unions, but he never translates the power of unions into the power of union leaders in serving their self-interest; he somehow equates their power with the interests of the workers. He talks about the media and the intellectuals as though they are somehow elevated in their concerns in a way different from businessmen. Few congressmen would agree that either the educational establishment or the media fight any less fiercely for their interests than do businessmen. Those of us who argue for the national importance of spending more on research differ not at all from a businessman arguing for more favorable treatment of his industry. Both are serving a mixture of legitimate special and general interests.

Lindblom compiles a long list of supposedly unique features of the political influence of business, but the only one in which business really differs from the rest is one that Lindblom does not mention: its aggregate percentage of our economy. He claims that business is the only interest group that finances its political activities with other people's money, that is, out of the treasuries of business. But who finances the trips of academics to Washington to sit on panels about national research needs? Who financed journalists who exposed the Nixon administration's attacks on the networks? Every organized institution uses its treasury to promote policies that are in its interest, and in a free society it should not be otherwise.

Initiator or Saboteur?

Lindblom comes up with another revelation, that all government regulation of business is a sham. But he tries to have it both ways. First he describes how business resists new regulatory legislation, uses back-room influence in both executive and legislative branches to weaken it, and sabotages it to some extent when it is enacted. No doubt there are examples of all such activities; to some extent that is what is known as politics. But if affected businesses fight regulation so savagely, then how are we to believe Lindblom's other argument, that regulation is really initiated by business to achieve special privileges, and only camouflaged as action in defense of the people? "A new group of historians," Lindblom tells us, "believe they are finding evidence of a common pattern. Policy is changed in response to business controls and is then paraded as democratic reform." He cites revisionist historians on food and drug legislation, municipal reform, and banking reform, and then says: "To none of these reforms was popular demand an important contributor" (p. 191).

Once more, there is a germ of truth to these discoveries. The old naive view was that business was a unified devil that brave reformers subjected to regulation in the public interest, though sometimes, admittedly, business later recaptured the regulatory agency and reversed its true purpose. But the reality was always more complex. When there were abuses that significant elements of the public wanted regulated, some of the more "responsible" elements of business saw that it would be in their interest to have these abuses controlled. Indeed, they sometimes even saw ways to gain monopoly advantages out of the regulation. So the real fight was not the people against business but some public interests aligned with some business interests against other public and business interests. Now the new naive view comes along: it is really business that is pulling all the strings; reformist movements have played no role in "reform."

Two decades ago I collaborated on a study of business activities in regard to foreign trade legislation (Raymond A. Bauer, Ithiel de

Sola Pool, and Lewis A. Dexter, *American Business and Public Policy*, Chicago: Aldine, Atherton, 1963). I began with no particular presuppositions about how business operated in politics, except for an assumption that businessmen would fight hard in politics for their particular economic interests.

With research came some surprising discoveries. In the first place, businessmen's economic interests were rarely clear to them: even when expectations could be clearly defined there were many different ways in which they could use their money and resources. Second, being specialists in the private sector, businessmen were often extremely maladroit and uncomfortable in the unfamiliar world of the public sector. Third, in the interaction between businessmen and politicians, politicians mobilized businessmen to serve the politicians' interests as often as businessmen mobilized politicians to serve business interests. Fourth, conflicts of interest within business often served to preclude action by major business interests, while quite minor business interests might prove effective if not checked by such conflicts. (Lindblom cites this book only to document the point that legislators use research provided by businesses and trade associations. He makes no mention of the main points we were making—that business interests moderate their stands to win this sort of acceptance from politicians, and that the result is two-way influence.)

In the end, the conclusion has to be that the process of politics is a complex set of two-way influences, with constantly shifting alliances. No one wins all and no one loses all. The attempt to reduce this to a simple theory of hidden monolithic control is bound to be wrong.

And it is not only wrong but also dangerous. Lindblom uses this theory for an attack on the corporation. Clearly there can be many arguments about the rights and wrongs of current corporate structure or legal status. But the premise from which we need to start in a free society is that of freedom of association. If a group of persons wish to pool their resources to engage in an enterprise, society should encourage, not discourage, them. It should certainly not subject them to more control than necessary.

Lindblom's attack on the corporation is an attack not on particular abuses that may occur from time to time but on the basic idea of freedom of association in a free society.

14

Human Subjects Regulations on the Social Sciences

Quietly, without a great deal of fanfare in the media, certainly without much awareness by the general public, the universities in the last years have survived an onslaught fully as dangerous as McCarthyism in the 1950s. Indeed, one could argue that in this century, no attack on academic freedom has threatened its destruction as much as the proposed, but now defunct, IRB regulations of August 14, 1979. On that date the then Department of Health, Education and Welfare published a set of regulations in the Federal Register, under which all of the following things would have been true.

A scholar, like Charles A. Beard, exploring eighteenth-century records to examine the economic interests of the founding fathers would have had to first get permission from an Institutional Review Board (IRB), since his research might have harmed identifiable individuals. (The regulations did not exclude dead human subjects from protection.)

A visiting scholar on sabbatical, using a university library to study Watergate would have had to ask permission of the local IRB. The regulations covered not only research sponsored by the university, but also all research at the university.

A student writing a paper, would have had to get permission before interviewing a candidate for political office.

None of this was intended, of course.

So it was inevitable that the Department of Health and Human Services (HHS) would modify the regulations somewhat before issuing them, but restrictions close to those ludicrous ones were fully intended.

A social scientist informally interviewing a Soviet dissident would first have to ask him to give explicit informed consent—in disregard of

First published in *Annals of the New York Academy of Sciences* (1983).

the consequences that would have followed if the Soviet secret police got their hands on such evidence that it was not just a conversation.

A sociologist before observing a demonstration on the street would have to satisfy an IRB that any potential harm that his observations might do to those he observed was justified by the value of his research. If he were a journalist or an ordinary citizen it would have been his right to watch—but not if he were a university scholar doing social research.

On January 22, 1981, a new revised set of regulations was finally issued by HHS, which drew back from almost all of those positions. For one thing, the new regulations apply substantially only to research funded by HHS itself. Even if some of the procedures remain a bit silly, they are simply part of HHS's procedures in deciding how to spend its own (rapidly declining) funds. A scholar without HHS funding can look at the founding fathers, Watergate, or whatever he wishes without IRB permission.

For another thing, a variety of particularly harmless kinds of research, such as most library research and most interviewing, have been exempted from review.

Also, a particularly obnoxious clause that required IRBs to review not only the potential harm to subjects which a researcher might do, but also to evaluate his research methods, has been struck.

In short, the protests of the social science community, the representations of its professional associations, and the advice of lawyers and Congressmen have been heard, and HHS yielded. A victory has been won; so perhaps this is now all history. True, but not quite! There remain a couple of aftershocks that need to be dealt with.

Other departments are now drafting their rules, and some of the same issues rise over and over. The Department of Energy, for example, published proposed rules containing the intolerable clause requiring IRBs to pass on research methods.

More important, there is a major job to be done of educating universities themselves about the proper functions of IRBs. The HHS regulations not only require IRB review of any research that it funds, but also a "general assurance" from the university that any research it conducts, however funded, will be done with proper regard for the rights of human subjects. The university must describe to HHS how it will protect them. A harried administrator, aware that there is an IRB procedure that is used with HHS-funded research is likely to respond, with a letter saying "we will do the same thing with the rest of our research." Then, voluntarily, social research will be back in the same mess all over again. Although HHS has the right to enforce these rules for research that it funds, they are neither appropriate nor intelligent for all research.

The reasons why these rules are improper will, I hope, be made apparent in this presentation, but for the moment let me simply say that the American Council of Education drafted appropriate language that universities can use in their general assurances. They should beware of the temptation to make of HHS's procedures their own voluntary prison.

While some problems thus remain, in general social researchers have won, so I cannot do the easy thing of giving you an agitational speech, calling on you to man the ramparts. Something more thoughtful, more analytic is called for.

Perhaps we should ask: What is there that we have learned from this experience? How could it all have happened? How could it be that in free universities in a free society we came so close to a major debacle, with little awareness of what was going on, and with relative quiescence by students and faculties alike? We can see in these events a pattern that is quite characteristic in the expanding organizations of our ever more institution-ridden and bureaucratized society. It is a pattern of intellectual failure of a new and enlarged populace of decision makers to appreciate the credenda earlier held sacrosanct by a guild whose members had absorbed those canons during their professional training, and had assimilated them into their cadre identity. When institutions pass from being such sectarian enclaves of an idiosyncratic culture to being encompassed into more comprehensive social decision processes, important special perspectives can get lost. That can happen to a newspaper or magazine bought by a conglomerate. It can happen to a university brought under the influence of politics.

Two great principles were at stake in the debate over IRBs. These were (1) anathema to prior restraint and (2) the nature of the university.

Prior Restraint

The doctrine of "prior restraint" is a legal concept. To constitutional lawyers it is fundamental. The constitution in Article I and the First Amendment draws lines among a set of domains in which Congress is free to act and domains in which it is without authority. One domain, called speech, is explicitly denied as a subject for regulation. But what does this denial mean? It has long been established that the denial is not absolute. We have libel laws. We prohibit fraud in advertising.

Somewhere lines are drawn in the gray area where speech shades over into action. Is picketing speech? Is parading speech? Is spending money on campaigns speech? These are the kinds of lines that Courts have to draw.

The first line that came to be drawn was a procedural one—the ban on prior restraint. A person can break the law by saying things; if he does so he can be sued in Court. But, so said the lawyers in the dawn of our country, what the First Amendment prohibited Congress from doing was setting up censorship, requiring a person first to submit what he proposed to say, so that its legality may be reviewed.

In the domain of speech, the state must suffer the disadvantage (so our forefathers concluded), of waiting till unrestrained speech was expressed, and then, but only then, if the outcome was illegal, to bring the speaker into Court.

That was a consensus among Constitutional lawyers. Indeed in the nineteenth century, conservative jurists who wished to limit the First Amendment argued that it was nothing but a ban on prior restraint. Congress, these conservatives argued, could prohibit various kinds of evil statements, but the one thing they conceded it could not do was to set up a review before publication.

Justice Parker in *Commonwealth v. Blanding* (3 Pick 304, 15 Am. Dec. 214) asserted the whole meaning of the First Amendment to be "to prevent all such previous restraints upon publication."

Today in the twentieth century (since the days of Holmes and Brandeis, Douglas and Black), we have defined First Amendment rights much more broadly, but the principle of no prior restraint remains at the heart of the bundle.

True, the prohibition on prior restraint has never been absolute. Some, but not all lawyers have argued that there could be dangers so overwhelming as to justify the setting up of prior review and the licensing of speech in some domains. The First Amendment absolutists do not agree, but others argue that freedom of speech is just one consideration to be balanced with others. That is an issue among constitutional lawyers. So be it.

But what are the kinds of cases asserted to be so horrendous as to be exceptions? The most important case in which the courts have had to grapple with the problem, and in which in the end they came down on allowing publication, was the Wisconsin *Progressive* case, brought about when that magazine proposed to publish information on how to build an H-bomb.

That is an issue on which reasonable men could perhaps disagree. I am ready to listen to an argument that the dangers of that publication were sufficient to justify some quite exceptional measures. I do not know if that is true, but it is at least arguable. To worry about the diffusion of thermonuclear knowledge is not absurd.

But to put the harms done by a sociologist asking questions into the same exceptional category is absurd. There is no denying that we can all do harm by the questions we ask and the things we say. We can offend, we can embarrass, we can annoy. But these are precisely the harms that 200 years ago the framers of the Constitution decided had better be suffered rather than controlled. To require prior approval before a social researcher engages in an interview is as patently unconstitutional as it would be to require it of a reporter or of any ordinary citizen. To any student of constitutional history that is clear.

How remote those ideas of constitutional lawyers are from those of other intelligent people who do not share the guild acculturation of the legal profession first came to my attention some years ago when I served on a committee at MIT to review the procedures used by our IRB. It was my first exposure to the problems. When I learned about the practice of reviewing informal interviewing and library research by the IRB it was obvious that that was prior restraint on speech and quite unacceptable under United States law. The issue seemed to me obvious on the face of it. I wrote up a short memorandum and explained the issue to the committee, assuming that there would be no disagreement. How wrong I was!

Some of my colleagues—including behavioral scientists—were utterly puzzled by the whole argument, as was the chairman of the IRB. How could the IRB learn about the risky projects if they received no form describing the projects to be done. Granted, they would approve the non-risky projects quickly and without fuss, still, they asked: how could they do their job if no project descriptions were submitted to them.

The idea that some ancient lawyers and philosophers had concluded that in certain fields the burden of ascertainment had to be put on the enforcer seemed absurd to them. Making enforcement hard by saying one had to wait to discover a violation that had already occurred, rather than clearing up the matter by consulting in advance seemed to them to be doctrinaire foolishness.

We came out with a good majority report, but certainly no consensual understanding of the philosophy of the historical battle against censorship. There was no shared understanding of the notion that speech and action should be controlled by different standards; that the ethical norms of the medical profession might be different from the ethical norms of social investigation; that all harms are not the same; and that the harms imposed by verbal conflict are the price of a free society. The notion familiar to lawyers, economists, and social scientists that adversary combat is socially desirable and the injuries suffered in the process socially useful, was puzzling.

What was familiar to them were the canons of a different guild—the biomedical one. That is where the whole system of human subjects review began. It started with a 1963 incident in which Sloan-Kettering researchers injected live cancer cells into patients for an experiment. This led the United States Public Health Service to seek ways to protect itself from scandalous behavior by its grantees. When it made grants, the Public Health Service required the recipient institutions to set up review boards to check that subjects in the experiments it was supporting not be subjected to untoward risks.

Then in the late 1960s and early 1970s application of the procedures was extended from Public Health Service grants and contracts to grants and contracts by any part of the Department of Health, Education, and Welfare.

By that time, "harm" to human subjects had been construed to mean not only physical harm but "psychological" and "social" harm as well. Possible breaches of confidentiality were increasingly treated as justifying Institutional Review Board control, as much as did risks of bodily harm.

After 1974 the rules were broadened in still another way. HEW's obligation to protect human subjects was interpreted us requiring the Department to withhold grants from institutions that mistreated human subjects, whether or not the abuse took place in research the HEW was supporting. Thus, as in affirmative action cases, HEW-aided institutions were told that they had to apply IRB procedures to all research on human subjects, not just to research done under HEW grants.

By 1974 there was enough confusion as to just what the scope of the regulations was, or what it should be, that Congress mandated the establishment of a National Commission for the Protection of Human Subjects of Biomedical and Behavioral Research.

The Secretary appointed to the Commission three M.D.s, three lawyers, a physiological psychologist, a behavioral biologist in a medical school, a professor of bio-ethics at a medical school, and a professor of Christian ethics. No social scientists were included, a clue perhaps to what the Secretary assumed was the Commission's field of action. But the Commission saw its task in grander terms. Unrestrained by humility or wisdom, the Commission chose not to limit itself to protecting subjects from the medical risks with which the whole discussion began, but instead set out to assure the "ethical" conduct of research. Furthermore, it seemed obvious to the Commission that there should be no double standard. The ethical principles that applied to HEW-sponsored research should be applied to all research using human subjects. The Commission also concluded that harm was not just a medical matter; researchers could also do psychological and social harm to their subjects. Accordingly IRBs should not be limited to biomedical or experimental research but should also review social research. The Commission showed no awareness of the fact that the risks involved in social research are fundamentally different from those in biomedical research.

The most frequent risk to subjects of social research is that information about them which they would rather keep secret may become known to others. A risk of bodily harm is something quite different. Biomedical research often places the subjects at risk of physical harm, and possibly even death. Social science research causes harm to subjects by breach of confidentiality, embarrassment or exposure. To treat embarrassment by breach of confidentiality by the same set of regulations as are designed to control physical harm can lead only to absurdities and chaos. Breach of confidentiality can, of course, under some circumstances be an actionable matter. That occurs when there is an explicit (or sometimes implicit) contractual obligation of a person not to reveal what has been told him. Proprietary information is often given under pledge of secrecy. Pollers typically assure their respondents that their answers will be kept confidential; violation of such a promise could create a legal claim.

That is an ethical concern, and social science professions take it very seriously. They recognize an obligation to their informants to protect their confidences. But for the rest their relation to their subjects is not one of protection. It may indeed be the opposite.

In medicine or in clinical psychology the subject of research is often also a client. In these helping professions, though the potential harm done can be great, the researching professional may also be the subject's helper. The researcher may have a therapeutic obligation to his client.

It is not so in journalism or in the social sciences. Their clients if they have any, are the public whom they inform, not the persons on whom they collect information. The HEW proposed regulations, however, tried to treat them all as though their ethical professional obligation was like that of a physician whose primary obligation is to do good to his patients. But the ethics of some of the social sciences, like journalism, may require practitioners to strip the concealing shroud from people whose behavior needs to be exposed for the good of others. Social scientists, like journalists, are engaged in what Sullivan has called "uninhibited, robust and wide open debate." Historians, political scientists, economists, and many sociologists are in that role. Their professional ethics are in no way inferior to that of the service professions; they are simply different.

Probably the majority of all social research examines situations in which people's behavior deviates from desired norms. As such it generally puts the persons studied at some risk of embarrassment and exposure. Whether the persons studied are brutal dictators, or corrupt politicians, insensitive employers or featherbedding workers, low achievement students or television viewers, whatever they may be they are people involved in some social problem, and so by definition not conforming to society's preferred ideals. Social science could not exist if that kind of critique had to be defended at all times before committees whose main assignment was to take the side of the persons being studied.

It was to protect this practice of investigation, exposure, and criticism—what the Supreme Court in the Sullivan case called robust, wide open debate—that censorship or prior restraint was prohibited in the domain of speech. Those who work in that style cannot live with a system of regulation designed for helping professions operating in areas of high risk.

The Nature of the University

If constitutional doctrines about prior restraint were puzzling to those who did not come out of that tradition, the concept of the university has been even harder for modern bureaucrats to appreciate.

There is an anecdote, and I believe a true one, from the time when General Dwight D. Eisenhower became president of Columbia University. At this first meeting with the faculty the new president told them about various plans to do good things for the "employees" of the university. At the end the Nobel Prizewinning physicist, I.I. Rabi, rose and said: “Mr. President there is just one point: we are not the employees of the university, we are the university.”

A university is not a bureaucratic structure of bosses and employees, but rather a loose confederation of independent scholars, each of whom decides for himself what he will study and how. The United States Supreme Court has reaffirmed that point in a different context; faculty members, the Court held, are not employees who must be bargained with collectively; they are autonomous decision makers.

If faculty members are not employees subject to university control of their research, *a fortiori* students are not. They pay to be members of the university; they are not paid by it. They may be members of the university with the right to do research in it, but they are not controlled by it.

The concept of the university as a loose collectivity of independent scholars is an ancient one—a thousand years old. The university antedates the modern forms of bureaucratic organizations that emerged first in government in the nineteenth century and more recently in private corporations.

This new bureaucratic structure is so characteristic in our society that those who do not come from the university find it hard to understand that it is a very different kind of organization, and one that cannot direct its members.

Max Weber has given us the classic description of a bureaucracy, converting some Marxist concepts to the realm of information. The bureaucrat, like the proletarian, comes to work in an institution that he does not own, and where he owns none of the files, papers, or other means of operation. There he is part of a hierarchy of command, carrying out policies set at a higher level, and instructing those below him.

As Weber stressed, a bureaucracy can be a marvelously effective organization. It can have enormous power. But it is the power of the organization, not the power of the individual.

Compared to the notable in the public sector, or the entrepreneur in the private sector, whom the bureaucrat has replaced, this new man in the gray flannel suit, is a far weaker, less autonomous character. The power of the bureaucracy is in gearing men, whom individually it reduces, into a powerful collectivity.

A university is a more feudal and more entrepreneurial type of organization that preserves the ego and the autonomy of its individual members far more. As in the case of the First Amendment issues that we discussed above, the condition for that privilege which scholars enjoy is that, unlike bureaucrats in large organizations, they have very few resources of power besides their words. They do not control much by way of money or cadres. So they can be allowed to continue to enjoy far more autonomy than an employee.

That is the essence of a university: it is a collection of autonomous, independent scholars, deciding for themselves what they will do, and exercising an uncontrolled creativity. Our bureaucratic society needs that kind of organization, so out of keeping with its normal operation.

The human subjects regulations are not designed for that kind of organization. They are predicated on the assumption that the university as an institution has responsibility for what goes on in its premises. They presume that the university can instruct its students and faculty what research they may or may not do!

Those who favor such regulations have a point that they sometimes make. The university they say has changed. The university that I have been describing is already, they say, long since dead. Today they say, the university is a collection of bureaucratic teams, conducting funded research on contracts and grants, with principal investigators directing their staffs.

Yes, it is true that universities have absorbed much of this bureaucratic productive type activities. Medical schools are, above all, the place where this change has gone the furthest. They run hospitals, feed and care for patients, have hundreds of nonacademic employees, and have a classic bureaucratic hierarchy. There is much of it elsewhere in universities too.

I am not against such collective group research. It is what I do myself. For thirty years now I have always had in my title director or assistant director of some research program or other. Social scientists too engage in big science that takes teams to carry out.

But it we accept the notion that that is all that is left in universities, then the university is indeed dead. Its creativity, its intellectual contribution requires the careful nurturing within it of that sector that preserves a turf for the uncontrolled individual scholar.

Granted, sponsored research puts a responsibility on the institution and its central administration for accounting for the money received, and for fulfillment of the terms of the contract. But side by side with that activity, in any university worthy of the name, there resides still the ancient university which cannot even know what its members are doing with their time, much less controlling it. If the HEW-proposed regulations had ever been implemented, that would have been the end of the university as it has been for a thousand years.

I am not asserting that the human subjects regulations if they had been enacted would have been enforced very repressively. I do not believe so. They would have completed the process of bureaucratizing controls over virtually all university research. That is not the same thing as saying the bureaucratic controls would have been harsh.

Among social scientists, voices of moderation have suggested that a system of IRB censorship would not hurt because in the end they themselves would have run it. That is true. Just that has happened to a large extent in biomedical research. IRBs, when surveyed by the National Commission for the Protection of Human Subjects of Biomedical and Behavioral Research, were found more often to be deficient in favoring their medical constituency, rather than deficient in being too restrictive on them.

The same would surely happen in the social sciences. Senior establishment social scientists working the main stream would have had no trouble at all getting their activities approved. That would allow them to see the whole thing as no more than an administrative formality. The regulated would have captured the regulatory mechanism.

Yet "capture" is only a partial description of what happens in such circumstances. Graduate students and assistant professors, dissidents, and investigators of genuinely upsetting social issues would be the ones to find themselves censored. A simple capture theory neglects the fact that it is only a core elite group within an industry or profession that consummates the capture. The variety and diversity of tendencies that characterizes an unregulated profession gives way to discipline by a conformist center.

That is how a bureaucratic organization functions. It controls its members to assure effective implementation of the policies set at the top. That is not the way a university functions.

Let me close by asking what lessons we can draw.

The first lesson is a very practical one. I would urge on those of you who are in universities to make sure that when your institution submits its "general assurance" it does not promise to subject all research to the IRB process. There is research that carries risks and that should be so treated. The American Council on Education has drafted language that it is urging on the universities which defines the kinds of research which should be subjected to IRB review. Universities should use that language in their general assurances. It promises that review will be required for research that involves intrusion on the subject's person (the medical case) withholds usual or necessary resources from the subject (certainly a class of actions not protected by the First Amendment), or which uses deceit.

For the rest, if our universities are to remain universities, no one should ask to review and authorize what a scholar does in unsponsored research.

The second lesson I would draw is a theoretical one. As institutions grow, and as centralized decision making increases, we have much to fear from failure to understand the principles which specialized cadres have created with their unique perspectives.

For those committed to freedom there is always much to fear from recurrent attacks. We have all heard that "eternal vigilance is the price of liberty." It is not a slogan that I like very much. If one has to be eternally vigilant one is not very free. To be free is to be able to relax and assume that no one will take one's rights away. Unfortunately it is not that way. I am afraid that it is true; we do have to be eternally vigilant. The freedom to relax and assume that our freedoms are safe is one we do not have.

15

What's Next? The Intellectual Legacy of Ithiel de Sola Pool

Lloyd S. Etheredge[1]

Good afternoon. It is a pleasure to return to MIT and speak about my former colleague, Ithiel de Sola Pool.

A discussion of Ithiel Pool's intellectual legacy is a large task. He was a pioneer in the development of the social sciences who continued to grow and explore new issues with new methods across more than forty-five years of professional work. He wrote, co-authored, or edited two dozen books and several hundred articles. He seldom repeated himself.[2]

This afternoon I will proceed in two steps. First, I will discuss Ithiel's major enduring contributions to the development of the social sciences. Then I will address Ithiel's legacy as a pioneer who always was engaging the question "What's Next?," and I will discuss what I think he would be doing today.

Contributions to the Social Sciences

Ithiel contributed to almost every field of political science and to the broader development of the social sciences. In the early 1970s the late Karl Deutsch assembled a list of sixty-plus "Major Advances in Social Science Since 1900." Ithiel was cited for his contributions to three major advances (figure 15.1).[3] I once discussed the list with Ithiel, and he said that he agreed with Karl Deutsch's judgments. It is a good place to begin.

The three contributions were research methods that Ithiel helped to pioneer and where his sensible discussions and early examples remain touchstones:

1. The quantitative analysis of communications content—which he helped to pioneer, with Lasswell and others, during World War II in the study of Nazi and communist propaganda and symbols of freedom in the speeches of political leaders.

1. Karl Deutsch's list
    - Content analysis
    - Elite studies
    - Computer simulation of social and political processes
2. Additions (Possible)
    - Contact nets
    - *Technologies of Freedom* and *Politics in Wired Nations* analysis of impacts of new communication technologies

Figure 15.1. Ithiel Pool's Major Contributions to the Social Sciences.

2. The rigorous analysis of political elites, who gets into power, from what backgrounds, by what routes.

3. The computer simulation of social processes, including the first computer simulation of decision making in international crises—the outbreak of World War I ("The Kaiser, the Tsar, and the Computer"; reprinted at pp. 99–119 in this volume) and the first major computer simulation of the American electorate based on public opinion data and used to advise President Kennedy's campaign for the presidency in 1960.[4]

I think there are two possible additions to this list:

4. Contact Networks and Influence.

Ithiel pioneered the rigorous study of contact networks and influence, a line of work that become known as "the small world" phenomenon.[5] One way to pose the question is to ask the probability that any two people, selected at random from a population, will share at least one acquaintance. Another version of the problem is to ask how many steps it would take a person to get a message to the President of the United States (or another target person) through chains of personal relationships. Ithiel's original work inspired a play and a movie "Six Degrees of Separation" and more recently an Internet Web site and game, "The Six Degrees of Kevin Bacon."

Ithiel began this work, with the mathematician Manfred Kochen, in the 1950s when the standard view of political influence was group-based. American politics, for example, was seen as an arena of interest groups and organizations like political parties, who interacted to set the political processes. Today, the verb "to network" has become standard at the Kennedy School, or Yale's School of Organization and Management, and throughout the professional and policy world. We speak readily of "policy networks."

"Most movements that are self-described as radical are highly urbanistic, or nationalistic, or oriented to obsolete class structures, or to central bureaucratic planning. The changes that we can see on the horizon are much more drastic than that . . . People who think about social change in traditional political terms cannot begin to imagine the changes that lie ahead. Conventional reformers case their programs in terms of national policies, or in terms of laws and central planning. But in the end, what will shape the future is a creative potential that inheres in the new technologies . . . "

—Ithiel Pool, "Development of Communication in the Future Perspective" in S. Aida (Ed.), The human use of human ideas (New York: Pergamon Press, 1983), pp. 237—238.

"With each passing year the value of this 1983 book (Technologies of Freedom: On Free Speech in an Electronic Age) becomes more evident. Like no one before or since, Ithiel de Sola Pool saw the world of communications whole and with up-to-the-second knowledge in depth . . . Technologies of Freedom . . . I've seen this book convert liberals away from government control of broadcast media toward a guided marketplace approach . . . I've seen technology skeptics . . . begin to get a gleam in their eye."

—Stewart Brand. Review, 9/89, http://www.gbn.org/BookClub/Technologies.html

Figure 15.2. Ithiel Pool as a Communication Technology Theorist and Science-Based Revolutionary.

Right now, social scientists are still lagging in the formal study of these new realities. As they begin, specify dependent variables, and this research becomes more prominent, I think Ithiel's conceptual and mathematical foundation will be seen as a major advance.

5. The last possible entry is Ithiel's analysis in *Technologies of Freedom,* and his broader work on the social and political impacts of new communication technologies that will be drawn together in an edited volume, *Politics in Wired Nations.*[6]

The key claim is Ithiel's argument (figure 15.2) that "*people who think about social change in traditional political [even radical] terms cannot begin to imagine the changes that lie ahead.*" If Ithiel is right, and his work *does* offer a reliable guide to the effects of communications technology on social, political, and economic life, then his work will have fulfilled, rather splendidly, the dream of the pioneers of the social sciences to provide an independent, steadier, truer, and more realistic alternative to the frameworks and choices (e.g., ideologies, election speeches, or policy argument television) that the political world provides. Clearly, it is an achievement that would be featured prominently on a list drawn a hundred years from now.

Actually, Ithiel's work may rate a double billing, since Karl Deutsch gave separate entries for revolutionaries who created new political movements. In this respect, I draw to your attention the quotation from Stewart Brand (figure 15.2, also), a leader from the counterculture left of the 1960s.

If Stewart Brand is correct, then Ithiel pulled off an almost unequaled historical feat of consensus building for worldwide public policy. The AT&Ts of the world were enrolled (from enlightened self-interest), and almost everybody else.

In suggesting a double nomination, I want to draw to your attention one of Ithiel's last writings that discusses the "unnatural institutions" that he expects—with the communications policy changes underway—now will begin to change.[7] It is a remarkable list—the nation-state, large hierarchical bureaucracies, the "unnatural" entrapment of human beings into megacities, etc. I am reminded that Ithiel was a passionate student leader and Trotskyite in his youth, and at this point I just want to draw to your attention that (surface appearances not withstanding) I am not sure, in some ways, how much he changed. Any leftist revolutionary would be thrilled by the hit list.

And of course if we consider Ithiel's legacy, there are the obvious points in his favor that he might be more effective than Mao or Lenin and that his science was better than Marx. Time will tell.[8]

Today, I list this achievement as a "maybe" because Ithiel did not live to write the equivalent of *Das Kapital.* I do not think people fully understood, even in his own Department, the pieces that were coming together. And we still need to see how many predictions and causal pathways turn out as forecast.

Let me just illustrate this legacy. On my desk is an announcement from Yale Medical School discussing a new global Internet research colloquium that our foundation has helped to develop that is connecting to desktop PCs of educators, public health professionals, students—and anybody else who is interested—in 110-plus countries.[9] It is designed to take a global framework and to accelerate scientific innovation worldwide. The public domain technology for compressed audio and graphics (Real Audio and QuickTime) is good enough to begin, and it is obvious that it will continue to improve quickly.[10]

For most of world history, this would have seemed almost inconceivable. Global, user-initiated and user-controlled television channels? Across national boundaries, without a license and without asking for permission? And building common frameworks for international cooperation to solve urgent global problems, with many of the people in the loop who could make this happen?

The Medical School initiative is about global organizing and influence, in addition to scientific information. The first global seminar in the Yale series was given by Dr. Ruth Berkelman, M.D. from the U.S. government's Center for Disease Control. She was able, so to speak, to address the troops (3,500+ leaders in international public health) worldwide and begin to explain new leadership in US policy: the audio and video technology began to create relationships that writing an article alone could not have achieved and saved her months of jet travel.

And once you begin to use this new global, interactive, user-controlled, and low-cost technology, contact networks become even more vividly alive as a new mechanism of policy cooperation and influence. Contact networks are not just sociological phenomena of people Dr. Ruth Berkelman (for example) has met, but the people she can interact with and work with—on a daily basis—wherever they are in the world.

II. What Ithiel Pool Would Be Doing Today

Ithiel was a pioneer who believed that he and his students should be creating the future. I think that this spirit and commitment were his greatest legacies. Forecasting what he would be doing today is easier than it may seem: Ithiel planned what he was going to do next, there is a written record of his criteria, and here are several major themes (figure 15.3).

1. Focusing upon the most important emerging trends, especially affecting freedom;
2. Addressing questions that were, jointly, of scientific interest and civic relevance for government and citizen decision making;
3. Assessing where he, given his background, could make the greatest contribution;
4. [Neat technology. Unstated, but probably relevant, was that Ithiel liked the challenges of developing new technology, especially for research.]

Figure 15.3. Ithiel Pool's Operational Code as a Pioneer.

Even with these questions to call forth a list there are many hazards to this kind of enterprise. As a preface it may help to recall Ithiel's own comment on forecasting, in a famous essay "The Art of the Social Science Soothsayer," [reprinted at pp. 135–154 in this volume], Ithiel wrote that if an analyst was faced with three possibilities, with probabilities p(A)=0.3 p(B)=0.3 and p(C)=0.4, he would predict option C (i.e., p(C)=0.4) as the most likely. But he also would predict that he would be wrong, that the probability was 0.6 that the actual outcome would be either A or B. The remark will, I think, introduce you to something about Ithiel—his intelligence, his capacity for self-reflection, his honesty, his humor. And although I was never entirely convinced that Ithiel believed he would be wrong, I will press forward in the same spirit (figure 15.4).[11]

1. Developing the Communications Framework as a Formal and Systematic Field in the Social Sciences

Ithiel believed that the study of communication systems could be as powerful as the study of economic systems.[12] He and several other pioneers (e.g., Karl Deutsch) worked in this direction—for example, in *American Business and Public Policy: The Politics of Foreign Trade,* Bauer, Pool, and Dexter created a model of scientific research to examine, with an anthropologist's astute observation and alert generalization, the details of a particular communication system.[13] Ithiel edited the *Handbook of Communication* to begin codifying the field.[14] And with Inose, Takasaki, and Hurwitz he began to develop a set of measures to

I. Developing the communication framework as a formal and systematic framework in the social sciences
- Measurement of trends
- Experiments to clarify and evaluate creative potentials (e.g., scientific innovation)

II. Nailing the Huntington Thesis

[Intermission: What Ithiel Pool Would Not be Doing]

III. Building Capacity for Empirically-Based Policy
- Domestic
  - The battle for social science in domestic policy
- International
  - Using the independence of the academic world to strengthen government analysis

IV. Travel (Japan, Russia)

Figure 15.4. What Ithiel Pool Would Be Doing Today.

monitor trends toward a global information society.[15] But the vision needs more work and refinement to develop the equivalent analytical power of the field of economics and other disciplines.

For example, there are flows of communication, just as there are flows of money. But we also can ask about the productivity of communications or of expenditures, about whether anything is happening or whether we are experiencing three percent to five percent annual growth in the intelligence and wisdom in what is being said; or the systems of feedback and government learning[16]; or citizen learning or intelligence as a result of the flows of communications in the mass media, etc.

There are many directions for the development of the field. My guess is that Ithiel would be updating and expanding his early measures of trends toward a global information society. And almost surely would be engaged in experiments to develop creative potentials of new communication technologies such as designing global discussions on the World Wide Web and expanded contact nets to aid the creative process in science. (Given his earlier interest in scientific creativity, communication technology, and international agricultural research, he might be drawn to this field for initial projects.)

2. Nailing the Huntington Thesis

Samuel Huntington at Harvard has recently written about the clash of civilizations as the new, emerging trend in world politics—especially the clash between Islam and the West. If true, these trends are important.[17] But I think that Ithiel would be drawn to studying these global processes for three additional reasons, especially because there is related work he began earlier in his life and that he set aside.

A. As you will recall, I mentioned that Ithiel and others pioneered the quantitative analysis of communication content. Eventually, they came to their senses and stopped because even inputting the data was taking too much time and they recognized that the deeper questions they wanted to ask were more sophisticated than their available technology to manipulate large data sets. For example, Ithiel worked on one study that coded 19,553 editorials from elite newspapers in five countries across sixty years. And each of the 19,553 editorials was coded by hand, word by word, for 416 symbols. In 1959 they called a temporary halt and Ithiel edited a volume that was a summary report in a time capsule, to scientists in the future, when the cause could again be picked up with newer technology. Now, almost forty years later, with scanning technology and the expanded capacity of computers, the time is arriving when renewed progress may be possible.

B. Ithiel was fascinated by cultures and tried to formulate an operational code that would capture and compare the deeper logic of political cultures. The passion was inspired by Nathan Leites, who fascinated his colleagues at Rand by *The Operational Code of the Politburo* and *A Study of Bolshevism.*[18] Ithiel started to do the same analysis for India, and in his basement is a trunk filled with note cards detailing classic Indian texts, stories of monkey kings, learned discussions of how the categories of Indian logic differ from Western logic, and other inputs into the creative process of explicating what made Indian sensibility distinctive.

(One of the most interesting contents are letters describing his bafflement at Indian movies—they are uniquely Indian because they are greatly beloved in India, but there is almost no market elsewhere in the world. And Ithiel could never quite grasp why Indian audiences were so drawn to the stories—and he was fascinated that he could not predict the plots!)

Ithiel never solved the problem, but he hooked himself on it. And this is a second reason why I think Ithiel would be engaged by the problem that Huntington has posed. He already would see a way—using operational code analysis—to make a deeper analysis of whether (for example) the Islamic world was becoming more Western in its sensibilities.

C. There is a third reason why Ithiel might be drawn to the problem and think he could do a better job of empirical grounding: Forty years ago, he had already anticipated that there were many more interesting stories to be told about cultures than an analysis of traditional religious/ethnic cultures as the organizing principles in global human affairs. He wrote, for example, about different languages and cultures that might be cross-cutting universals: "Formal language, colloquial language, rude language, mothering language, upper-class language, lower-class language, men's language, women's language, children's language."[19] It would not escape Ithiel's notice that MTV is now a global channel and that a global teenage culture would be a consequential phenomenon to recognize, even if its current relevance is beyond the ken of national security elites. The study of global cultures could reveal a much more interesting and pluralist world, and perhaps—rather than a clash of cultures—a much more interesting set of interactions. And I think it is a story he might like to begin to tell.[20]

* * *

At this point, I just want to take a brief intermission and suggest one thing that Ithiel would *not* be doing. He would not be writing a single word about Israeli or Middle Eastern politics or about Israeli-Palestinian relations.

On its face, this may seem unexpected, coming from a political scientist whose ancestors, on both sides, included centuries of distinguished rabbis. In fact Ithiel's father, Rabbi David deSola Pool, was the spiritual head of the Sephardic synagogue in New York City and his mother was a passionate Zionist.[21] But across two dozen books and several hundred articles there is a loud silence about Israel and the Middle East.

* * *

3. A third prediction is that Ithiel would be involved in research to improve decision making by governments and citizens concerning important issues.

3. The Battle for Social Science in Domestic Policy

In domestic policy I think his priority would be easy to predict. Ithiel belonged to a generation of pioneers who believed that ideology was on the decline, being steadily replaced by social science, and that we were entering a period of empirically based, rather than belief-based, public policy. Ithiel was passionately committed to free speech and democratic processes, and he also believed that the schema of hypothesis and evidence, introduced by our scientific institutions into democratic processes, could save us from the endless recycling of similar ideological arguments, give us real historical leverage, and genuine progress. The aggressive resurgence of ideologues such as Ronald Reagan or Newt Gingrich was completely unexpected.

In this regard, Ithiel shared the views of his Harvard colleague Daniel Bell, whose famous pre-Reagan and pre-Gingrich book was *The End of Ideology.* Ithiel, for his own part, believed that the American people were not highly ideological and the policy differences between Republicans and Democrats often could be resolved, in practice, by testing empirical claims. He wrote:

> The interesting issues in normative political theory are in the end generally empirical ones. Only rarely do arguments over policy turn on irreducible conflicts of values. More often they are arguments about the facts of situations to which the values are applied. Most men agree in valuing freedom and also equality, and order and also

> progress. . . . [There is a fundamental problem, clarified by Arrow and others of value mixes but] "for the rest, when men differ in their policy conclusions it is usually because of differing empirical judgments about how a chosen package of values may be achieved."[22]

The difficulty, as you may know, is that we made good progress in evaluating liberal assumptions of the Great Society until the first election of Ronald Reagan. Then David Stockman launched a pre-emptive strike to zero-out all behavioral science research in the federal budget and our major agenda-setting institutions in science suddenly shut up. And the accommodations have become permanent.[23]

I think that Ithiel would have fought back for social science, and a more politically independent undergraduate curriculum. I think he would have advocated tests of theories of the political right, on an equal footing with evaluations of the Great Society programs, and an independent and respected role for empirically-based social and economic policy. And I think he would have been outraged that distinguished scientific panels (such as the Luce Commission quoted from private correspondence in figure 15.5) were quietly compromising the political independence of science and university-based inquiry, a challenge that he fought fiercely when the Department of Health and Human Services sought to impose requirements for prior review of research involving human subjects.[24]

Concerning figure 15.5, let me add a current illustration from the new President's Committee of Advisers on Science and Technology. They have recently discussed the question of restarting progress in testing ideological assumptions. The meeting to discuss these issues acknowledged the distinction between "belief-based rather than empirically based" social and economic policy, but the members expressed doubt about "the relative important of these issues to the broader public." And they decided to continue the *de facto* policy of quietly deferring initiatives to obtain evidence that might be too politically significant.[25]

Here is an example of the current breakdown: if you listened to the televised selection from the Markle Foundation's experiment during the last election (bringing a sample of American voters together to discuss the issues), it was striking to hear the citizen group ask an expert panel of economists to address their concern of how much government should do for people versus how much people should do for themselves? In answer, Lester Thurow of MIT—one of the experts—changed the subject and said that the citizens were asking the wrong question—

"A number of criteria should be applied in the selection of research projects, among them the criteria of scientific merit and political significance (sic)."

—Speier, Hans; Bruner, Jerome; Caroll, Wallace; Lasswell, Harold D.; Lazarsfeld, Paul; Shils, Edward; Pool, Ithiel de Sola (secretary). "A Plan of Research in International Communication." Condensation of the Planning Committee Report, Center for International Studies, MIT. *World Politics* 6, no. 3 (April, 1954): 358–377, p. 359.

"I very much doubt that a cleaned up version [of the proposal to restart the testing of ideological assumptions] would be acceptable in the near term even if it came from another source and were backed by a number of Academy member."

—R. Duncan Luce [Co-Chair of the National Academy of Sciences agenda-setting Commission for the social and behavioral science in the 1980s and early 1990s that (without public disclosure) quietly killed recommendations for restarting progress in testing ideological assumptions on the grounds that the research would have too much political significance. Letter to the author, May 14, 1992.]

Figure 15.5. The Retreat of Social Science, 1954—Present.

the real question is not what people (v. government) should do, but the total amount of investment made by both. . . . And the questioner nodded politely and, five minutes later, another member of the citizen group persevered and said, still politely: "Yes, we understand Professor Thurow's point, but what we *really* wanted him to talk about was how much government should do for people versus what people should be expected to do for themselves . . .?"

What is involved in this non-exchange is a narrowness of social science. Academic economists assume autonomous individuals with fixed motivation—there is no group psychology or capacity of government to energize people or otherwise affect their personality, motivation, or moral character by its size, subjective prominence, or the comprehensiveness of its role. But I think there is very suggestive evidence—which is beyond the scope of this discussion—that Ronald Reagan and a core of other Republicans (and members of citizen panels) worry about the possibility of a clinical-like, hierarchical relationship to a prominent government that induces dependency and affects motivation and responsibility in a zero-sum fashion. As government takes more responsibility, people take less . . .

In candor, Lester Thurow mis-answered the question, and he should have said that he and his colleagues had no scientific basis to give advice about economic policy if you framed the question this way. Economic theory and econometric measurements have—and I intend this as a technical comment—no imagination. When Ronald Reagan was asked about economic policy, he talked about how alive and wonderful it felt to ride the open range on horseback: *He was not talking in metaphors.* Rather, he was trying to change a sense of reality that originates in a different universe than Lester Thurow and his colleagues inhabit.

I think that Ithiel would have gone after the challenge to social science by broadening an empirically based dialogue and starting to test the truth claims of these models. Especially, Republican beliefs that they can change (and have been changing) national modal personality by their policies.[26]

There is another reason Ithiel would have done this. He went through psychoanalysis and was engaged by the study of imagery as a way to incorporate depth psychology into policy analysis. In fact, one of his most original and gifted studies was "Newsman's Fantasies, Audiences, and Newswriting"—using terms like fantasy, audiences, and reference groups to discuss projection and transference in a more acceptable vocabulary. I think he would have been especially interested to develop the study of hierarchical imagery to help evaluate the concerns and claims of ideology.[27]

Improving Government International Policy: Forecasting

I am quite sure that Ithiel would be actively engaged by issues of international policy, both intellectually and because the engagement could contribute to the continued strength of a political science program at MIT.

A word of context: As many of you know, the Political Science Department at MIT was always an unnatural institution. The Center for International Studies, the Research Program in Communications, and the Political Science Department were created when James Killian from MIT was science adviser to President Eisenhower, and then Jerome Weisner was science adviser to President Kennedy. They were created during the Cold War to build national capacity and demonstrate the contribution that first-rate social science might make to understanding the major forces of change in the world. The original research program was created by a distinguished Ford Foundation-supported panel of which Ithiel was the secretary before being hired to implement the agenda.[28] The *quid pro quo* for a Political Science Department at MIT has always been that first-rate scientific analysis of global trends and international policy questions should be the defining agenda.

Ithiel also believed strongly that foreign policy was too important, and the assessment of reality required too much capacity for independent thought, to be left to the kinds of people who chose careers as spies, KGB or FBI operatives, or diplomats. He campaigned very hard to open-up the CIA's analyses to rigorous vetting by outside science-based research.[29] If you look at the structure of the new National Intelligence Council at the CIA—which had, as its first directors, Joseph Nye and Richard Cooper from Harvard—it is the kind of institutional innovation and meeting ground that his writings would support.

Just to indicate briefly: I think he would pick forecasting as a critical focus for this dialogue. He was interested in the development of the methodology and—like "international communications"—it is a wide-ranging entré and seems devoid of a partisan agenda. And he would surely have credibility, as he was one of the only social scientists to forecast the breakup of the Soviet Union and the resurgence of nationality- and ethnicity-based conflicts as part of this extraordinary development.[30]

Concerning specific forecasting: Ithiel almost surely would be interested in ethnicity-based conflicts, since he had been involved in the programs of Radio Free Europe/Radio Liberty and Voice of America to affirm, among minorities in the USSR and in Eastern Europe, that their identity was their ethnic or national identity. This was a strategy to encourage the breakup of the Soviet Union and the Warsaw Pact. Having helped to turn the dial in one direction, I think he would be especially engaged by the possible use of communication technology to turn the dial in the other direction.

My guess, too, is that he might be interested in the study of contact nets and the remarkable growth of a cluster of global humanitarian politics movements—environment, human rights (including women's rights), and support for humanitarian interventions in Africa and elsewhere—as an expression of new communication networks and organizational patterns.

IV. My final thought is that Ithiel did like to travel. And I suspect that he would manage to be developing projects in Japan, which he was beginning to know and admire greatly at the time of his death. And Russia, since the political transition there is surely one of the most interesting and consequential processes in world politics and reality-based policy would be very helpful.

Notes

1. Director, International Scientific Networks Project, Policy Science Center 127 Wall St., Room 322, P.O. Box 208215, New Haven, CT. 06520-8215. lloyd.etheredge@yale.edu (Internet). Paper prepared for a panel sponsored by the Communications Forum at MIT and the Markle Foundation. Cambridge, MA, May 10, 1997.
2. And he had a secret edge—at least in the eight years I knew him as a member of the MIT faculty, Ithiel was blessed with the most remarkably efficient secretarial staffs I have ever seen in universities.
3. Deutsch, Karl W., Platt, J. & Senghaas, D., "Conditions favoring major advances in social science." *Science,* 171 (1971): 450–459.
4. Pool, Ithiel de Sola, "The Kaiser, the Tsar, and the computer: Information processing in a crisis." *American Behavioral Scientist* 8, no. 9 (May, 1965): 31–39; Abelson, Robert; Pool, Ithiel de Sola; Popkin, Samuel, *Candidates, issues, and strategies: A computer simulation of the 1960 and 1964 elections.* (Cambridge, MA: MIT Press, 1965).
5. Kochen, Manfred, (ed.), *The small world: A volume of recent research commemorating Ithiel de Sola Pool, Stanley Milgram, and Theodore Newcomb.* (Norwood, NJ: Ablex Publishing Company, 1989.)
6. Harvard University Press, 1983; Etheredge, Lloyd S. (ed.), *Politics in wired nations: Selected papers of Ithiel de Sola Pool.* (New Brunswick, NJ; Transaction Publishers, 1998).
7. In Aida (ed.), *op. cit.*
8. The URL is http://info.med.yale.edu/EIINet. The subject concerns emerging infectious diseases, a problem that has both scientific and organizational challenges. An early source of inspiration was Ithiel Pool's work concerning the potential contribution of satellite technology to the creative process in international agricultural research. See, for example, Pool, Ithiel de Sola and Corte, A. B. "International data communication capabilities and information revolution." *Proceedings of the American Society for Information Science* 12 (1975): 1–2; Pool, Ithiel de Sola, Freedman, Elliott H., and Warren, Colin John, "Low cost data and text communication for the less developed countries: A study with special reference to the needs of the international agricultural research centers." A study completed for the US Agency for International Development. (Cambridge, MA: MIT Research Program on Communications Policy and others, 1976).
9. Once a lecture series is organized, the added cost to Yale to make it available globally also is remarkably small: after a lecture is recorded by conventional means, it requires about 1.5 hours of a technician's time to digitize one hour of audio, and about 0.5 hours to digitize 20–30 slides, at $65/hour (Yale Medical School rates).
10. Pool, Ithiel de Sola, "The art of the social science soothsayer" in Nazli Choucri and Thomas W. Robinson (eds.), *Forecasting in international relations:*

Theory, methods, problems, prospects (San Francisco: W. H. Freeman, 1978), pp. 23–34.

11. E.g., Pool, Ithiel de Sola, "Political communication" in David Sills (ed.), *International encyclopedia of the social sciences.* Vol. 3 (New York: Macmillan-Free Press. 1968), pp. 90–96.
12. Bauer, Raymond; Pool. Ithiel de Sola; Dexter, Lewis A., *American business and public policy: The politics of foreign trade.* (New York: Atherton Press of Prentice-Hall, 1963).
13. Pool, Ithiel de Sola; Schramm, Wilbur; with others, (eds.) *Handbook of communication.* (Chicago: IL: Rand McNally, 1973).
14. Pool, Ithiel de Sola; Inose, H.; Takasaki, N.; Hurwitz, R., *Communication flows: A census in the United States and Japan.* (Tokyo: University of Tokyo Press, 1984).
15. E.g., Etheredge, Lloyd S., *Can governments learn? American foreign policy and Central American revolutions* (NY: Pergamon Press, 1984); *idem.*, "Government learning: An overview" in Samuel Long (ed.), *Handbook of political behavior,* vol, 2 (NY: Plenum Press, 1981), pp. 73–181.
16. *The clash of civilizations and the remaking of world order.* (New York: Simon and Schuster, 1996).
17. *Operational code of the Politburo* (NY: McGraw-Hill, 1951) and *Study of Bolshevism* (Glencoe, IL: Free Press, 1953).
18. Pool, Ithiel de Sola, "Trends in content analysis today: A summary" in Ithiel de Sola Pool, (ed.), *Trends in content analysis.* Chapter 7, 189–233. (Urbana, IL: University of Illinois Press, 1959), p. 233.
19. Just to suggest a couple of elements: *Baywatch* is the most popular television series in the world and this (coupled with the prominence of X-rated Web sites) suggests a cross-cultural universal (one of the questions that engage social scientists). And *Aladdin* was a charming Islamic folktale until it was transformed by Hollywood and the Disney Studios into a planetary mega-hit. Not all interactions among cultures are clashes, in other words. Although even if Huntington is wrong generally, he may be right about the simple dramatic stories of zero-sum clashes that power-oriented national security elites begin to tell one another—and, if so, it may be especially important to have a more complex and refined picture, with an empirical base, available as a counterweight.
20. Also, Ithiel would not be doing experimental studies involving undergraduates. He worked with distinguished scientists, like Robert Abelson, who used much of their professional lives to build what they viewed as the foundation of social science by careful experimental studies. Ithiel, by contrast, viewed the real world and the laboratory as two distinct social contexts. He was delighted by happy convergences of results between the two settings, but in his view you would never really know what was happening in the real world unless you studied behavior in the real world. For him, field work was the priority.
21. Pool, Ithiel de Sola, "The Public and the polity" in Ithiel de Sola Pool (ed.), *Contemporary political science: Toward empirical theory.* (NY: McGraw-Hill, 1967), pp. 22–52, pp. 23–24.
22. E.g., Lloyd Etheredge, "Commentary: The scientific scandal of the 1980s" *Political Psychology,* 15:3 (1994), pp. 531–539 and "Problems of Scientific

Integrity that Affect Unfunded Research." Testimony to the US Commission on Research Integrity, April 10, 1995. Harvard Medical School. Boston, MA. Xerox.

23. E.g., Pool, Ithiel de Sola, "Human subjects regulations on the social sciences." *Annals of the New York Academy of Sciences* 403 (26 May 1981)** 101–110.
24. Letter on behalf of Norman Augustine from Angela Phillips Diaz. Executive Secretary, October 26, 1995. Three votes on PCAST were by members of the MIT faculty: President Charles Vest, and Profs. Mario Molina and Philip Sharp.
25. I.e., reducing dependency and increasing achievement motivation by cutting back the size and subjective prominence of government, a backward linkage between events in the public sphere and individual personality that is not measured by standard macroeconomic models that deny hierarchical group psychology and assume autonomous individuals with fixed motivation. See Etheredge, Lloyd S., "President Reagan's counseling," *Political Psychology,* 5:4 (1984), pp. 737–740.
26. Pool, Ithiel de Sola; Shulman, Irwin, "Newsmen's fantasies, audiences and newswriting." *Public Opinion Quarterly* 23, no. 2 (Summer, 1959): 145–158.
27. Speier, Hans *et al.,* "A Plan . . .", *op. cit.*
28. E.g., Pool. Ithiel de Sola "Approaches to intelligence and social science" in Robert Pfaltzgraff Jr. et al. (eds.), *Intelligence policy and the national security* (Hamden, CT: Archon Press, 1981), chapter 3.
29. Pool, Ithiel de Sola. "The international system in the next half century" in Daniel Bell (ed.), *Toward the year 2000: Work in progress* (Boston, MA: Houghton Mifflin, 1968), pp. 318–323. Originally published in *Daedalus,* vol. 96. (1967): 930–935. See also his "The changing Soviet Union: The mass media as catalyst" excerpted in *Current* 67 (January 1966): 12–17.

Index

For Product Safety Concerns and Information please contact our EU representative GPSR@taylorandfrancis.com
Taylor & Francis Verlag GmbH, Kaufingerstraße 24, 80331 München, Germany

www.ingramcontent.com/pod-product-compliance
Ingram Content Group UK Ltd.
Pitfield, Milton Keynes, MK11 3LW, UK
UKHW021450080625
459435UK00012B/438

* 9 7 8 1 4 1 2 8 5 7 0 9 3 *